Television and the Family Ideal in Postwar America

Lynn Spigel

The University of Chicago Press

Chicago and London

The University of Chicago Press, Chicago 60637
The University of Chicago Press, Ltd., London
© 1992 by The University of Chicago
All rights reserved. Published 1992
Printed in the United States of America

01 00 99 98 97 96 95 94 93   5 4 3
ISBN (cloth): 0-226-76966-6
ISBN (paper): 0-226-76967-4

Library of Congress Cataloging-in-Publication Data

Spigel, Lynn.
    Make room for TV : television and the family ideal in postwar
America / Lynn Spigel.
        p.   cm.
    Includes bibliographical references and index.
    1. Television and family—United States.   I. Title.
HQ520.S75   1992
306.87—dc20   91-32770
                                                        CIP

To
Bill Forman
and to my parents,
**Roslyn and
Herman Spigel**

Contents

Acknowledgments

This book is a product of a dialogue with friends, family, and colleagues who gave me their support and encouragement. The people I want to thank will recognize their particular contributions.

I first wish to express my deepest gratitude to Bill Forman for his editorial suggestions. He saw this project through its six-year span and lived through the numerous forms it has taken. His willingness to re-read chapters and provide new thoughts is a true act of kindness.

I also want to thank the numerous people who helped foster and spur ideas for this project. Janet Bergstrom was irreplaceable, both as a friend and as a teacher. Her intuitive intelligence and nonconformist scholarship have greatly influenced this work and my general under-standing of feminist collaboration. Nick Browne devoted many hours to the formation of this study when it was first conceived in graduate school. His efforts have had an enormous impact on this book and on my thinking in general. George Lipsitz had a special role in the book's formation, both through his own imaginative writings on American popular culture and through his direct support of my research. Robert Allen read numerous drafts and inspired me with his vision of American cultural history. Lary May encouraged the transformation of my re-search into a book and influenced its contents with his own writings on American cultural history. Douglas Mitchell, my editor at the University of Chicago Press, had faith in this project from the start and always offered guidance and encouragement. Kathryn Montgomery, Paul Ro-senthal, William Roy, and Kathryn Kish Sklar all provided insights in the early stages of this study. I also extend my warmest gratitude to other family, friends, and colleagues, including Marcia Untracht, Margie Sol-ovay, Chris Berry, Denise Mann, Mary Beth Haralovich, Constance Pen-ley, Elisabeth Lyon, Henry Jenkins, William Lafferty, Thomas Streeter, Michael Curtin, Jackie Byars, David Eason, Cory Creekmur, Beatriz Colomina, Patricia Mellencamp, Lauren Rabinovitz, Lisa Freeman, Char-lotte Brunsdon, David Morley, Richard deCordova, Matthew Geller, William Boddy, and Mary Carbine.

Certainly, this book would not have been possible without the col-legial support, insights, and goodwill of my colleagues at the University of Wisconsin, Madison. I especially want to thank Julie D'Acci, John

Fiske, David Bordwell, Kristin Thompson, Tino Balio, J. J. Murphy, and Jeffrey Sconce for their willingness to discuss ideas, make suggestions, and provide a context of generous collaboration. I am also indebted to Maxine Fleckner and Don Crafton at the Wisconsin Center for Film and Television Research; Eleanor Tannin, Robert Rosen, Steven Ricci, and Dan Einstein at the UCLA Archives; William Bird at the Smithsonian Institution; and my research assistants Aimee Lefkow, Reg Shrader, Shelley Happy, and Paul Seale.

Finally, I want to express my gratitude to my mother Roslyn and my father Herman Spigel, with whom I did my first fieldwork. A TV repairman for Macy's department store, my father took me out to his customers' homes where I sat curiously watching him tinker with the tubes and wires of TV consoles located somewhere in the outer limits of postwar suburbia. Memories like that always make for odd connections between history and life.

In 1927, the American modernist architect R. Buckminster Fuller built his famous Dymaxion House, a glass octagonal structure supported by a steel frame, one of the first in a history of "homes of tomorrow" to include a television set. When Fuller's house was first displayed to the public in 1929 at Marshall Field's department store in Chicago, it was scarcely more than a science fiction oddity to the curious onlookers who were told that the home would one day be produced on assembly lines across the nation. The television set, placed in what Fuller called the "get-on-with-life-room" along with a radio, phonograph, and numerous domestic office machines, seemed to be, like the house itself, an alien contraption to the customers at the Chicago store. Twenty years after the Marshall Field's exhibit, Fuller's dream for mass-produced housing would become a reality, albeit in a completely transmuted form. In 1949, on the unlikely spot of a potato field in Hempstead, Long Island, more than 1,400 people lined up on a cold March morning anxiously waiting to purchase their very own home of tomorrow, a prefabricated Cape Cod/ranch-style cottage filled with modern labor-saving appliances and located in the most famous of the mass-produced suburbs, Levittown. Although these eager consumers were the first on their block to become Levitt families, it wasn't until the following year that the developer introduced his newest "built-in" feature, an Admiral television permanently embedded in the living room wall. In less than a quarter of a century, the television set had become a staple fixture in the American family home.

This book is a cultural history of American television, concentrating upon its installation into domestic space in the years following World War II. During this period, the primary site of exhibition for spectator amusements was transferred from the public space of the movie theater to the private space of the home. Americans purchased television sets at record rates—in fact more quickly than they had purchased any other home entertainment machine. Between 1948 and 1955, television was installed in nearly two-thirds of the nation's homes, and the basic mechanisms of the network oligopoly were set in motion. By 1960, almost 90 percent of American households had at least one receiver, with the average person watching approximately five hours of television each day.[1]

1

How, over the course of a single decade, did television become part of people's daily routines? How did people experience the arrival of television in their homes, and what were their expectations for the new mass medium? Routine events such as television viewing are part of the often invisible history of everyday life, a history that was not recorded by the people who lived it at the time. In order to understand such historical processes, it is necessary to examine unconventional sources, sources that tell us something—however partial—about the ephemeral qualities of daily experiences. This study originated some five years ago when I began to look in popular women's magazines in order to see how television had been advertised to its first consumers. I did find advertisements, but I also found something else—a wealth of representations of and debates about television's relationship to family life. These popular sources expressed a set of cultural anxieties about the new medium as they engaged the public in a dialogue concerning television's place in the home. This book investigates that dialogue by examining how popular media introduced television to the public between 1948 and 1955, the years in which it became a dominant mass medium.[2] During this period, magazines, advertisements, newspapers, radio, film, and television itself spoke in seemingly endless ways about television's status as domestic entertainment. By looking at these media and the representations they distributed, we can see how the idea of television and its place in the home was circulated to the public. Popular media ascribed meanings to television and advised the public on ways to use it. While the media discourses do not directly reflect how people responded to television, they do reveal an intertextual context—a group of interconnected texts—through which people might have made sense of television and its place in everyday life.

Discourses on television drew upon and magnified the more general obsession with the reconstruction of family life and domestic ideals after World War II. The 1950s was a decade that invested an enormous amount of cultural capital in the ability to form a family and live out a set of highly structured gender and generational roles. Although people at the time might well have experienced and understood the constraining aspects of this domestic dream, the new suburban family ideal was a consensus ideology, promising practical benefits like security and stability to people who had witnessed the shocks and social dislocations of the previous two decades. As Elaine Tyler May has suggested, even while people acknowledged the limitations of postwar domesticity, they nevertheless often spoke of their strong faith in the overall project of family life.[3] In this social climate, television was typically welcomed as a catalyst for renewed domestic values. In many popular sources, television was depicted as a panacea for the broken homes and hearts of wartime life; not only was it shown to restore faith in family together-ness, but as the most sought-after appliance for sale in postwar America, it also renewed faith in the splendors of consumer capitalism.

By the same token, however, television was also greeted in less eu-phoric terms. The discourses that introduced television to the public ex-pressed multiple anxieties about the changing nature of everyday life and television's place within it. Utopian statements that idealized the new medium as an ultimate expression of technological and social prog-ress were met by equally dystopian discourses that warned of television's devastating effects on family relationships and the efficient functioning of the household. Television was not simply promoted; rather, it was something that had to be questioned and deliberated upon. For ex-ample, how would television affect romantic and marital relations? Would it blend with interior decor? Would it cause eyestrain, increase the risk of cancer, or even, as one orthodontist suggested, lead to "mal-occlusion—an abnormal arrangement of the teeth likely to be caused by Junior's cradling his jaw in his hand as he watches television?"[4]

The ambivalent response to television is part of a long history of hopes and fears about technology—a history that dates back to the late nineteenth century when new forms of electrical communications were innovated for everyday use. As cultural historians have shown, commu-nications technologies such as the telegraph, telephone, and radio were all met with a mixture of utopian and dystopian expectations—both in intellectual circles and in popular culture.[5] Radio, for example, was praised for its ability to join the nation in democratic harmony through the mass dissemination of culture, but at the same time it was feared as an instrument of supernatural power that might wreak havoc on the public. According to Warren Susman, such hopes and fears about tech-nology are part of the cultural context in America, and they help to shape the form and content that communications media take. He writes:

> One of the reasons we talk so persistently about the impact of
> media is because thinking and talking about its role, and about
> the role of technology generally, have become cultural charac-
> teristics. In a sense, we are hardly able *not* to think and talk
> about the media. And we engage in this enterprise with a par-
> ticular set of questions and a special language provided for us
> from the start. Not only do the media help shape the way we
> think about the media, but thinking about the media also
> helps shape the way the media operate within the culture.
> There is a complex relationship between the way the media are
> used and the way we think about those uses.[6]

What Susman describes is what I will call a dialogical relationship ¹ tween communication technology and culture, a relationship tha⸍

3

explains the connections between popular discourses and television in the postwar period. Television spurred a host of debates in popular media, and what was said about the medium in turn affected television's ultimate cultural form.

As Susman suggests elsewhere in his essay, it is important to be aware of the pitfalls of technological determinism. Technologies such as automobiles, radios, and computers do not simply cause social change; instead, their uses are shaped by social practices and cultural expectations. Using the example of Ford's Model T, Susman argues that the genius of Henry Ford lay not in his invention, but rather in his ability to create a specific cultural form that meshed with central values of American social life. Ford did not just provide a means of transportation; rather, he helped devise the idea of the family car to be used for leisure pursuits. Furthermore, Susman argues that the public often resists new technologies. I would add to this that resistance can also help determine the form that communications media take. A contemporary example is the Apple computer, which designs its user-friendly product according to cultural reactions against difficult, high-tech machines. Above all, then, technologies are part of a cultural and social context, and we need to analyze them as such.

This book examines popular discourses on television in the context of wider cultural and social events of the postwar period. If America's response to television was highly contradictory, this should be seen in relation to tensions within the culture at large. This proposition necessarily calls for an interpretive approach to media history because it assumes that these discourses were part of a complex orchestration of social forces—some of which are not immediately observable at the level of content. If television was believed to cause childhood maladies, might this not in part be symptomatic of the country's larger concerns about problem children and juvenile delinquents? Conversely, how can we account for representations of television that seem to defy the social realities of postwar life? For example, at a time when increasing numbers of married women were entering the labor force, why did representations of television neglect their roles in the public world? In this study, I examine discourses on television and the family *in relation* to other aspects of the postwar world. The problem is to analyze this relationship, to ask why television came to represent so much of the culture's hopes and fears.

The documents used in this book reflect a wide array of popular sources—magazines, advertisements, newspapers, television programs, and films—aimed mainly at the white middle class.[7] In particular, I focus on women's home magazines, which were the primary venue for debates on television and the family. The bulk of the study is based on an analysis of four of the leading middle-class home magazines—*Better*

Homes and Gardens, American Home, House Beautiful, and *Ladies' Home Journal*—which I examined in their entirety from the year 1948 to 1955.[8] All of the magazines had been popular with women readers since the late nineteenth century, and all addressed homemaking issues.[9]

Apart from occasional references, these magazines have been disregarded in television histories. Rather than focusing on the social and domestic context, broadcast history has continually framed its object of study around questions of industry, regulation, and technological invention—that is, around spheres in which men have participated as executives, policy makers, and inventors. Women, however, are systematically marginalized in television history. According to the assumptions of our current historical paradigms, the woman is simply the receiver of the television text—the one to whom the advertiser promotes products. This is not to say industrial history cannot contribute to our understanding of gender relations. Indeed, as other feminist critics have shown, the very notion of femininity itself is in part constructed through and by mass media images as they are produced by the "culture industries." Nonetheless, industrial history clearly needs to be supplemented by methods of investigation that will better illuminate women's subjective experiences and the way those experiences might, in turn, have affected industry output and policies.

By looking at women's magazines as a viable source of historical evidence, we find another story, one that tells us something (however partial and mediated itself) about the way women might have experienced the arrival of television in their own homes. These magazines, through their pictorial displays of television sets in domestic settings, advised women on ways to integrate the new medium into the traditional space of the family home. Moreover, through their debates on television's place in the domestic sphere, the magazines gave women opportunities to negotiate rules and practices for watching television at home. They addressed female readers not simply as passive consumers of promotional rhetoric, but also as producers within the household. In short, they engaged women in a popular dialogue about television's relationship to family life.

Although the magazines addressed their public as white middle-class consumers, the actual readers were no doubt more heterogeneous in nature. The category of class is difficult to pinpoint since its meaning is one of cultural identity rather than simply of income. We might imagine that many postwar Americans fancied themselves in the growing ranks of middle-class consumers, especially since the period was marked by the promise of social mobility in a new suburban commodity culture. Women's magazines certainly contributed to this sense of class rise by presenting an upscale fantasy lifestyle to which their readers might aspire. But most women who read these magazines did not enjoy the degree of wealth presented in the editorial copy and advertisements. Indeed, circulation statistics indicate that women consumers came from a range of middle-class income levels and, in fact, since the 1920s, these magazines had a significant lower-class constituency.[10]

The category "white" is also less than obvious. Numerous postwar suburbs welcomed Jews, Catholics, Protestants, and other Judeo-Christian faiths in their proverbial melting pot. Even while prejudices still existed—indeed, people of color were systematically excluded from these communities—the prefabricated postwar suburbs encouraged a flattening out of religious identities and also leveled ethnicity to the extent that the communities allowed second-generation European immigrants to sever their national and ethnic ties with urban neighborhood networks. Given this, the term "white middle class" as used in this study refers to a set of social identifications encouraged by the media rather than to real individuals whose identities were more fractured and complex. Still, the term has real meaning because it was the particular aim of the mass media—especially television—to level class and ethnic differences in order to produce a homogeneous public for national advertisers. In the early 1950s, as television became a national medium, the networks continually drew on the image of the white, middle-class family audience when devising programming and promotional strategies.[11]

In addition to looking at popular media, I have drawn on a number of social scientific studies conducted during the period, studies that measured social and psychological effects, audience size and composition, and viewing preferences. While this research presents a wealth of data on the early audience, its evidentiary status is limited. Since the findings often contradict one another, and since the studies use different sample populations and apply different methodologies, it is not possible to form an accurate composite picture of the television audience through them. For these reasons, I have chosen to look at audience research as a kind of machine for the production of discourse on television rather than as a repository of social facts. I have mined the studies for their personal testimonies—the voices of ordinary women and men—who often spoke about television's impact on their daily lives. Much of what people said in these studies was remarkably similar to the more general ways that the media spoke about television. This correspondence between social scientific studies and popular texts suggests that the discursive rules for speaking about the new medium were highly conventionalized.[12]

My book also draws upon the corporate records of the National Broadcasting Company and numerous industry trade journals that discussed television programming, advertising, and business strategies. These sources demonstrate how industry executives imagined their first audiences and how they fashioned television to suit that image. When read in conjunction with popular sources, they also reveal the limits of the industry's endeavor to win the consent of television viewers. In fact, popular media often spoke critically of the industry's attempt to glue viewers to the tube, and they suggested ways for people to resist this new temptation.

This book thus takes issue with the widespread assumption that television's rise as a cultural form was brought about solely by big business and its promotional campaign. While it is true that television was in the hands of large corporations, it would be a logical leap to assume that the sales effort determined the public's fascination with television. Instead, this fascination was rooted in modern American culture and its long-standing obsession with communication technologies. In these terms, the sales effort is no longer the fundamental cause—"the determination in the last instance." Rather, it is one among several factors leading to television's success in the early period.

This is especially important to keep in mind when considering consumer magazines and their advertisements. A popular assumption in advertising history and theory is that advertisements are the voice of big industry, a voice that instills consumer fantasies into the minds of the masses.[13] But advertising is not simply one voice; rather it is necessarily composed of multiple voices. Advertising adopts the voice of an imaginary consumer—it must speak from his or her point of view—even if that point of view is at odds with the immediate goals of the sales effort. In this respect, television advertisers did not simply promote ideas and values in the sense of an overwhelming "product propaganda." Rather, they followed certain *discursive rules* found in a media form that was popular with women since the nineteenth century. Advertisers often adjusted their sales messages to fit the concerns voiced in women's magazines, and they also used conventions of language and representation that were typical of the magazines as a whole.

The relationship between sales and editorial departments in the 1950s is particularly complex since some of the most popular consumer magazines were in a state of demise. While specialty periodicals such as the women's home magazines remained strong, the general weeklies found themselves competing with television for advertising revenue, and largely because of this some were eventually forced to go out of business.[14] Importantly, however, the magazines' ambivalent response to television was not simply caused by media competition. Instead, many of the magazines had symbiotic relationships with the television industry. Advertisements for television sets and promotional ads for programs brought new sources of revenue to the print media, and numerous magazines entered into cross-promotional campaigns with the television industry. Moreover, personal letters in the NBC Records show

7

that network executives encouraged cross-media ties by giving (or else selling at reduced prices) television sets to magazine editors.[15] Thus, the institutional relationship between television and the print media was often characterized by mutual relations of support rather than simple competition. For this reason, we cannot account for the print media's response to television solely through economic models of industrial competition. Instead, the ambivalence can be better understood as being symptomatic of wider cultural conventions for speaking about new communication technologies.

More than producing a singular discourse on television, popular magazines provided a site for a variety of discourses that originated in a number of social institutions. Television was debated throughout numerous fields of knowledge, including architecture, interior design, pedagogy, medicine, social science, psychoanalysis, and others. By looking at the popular magazines as discursive sites, we can better account for the diverse number and kinds of meanings attached to television during the period of its installation. This emphasis on the media as sites for the production of meaning helps to explain how mass media provide contradictory ideas and values. Since media absorb the discourses of different social institutions, they present a variety of positions and perspectives that are at times in direct opposition to one another. (In the home magazines, for example, notions drawn from psychoanalysis might stress the importance of talking to the problem child, while those based on jurisprudence might recommend punitive discipline). We can thus explore popular media as a ground for cultural debate, which is a very different notion from mass media as propaganda or even as "consciousness industries." While certain ideas might have been emphasized more often than others (I refer to the notion of dominant ideology), we should not forget that culture is a process that entails power struggles and negotiations among various social ideals. Thus, although the debates do not reflect a "happy pluralism," they do suggest that cultural changes take place within a framework of unstable power hierarchies in which different social forces must constantly reinvent their authority through the mechanisms of control at their disposal. Discourse and representation is one such mechanism of control.

Magazines, television programs, and advertisements give us a clue into an imaginary popular culture—that is, they tell us what various media institutions assumed about the public's concerns and desires. However, as Roland Marchand has demonstrated in the case of advertising, the mass media are distanced from the people to whom they speak, and their assumptions about the public can be quite off-base—even with the aid of market research.[16] Again, we should remember that these popular representations of television do not directly reflect the public's response to the new medium. Instead, they begin to reveal a general set of discursive rules that were formed for thinking about television in its early period.

This book begins by placing television's arrival in the home into a broader historical context of domestic recreation. Chapter 1, "Domestic Ideals and Family Amusements: From the Victorians to the Broadcast Age," traces domestic ideals for family recreation from the nineteenth century to the years following World War II. It explores how gender and generational differences have historically been related to middle-class ideals of family leisure and the innovation of domestic technologies, particularly entertainment machines such as the radio. Taking this up to the 1950s, chapter 1 summarizes key aspects of television's invention and innovation.

The remaining chapters are organized according to central themes in popular discourses on television. Chapter 2, "Television in the Family Circle," examines how the new medium was represented as both a unifying and divisive force in the home. While television was greeted as a vehicle for family togetherness, popular media also warned the public about its excessively unfamiliar qualities, presenting the new machine as a kind of modern Frankenstein that threatened to turn against its creator and disrupt traditional patterns of family life. Television, in these representations, came to threaten the very foundations of domesticity upon which American broadcasting was built. In particular, the new medium was shown to disrupt women's lives and the gender-based ideals of domestic labor. Chapter 3, "Women's Work," investigates television's place in the household economy, focusing on how the broadcasting industry attempted to woo housewives away from their chores with daytime programming. This chapter also considers how home magazines advised women how to respond to these attempts. Indeed, rather than simply promoting television as a pleasant diversion from household drudgery, the magazines cautioned women about its disruptive effect on the efficient management of the home.

The last two chapters concentrate on television's relation to popular conceptions about the changing nature of social space in postwar America. A new "window on the world," television was expected to bind public and private spheres, making trips into the outside world an antiquated and even redundant exercise. As cultural theorist Raymond Williams has argued, the dream of bringing the outside world into the home— what he terms "mobile privatization"—has been a long-standing fantasy surrounding electrical communications. Chapter 4, "The Home Theater," focuses on how this dream materialized in postwar home magazines, advertisements, and network promotional strategies, which suggested television would merge public amusements with the private sphere of the home. Popular media instructed people on ways to create a total theatrical environment in their living rooms, promoting the new family theaters as a substitute for traditional forms of community life and social relations. However, the media also expressed dismay with the new simulated community and instructed people on ways to resist television's homogenization of cultural experiences. Following this, Chapter 5, "The People In the Theater Next Door," explores how situation comedies fulfilled expectations about television's ability to transport viewers into the social world. I consider the way the industry addressed family audiences by offering them the chance to enter into a new electronic neighborhood where happy families invited viewers into their homes on a weekly basis. Against the popular truism that television presents a mirror reflection of family life, I argue that early sitcoms typically depicted the family as a theater troupe rather than as a "real" family. These situation comedies often reflected back on their own theatricality, self-consciously suggesting that family life itself was nothing but a middle-class social convention in which people acted out certain roles for each other. Situation comedies served in part to express anxieties about middle-class family life even as they worked to reinforce that lifestyle by their obsessive representation of it.

Together, the chapters are designed to reconstruct the dialogue between popular expectations for television and television's growth as a national medium. Above all, I show how a mass medium develops in relation to its social context and how subjective responses to it can help create a milieu of ideas that help to shape its cultural form. Given the fact that there is so little work done on the social and cultural history of television, the following discussion is meant to open up questions about the period of installation as much as it is intended to provide answers.

One

Domestic Ideals and Family Amusements: From the Victorians to the Broadcast Age

By the early decades of the twentieth century, the industrial revolution had found its way into the parlors of the American home. New machines, designed for domestic amusements, were marketed and sold to increasing numbers of middle-class families. Mechanized entertainment such as the phonograph and radio became part of a set of cultural ideals for domesticity, while also contributing to changes in the way family members spent their time at home.

Television's installation in the American home is framed by the history of family recreation. Broadcast historians have typically ignored the historical context of family life, favoring instead a model of invention that relies on economic and political causes to explain the arrival of the new medium. But such histories divorce television from its primary sphere of reception—the home—and thus cannot account for the social factors that helped to shape television's cultural form.

The rise of a distinctly bourgeois aesthetic of family life in Victorian America established a set of domestic ideals that had important implications for the ways in which leisure activities would be conceptualized in years to come. In particular, television's inclusion in the home was subject to preexisting models of gender and generational hierarchies among family members—hierarchies that had been operative since the Victorian period. Distinctions between man and woman, child and adult, organized the spatial environment of the home, and they also worked to justify the ideological divisions between public and private spheres. By the turn of the century, these domestic ideals were modified and sometimes even radically altered to suit the needs of an increasingly modern suburban consumer culture, but they often reemerged in representations of domestic technologies, and they worked to structure domestic spaces in ways that had important implications for television's arrival in the home.

This chapter shows how ideals of family life and domestic recreation supplied a framework of ideas and expectations about how television could best be incorporated into the home. It traces the development of domestic ideology in the Victorian era; the changes that took place within that ideology with the rise of suburbia and consumer-family lifestyles; and the corresponding innovation of domestic amusement machines. Finally, it details how the broadcast industry responded to the history of family ideals when introducing radio and television to the public.

The Cult of Domesticity and Ideals of Family Recreation

In the nineteenth century, the American family underwent a number of transformations. As the agrarian society of the 1700s gave way to a new industrial order, patterns of everyday life were significantly altered. While the eighteenth-century family was bound together primarily as an economic unit, working together on a farm, in the nineteenth century production shifted to the world outside the home, to an urban landscape of factories and office jobs. This shift had an important impact on the way family life was conceived and organized. No longer tied together by economic survival per se, the family took on a more overtly ideological function in relation to the marketplace outside the home. Beginning around 1820, America witnessed the development of a middle-class ideal that was predicated upon the division of public and private spheres. Middle-class Victorians represented the family as a site of comfort and rejuvenation while the public sphere contained the hardships of the workaday world. During the early Victorian period (about 1820 to 1860), architects, plan book writers, ministers, educators, physicians, and novelists advised on a new design for living based on the sharp separation of inside and outside worlds.

In this binary system, the home was organized as the antithesis of the urban centers, which were thought to be threatening and sinful. By the 1830s, American thinkers began to worry about the unpleasant effects of the factory system, effects that had already taken hold in Victorian England. Would the urban crime, poverty, pollution, and labor unrest of the English city be recreated on American soil? If so, in what way could the nation hope to maintain the pastoral ideals of the agrarian past? For many, the answer to this problem came in the form of a new utopian social space located on the periphery of the city, at once rural and urban, a space that was prototypically suburban.[1] As Margaret Marsh has argued, the ideal of a suburban retreat was mainly (although not exclusively) a male objective based on the Jeffersonian belief in agrarian landownership. In a world of industrial urbanization, the middle-class man could uphold the republic's agrarian values through owning a private home outside the city.[2]

The homes themselves were vernacular in style, recalling a preindustrial America. In his widely read book of 1850, *The Architecture of Country Houses,* Andrew Jackson Downing, the most famous of the plan book writers, extolled the virtues of the rural cottage.[3] Predicated upon the notion of private havens, each house stood as an entity unto itself, usually set in a pastoral landscape that suggested repose and moral sanctity. Often decorated with Gothic adornments, the cottages took on a godly mission. Ministers such as Henry Ward Beecher and Horace Bushnell wanted to make Americans aware of the influence of the domestic setting, and they preached about the family's role in building the American character.[4] In this way, the early nineteenth-century dwelling was intimately linked to rejuvenation of a *religious* order. Here, the tired worker could retreat to a world of higher spirituality and heavenly splendor. The home served a divine purpose in raising the consciousness of its residents above the everyday world of physical toil in the city.

The evangelical ethic also supported the division of gender and the separation of spheres. The "Cult of True Womanhood" ensured that middle-class women remained at home while the man of the house traversed the two spheres of work and family on a daily basis. According to codes of middle-class domesticity, women had a divine purpose in the home; they served as moral guardians who were ordained by God to instill the family with Christian values. Popular manuals and early magazines such as *Godey's Lady's Book* suggested that women be God-fearing, innocent, obedient to their husbands, and committed to a life based on their activities at home.[5] The woman's place within the home was part of an overall division of social roles at the core of domestic ideology. While the Victorian family was supposed to be tied together by love and affection, there was also a clear hierarchy of dominion and subordination. The family was organized as a microcosm of the American Republic, with power dynamics based on principles of governance.

Most explicit in this regard was Catharine Beecher's influential home manual of 1841, *A Treatise on Domestic Economy.* In this book, Beecher suggested that women's ability to make the family adhere to Christian doctrine would serve as an example for American society. She wrote, "The principles of democracy . . . are identical with the principles of Christianity." In this regard, Beecher thought that the tenets of True Womanhood could provide a model for civic life, and she suggested that traits like feminine submissiveness would serve a higher cause. "It is needful," she claimed, "that certain relations be sustained, that involve the duties of subordination. There must be a magistrate and the subject. . . . There must be relations of husband and wife, parent and child. . . . The superior in certain particulars is to direct, and the inferior is to yield obedience."[6] For Beecher, this hierarchy of social life was not at odds with democratic notions of equality and free will. As she suggested, in the case of parents and children, relations of subordination were "decided by the Creator," while in the case of husband and wife, "No woman is forced to obey her husband but the one she *chooses* for herself; nor is she obliged to take a husband, if she prefers to remain single" (emphasis added).[7] As numerous feminist historians have argued, Beecher's book and the more general domestic ideology of the time were intended to elevate women by making them the moral authority in the home.[8] The ideology of domesticity, in this regard, had a different meaning and function for women than did the more general family ideal supported by men like Downing. While the family ideal presented domestic life as a respite for the weary man, the domestic ideology provided women with a way to glean power in a world that systematically marginalized their input in civic matters. At home, the woman could invert the patriarchal rules of governance, staking claim to the family as her privileged domain. As Beecher wrote, "In matters of education of children, in the selection and support of a clergyman, in all benevolent enterprises, and in all questions relating to morals or manners, they [women] have superior influence."[9] Moreover, domestic ideology had an emancipatory function in a class-based social system: "Universally, in this Country, through every class of society, precedence is given to woman, in all the comforts, conveniences, and courtesies of life."[10] The "True Woman" of any class could thus expect privileged treatment in the public sphere.

Given the associations between domesticity, the tenets of Christian doctrine, and the preservation of the Republic, it is not surprising that Victorian ideals of family amusement were organized around these values. According to Foster Rhea Dulles, whose history of recreation remains the most comprehensive, the early 1800s witnessed a "renewed emphasis upon the importance of work," harking back to a puritanical "moral sanction for the disapproval of recreation." Even while commercial amusements such as variety houses, minstrel shows, legitimate theaters, dime museums, circuses, and dance halls became increasingly popular over the course of the century, Victorian "experts" warned against overindulgence, sanctioning forms of play that would instill moral and physical traits beneficial for the increased productivity of the nation.[11] Such warnings were intended especially for women and children; the growing sphere of cheap commercial pastimes was, until the later decades of the century, a specifically male domain into which only "lowly" and "fallen" women would venture.[12] While Dulles and other historians of recreation have primarily concentrated on public amusements, similar puritanical attitudes underscored Victorian views of family leisure. In *A Treatise on Domestic Economy*, Catharine Beecher found the subject important enough to include a chapter entitled "Domestic Amusements," but her text warned readers to remember that the purpose of leisure activities was to "prepare the mind and body for the proper discharge of duty," and that anything which interfered with that "must be sinful." In particular, the family had to avoid stimulation, especially when excitement was connected to temptations of a "pernicious" nature.[13] While gathering flowers and shells from the world of nature was healthful, dancing would lead not only to spiritual decline but also to physical ailments such as bad digestion. While reading narrative prose might be morally uplifting (the Scriptures were an early example), it was imperative to regulate the kinds of novels that children read. While piano playing and telling jokes (in moderation) promoted happiness at home, horseriding, cardplaying, and going to the theater were not permissible because they might result in evil deeds.

At the heart of this advice was a clear distinction between domestic and public amusements. Dancing, for example, was an activity that would have been associated with dance halls and brothels (places where only men and fallen women could go), while the novel often spoke too graphically of the sinful activities in the outside world. Beecher herself made this clear when she advised that "even if parents, who train their children to dance, can keep them from public balls (which is seldom the case), dancing in private parlors is subject to nearly all the same mischievous influences."[14] Thus, rather than incorporating the bawdy "masculine" amusements of the urban streets, the home was supposed to encourage genteel, "feminine" forms of play. Among the most important activities in the Christian home was piano playing, which was associated with the spiritual talents of the True Woman who played hymns in the family parlor. More generally, the sanctions against sinful, public forms of recreation particularly constrained women's sphere of amusements to the polite and spiritual activities of Bible reading and arts and crafts in the home.[15]

By midcentury, plan book writers were suggesting similar ideals for more elaborate middle-class dwellings based on styles of Italianate, Gothic, and Georgian design. Plan book writers were deeply concerned that the house remain a self-contained entity for a cohesive family unit, but they also stressed the social division of spaces within it. The back parlor and dining room allowed for family gatherings; however, recreation was divided according to highly formalized spatial laws. Women might read books or do needlework in their upstairs bedrooms, while men might read in their own libraries located near the back of the house, away from the commotion of everyday affairs. While children often shared space with women, they were also given special rooms, and youngsters of different sexes would ideally have separate bedrooms. Even in homes that did not include rooms devoted to separate family members, portions of rooms were allocated to specific individuals (e.g., the window seat provided a reading area for the mother).[16] Not only family activities, but social occasions were also carefully laid out according to spatial hierarchies. Here, the relationship between public and private areas took on special importance. While family life was relegated to the back parlor, guests were entertained in the more formally decorated front parlor and greeted in large hallways that allowed for elaborate visitation rituals.[17] These formal distinctions between rooms allowed Victorians to experience private, familial, and social life within conventionalized settings so that residents and guests would often know what kind of social situation to expect by the household space they occupied at any particular moment. In this way domestic space and recreational pursuits within the home were sharply differentiated from the chaotic urban environment where industrialization presented both spatial and social confusion.

In 1869, when Catharine Beecher published her revised home manual, *The American Woman's Home,* she still adhered to the principles of domestic recreation suggested in the earlier edition. The book, which she wrote with her sister, Harriet Beecher Stowe, depicted piano playing and Bible reading as particularly appropriate forms of domestic amusement. Their floor plan included a space for the piano, displaying that instrument as a permanent fixture in the family home, while the book's frontispiece depicted a grandfather reading a book (most likely the Bible) to his family. The religious metaphor was further suggested as a kerosene lamp, hung over the grandfather's head, illuminated him with rays of light.[18] However, even if *The American Woman's Home* took a Christian view of family leisure which adhered to that of the early Victorian period, it appeared at a moment of transition. Over the next three decades, domestic ideology would be revised, and ideals of recreation would also be transformed. While the change was never complete (indeed, some Victorian concepts of proper amusements still inform contemporary ideals), the home began to reflect the burgeoning consumer culture of the outside world.

Changing ideals of family leisure were integral to the middle-class suburbs that flourished after the Civil War. By the 1880s, cities such as Chicago, Los Angeles, and Boston experienced population booms that were offset by the growth of surrounding communities. Improvements in transportation helped provide easy access to the cities so that by the 1890s people could commute to work on electric trollies, street cars, and elevated railroads. In addition to these economic, demographic, and technological changes, there was an increased ideological emphasis upon the suburbs as an ideal cultural and social space for the middle-class family.

According to Margaret Marsh, it was in the later years of the nineteenth century that domestic ideology and the suburban ideal began to merge most fully. In the earlier decades of the 1800s, she argues, the suburbs were mainly supported by men such as Downing, whose main interest lay in the Jeffersonian concept of agrarian landownership. However, the domestic ideology promoted by female reformers and novelists tended to emphasize the urban milieu as the woman's preferred social setting. The city gave middle-class women access to shops, servants, better education for their children, and feminine social networks. Thus, even while domesticity was idealized in women's culture, it was not typically associated with suburbanization (even Catharine Beecher, who glorified the rural cottage, was not completely anti-urban). While female reformers feared the turmoil of city life, they advised that the proper home environment could shelter the family from vice and corruption even in an urban locale. By the later years of the nineteenth century, when cities became increasingly populated by European immigrants and Black Southerners and were also witnessing the growth of radical-socialist movements and women's rights advocates, it no longer seemed possible to raise a "proper" family in the urban environment. Meanwhile, the new railroad suburbs, with their increasing emphasis on community life and their access to urban centers, provided middle-class women with an alternative. By the turn of the century, then, ethnocentrism, resistance to political activism, and the increasingly urban nature of the suburbs themselves contributed to the ideological merger between suburbia and domestic bliss.[19]

As the suburbs became a privileged place of family life, the religious tenets of domesticity were increasingly accompanied, and at times replaced, by a consumer mentality. The suburban house of the late Victorian period took on an elaborate display function as domestic havens were infused with an increased emphasis on visual pleasures and bodily comforts that luxury goods promised to provide. Ornate finery (much of which was mass produced) was a sign of wealth and good taste at afternoon tea parties and other social gatherings. Most of the houses were built around a central fireplace that was usually lavishly decorated with carved mantels upon which sculptures and other ornate bric-à-brac were placed. Here family members might convene for a night of relaxation, gazing at the burning logs and artfully arranged objects in the room.[20] Other domestic amusements were meant to exhibit the residents' talents. Mothers and daughters were not only expected to play the piano, they also had to cultivate artisan skills such as doily-making and decorative embroidery, which were then displayed in the home. Fathers would ideally spend time collecting paintings and books, while children were given music and painting lessons so that they too could fill their leisure hours with artistic endeavors. Although many of these activities were ostensibly productive, they involved consumer purchases or at least an appreciation for worldly goods.

Suburban families were also given a wide array of technological improvements that promised physical comforts. Plumbing implements, including modern flush toilets and porcelain sinks, became standard fixtures by the turn of the century; basement furnaces or individual room stoves regulated domestic temperatures; and electric lighting offered new solutions to illumination (although the widespread diffusion of electricity took place over the second two decades of the twentieth century). All of these technological comforts were promoted in the home magazines that began to proliferate in the 1880s after Congress lowered the postage rates for periodicals. *Ladies' Home Journal* (1883), *Good Housekeeping* (1885), and *House Beautiful* (1896) spoke of the latest fashions in interior decor and extolled the new machines that promised the comfortable life of a modern era.

Modernity, Technology and the Comfortable Life

By the 1890s, a new conception of the home had begun to emerge, one that had important implications for ideals of family recreation. While the early Victorians believed that the home was a place of moral and spiritual rejuvenation, the late Victorians and Progressives felt the home should incorporate secular pleasures and physical comforts.

The ideological shift from the Victorian to the Progressive notion of domestic leisure was by no means a complete or smooth transition. The new model of domestic life was itself predicated upon the social, political, and economic tensions of Victorian America. The Panic of 1873 showed the public that an economy based on industrialization was vulnerable to breakdowns, a lesson that was learned again during the Depression of 1893–97. A nationwide railroad strike in 1876 was followed by another in 1885. Chicago's 1886 Haymarket riot and the 1894 strike at George Pullman's factory town in Illinois were vivid proof of the public's discontent with industrial working conditions. By the turn of the century, the social and political climate of the industrial world had caused a crisis in the basic tenets of Victorian ideology.

In addition to economic and labor problems, there was skepticism about domestic ideology itself. While the doctrine of two spheres called for a sharp division of public and private space, in reality the distinctions between these spheres were often blurred. Working-class women took piecework into their homes so that the domestic haven for them became a private sweatshop. In addition, tenement housing and severe poverty in ethnic urban areas served as constant reminders of the failures of bourgeois ideals. In fact, domestic ideology was plagued with so many internal contradictions that even middle-class families could not hope to live by its principles. For women, Victorian femininity was an impossible position, calling for a schizophrenic malleability that no woman could hope to maintain—at least not without considerable difficulty. While the True Woman was supposed to be innocent and pure, she was also asked to be a sexual partner and mother.[21] Given the contradictions entailed in this role, it is not surprising that a large number of middle-class women expressed their frustrations through a newly defined disease, hysteria. In many ways, as feminist historians and critics have suggested, women used their loud and visually aberrant hysterical symptoms as a form of rebellion against domestic ideology and the submissive femininity it required. Even psychiatrists began to see domestic life as the cause of the new disease. In the early 1890s, when Sigmund Freud and Josef Breuer wrote *Studies On Hysteria,* they blamed the illness on daydreams that counteracted the boredom of repetitive household routines like knitting and needlework.[22]

Given the considerable tensions in the increasingly modern home, it is not surprising that, by the 1890s, key aspects of domestic ideology were revised and, in particular, the sharp differentiation between public and private spheres became less distinct. The growth of factories, business firms, and department stores helped to create new kinds of jobs for single and working-class married women as clerical workers, saleswomen, and other forms of nondomestic labor. Although middle-class married women did not typically take jobs outside the home, they too had an increasing presence in the public sphere. The growing popularity of women's rights helped encourage participation in clubs, church work, and other female-oriented community pastimes. At the same time, the gender distinctions entailed by ideals of recreation were beginning to change.

A new emphasis on outdoor family recreation is a case in point. Advertisements for suburban developments displayed ornate homes with expansive front lawns where families played croquet, badminton, and other outdoor sports.[23] Since standards of femininity had traditionally governed against exercise for women and had placed women's amusements within the confines of the home, such lawn games were a significant change from the past.[24] As women took on traditionally male forms of pleasure, leisure activities tended to become more centered around couples. Men's clubs temporarily dwindled while games such as golf were promoted as pursuits for married couples rather than male business associates.[25]

The emphasis on consumer lifestyles in the Victorian suburbs also created a blurring of traditional gender divisions entailed by the doctrine of two spheres. It was fashionable for women to spend a day in the city at theaters, museums, or the new department stores that had begun to flourish in the 1880s. The stores, with their palatial decor, offered women a new kind of spiritual experience among an array of luxury goods. Moreover, they connected shopping with other feminine needs and interests, providing such enticements as child-care services, public lectures, amateur shows, restaurants, beauty salons, and reading lounges, thus offering consumers the chance to be part of a female social network in a public place where women—typically of the working class—were employed.[26] In addition to their presence in department stores, women were becoming consumers of commercial amusements as showmen began to entice them into their traditionally male spaces, hoping to expand business by advertising their entertainment as suitable for a family audience. As early as the mid-1800s, P. T. Barnum and Moses Kimball welcomed women into dime theaters and, by the 1860s, legitimate theaters refined their clientele and instituted codes of respectability so that middle-class families would not have to mingle with the likes of prostitutes and drunkards. Variety theaters, with their traditionally racy and rowdy entertainments, also evolved into polite vaudeville circuits geared to a middle-class family audience.[27] Even though, as social historian Kathy Peiss argues, "entering certain commercial leisure spaces continued to trouble many women in the late nineteenth century," the efforts of commercial showmen did meet with success. By the turn of the century, as Peiss also claims, commercial amusements had become much more "heterosocial," incorporating women into public spaces by dividing those spaces along class and gender lines. For example, amusement parks such as New York's Coney Island and Chicago's Riverview Park contained spatial barriers that divided wholesome family amusements from the more rowdy and sexually illicit spaces of the sideshows and dance halls.[28] In the 1910s, motion picture exhibitors used similar appeals to female audiences. By building theaters near downtown shopping districts, they linked women's more general role as family shopper to their participation in the world of commercial amusements, and, like the department stores before them, they offered such conveniences as child-care services and plush lounges where mothers could relax. Women thus played a critical role in the new consumer economy; their presence at the marketplace came to have just as much importance as their work at home.

While middle-class women were increasingly present in the public sphere, men were becoming more involved in family life. What Marsh has called the new "masculine domesticity" made it more acceptable for men to be "chums" with their families and to participate in household functions—including housework, childrearing, interior decorating, and family amusements. Although fathers had previously been involved in matters of family governance, by the turn of the century, advice literature for men recommended that they have more compassionate marriages by taking increased responsibility for the home and forming closer ties with their children.[29]

The compassionate household was further encouraged by new consumer technologies and mass-production techniques. In the early 1900s, building expenses entailed by plumbing fixtures and electrical wiring were offset by a reduction in domestic square footage. In the smaller homes, it was difficult to maintain the formal distinctions between rooms as well as the social hierarchies of space that Victorians had cultivated. Entrance halls were diminished to small vestibules or else entirely eliminated, thus allowing for more informal relations with visitors. Front parlors were often removed, and in their place one central living room emerged as a place where family and friends could convene under less formal circumstances.[30] Human relationships in the home still retained the mix of patriarchy and democracy suggested by Beecher in her *Treatise,* but now social contact between family members was supposed to be more casual. Elaborate dinners gave way to lighter and less time-consuming meals. In addition, the fixtures of the home became less ornate, more geared toward physical comfort and well-being. Simple easy-to-clean surfaces were advocated by physicians, housing reformers, and domestic scientists, who warned that Victorian ornamentation would gather dust and lead to unhealthy conditions. More generally, the domestic scientists promoted women's freedom from household drudgery, devising scientific methods by which to reduce the labor involved in daily chores. Most famous in this regard was Lillian Gilbreth, who used time-motion principles of factory production to calculate the movements and energy required to perform simple tasks like boiling eggs. Women like Gilbreth embraced the labor-reducing technologies offered by big business, extolling such items as washing machines and convenience foods for their potential liberation of the housewife. The new liberal household was thus structured on the quite paradoxical nature of freedom in twentieth-century life: consumer products promised people the everyday experience of liberation in return for their increasing dependence on corporate production.

Thus, while the concept of domesticity formed in the Progressive era was in many ways a continuation of the Victorian model, significant changes had taken place. Although social hierarchies remained, relationships among family members had become more informal, and, at least in advice literature, closeness between members was more strongly emphasized. Similarly, while domestic ideology was still predicated on the division of private and public worlds, the separation between the two spheres was less distinct. New forms of recreation that included men, women, and children both reflected and helped promote the increased importance of the compassionate family, and they also were symptomatic of the merging of domestic life with the public world of commercial amusements. In the modern industrial world, the home was figured as a well-run machine rather than a shrine for spiritual welfare. In addition, the homemaker was no longer seen primarily as a moral guardian; rather, she became a lab assistant and efficiency expert who knew how to manage modern technology. Her expertise in this regard ensured that the physical labor entailed by housekeeping could be done with a modicum of effort. The more efficient she became, the more likely she would find liberation from a life of household drudgery.

The new domestic ideal rewarded the technologically liberated housewife with the practical promise of pleasure and recreation. The woman, freed from her tasks, would now have time for club meetings, tennis, golf, and other leisure-time pursuits in the public sphere. By the 1920s, industrialists had adopted the rhetoric of domestic scientists, using it for their own merchandizing purposes. In her 1929 book, *Selling Mrs. Consumer,* Christine Frederick offered businessmen a practical guide for selling products to the modern housewife who, she argued, was responsible for 80 percent of the family purchases. Considering the top ten advertising appeals for the sale of household equipment, Frederick suggested that "Mrs. Consumer buys" appliances in order "to gain leisure for chosen activities and pursuits."[31] Meanwhile, advertisers circulated images that encouraged women to believe that machines gave them leisure time. Sleek female figures were shown holding tennis rackets while standing next to washing machines and refrigerators.[32] Even if, as Ruth Schwartz Cowan argues, this message was more myth than reality, the imagery of leisure-class lifestyles was still seductive, and the ideals it set forth helped shape modern notions of the comfortable life.[33]

Architectural trends reinforced the changing domestic ideals. By 1910, the bungalow cottage had become the ideal house. Modeled on the "California lifestyle," it still promised refuge from the industrial city, but it also placed an exaggerated emphasis on the resident's relationship to the outside world. The bungalow was intended to provide an Arcadian view of scenic landscapes, and the outdoor setting was just as important as the home itself. The recreational aspect of this nature aesthetic was nowhere better stated than in the *Sears, Roebuck Catalog,* which displayed cottages in lakeside and treelined landscapes. Some models even bore the names of scenic vacation areas like "The Alps" and "The Yellowstone."[34] What is most paradoxical about this nature ideal is that it was predicated upon new technologies. The bungalows (like the late Victorian homes before them) were based on factory methods of construction, and some were even sold in ready-to-assemble kits. Moreover, they incorporated a host of consumer technologies, including such new amusement machines as phonographs, player pianos, telephones, and family cars—all of which were increasingly marketed to middle-class families during the early decades of the twentieth century.

This new influx of household machines thus contributed to a redefinition of family leisure from the Victorian concept of spiritual uplift that prepared the individual for everyday duties to the more modern notion of leisure as a set of secular and liberating activities that served as a distinct counterpart for work. In the Progressive household, machines were the ideal vehicle through which to maintain the separation between leisure and work because they symbolically freed people from the toil involved in producing their own entertainment. Still, the domestic amusement machines had troubling side effects. The prospect of having machines govern family relations was met by ambivalent responses as long-held agrarian ideals returned with a vengeance to haunt the modern, mechanized world. Progressives worried about the dehumanizing effects of machines, and although middle-class culture celebrated their pleasurable aspects, it also expressed anxieties about their less desirable elements.

When viewed in this framework, it appears that the pastoral ideal expressed by bungalow cottages and other Progressive fashions provided a powerful antidote to the new world of mechanization. As T. J. Jackson Lears claims, the return to nature was one in a series of reactions to the mounting confusions of the secular industrial society. As such, it was intended to serve a therapeutic function, to soothe the painful ambiguities of modern life.[35] However, it wasn't just that the nature ideal provided an escape from the effects of new technology. Instead, the new technology was often depicted in ways that recalled the traditional values of a simpler age. The new machines of leisure were incorporated into the imagery of a perfect past, which was less a concrete historical period than a confused pastiche of ideal moments. At times, the discourse evoked a preindustrial America of pastoral beauty and natural harmony; at other times it recalled the early Victorian age when family values were rooted firmly in Christian doctrine.

The connection between household machines and the pastoral ideal was part of a larger history of American discourse on technology. As Leo Marx demonstrates, by the 1830s politicians, novelists, and artists were trying to ease cultural tensions about industrialization by forging links between nature and machines. George Inness's painting, "The Lacka-wanna Valley," which was commissioned by the Lackawanna Railroad Company in 1854, is a good example. The canvass displays a train nestled in the rolling hills of the countryside, and, since the track is rendered in a circular pattern, the train appears fully harmonious with the natural setting. Here, as Marx claims, anxieties about technology are tempered by placing "the machine in the garden." [36]

Industrialists who manufactured household appliances began to see the advantage of designing and promoting machines in ways that evoked traditional values. Labor-saving appliances were made to appear as if they fit naturally into the rhythms of family life; rather than sug-gesting work, the products were marketed as family pastimes. One of the first to employ this strategy was the Singer Sewing Machine Com-pany, which offered its first "family" model in 1858. Singer set up dem-onstration agencies in which women machine operators showed the public that the average housewife was capable of using machines, and the machine itself was designed with ornate trim and advertised with scenes that suggested family values. One of the early advertisements em-ployed the same kind of familial imagery used in the frontispiece of *The American Woman's Home*, only here the family was gathered around the sewing machine. Following Singer's lead, other companies designed sewing machines in shapes suggestive of older values. One company gave modern technology a natural look by designing its product in the shape of a squirrel. Another recalled values of the Christian home by fashioning its machine in the form of a cherub. [37]

By the turn of the century, entertainment machines were following suit. When the Victor company marketed its domestic gramophone in 1900, it evoked familialism and naturalism by using various mascots for the machine. Among these were a monkey, a beautiful woman holding a rose, and the more successful fox terrier with ears perked up to the sound of his master's voice. [38] Some early gramophones evoked nature with floral patterns on their large megaphone speakers, a design strategy that not only associated the machine with the garden, but also made it more suitable for domestic life by transforming it into decorative fur-niture. Later, in 1929, one home manual even suggested that the pho-nograph might replace the piano as a center for family recreation. Mary Hinman Abel noted: "In very many homes supported on an income of no more than $2,500 the very first outlay beyond necessities is for a piano. And in some miraculous manner they learn to play it, at least for dance music and to accompany singing. A phonograph is second choice, or it may come first in those families whose members do not easily learn to play an instrument, and they can both sing and dance to its accompaniment."[39] In this way, entertainment technology was given traditional family functions.

Although the new amusement machines were fashioned to reflect the order of an older lifestyle, they were also part and parcel of an increasing move toward modernity. When Robert and Helen Lynd visited Muncie, Indiana, in 1924, they found numerous "inventions re-making leisure." Their famous Middletown study showed that the leisure activities in this industrialized town had changed significantly since the 1890s. Many families believed new mechanical entertainments had significantly altered patterns of everyday life; the most striking among these inventions was the automobile. Although the Lynds observed that families believed the automobile gave them ways to spend time together, they also warned that "signs in the other direction are almost equally prominent."[40] Summarizing popular sentiment, they claimed, "When auto riding tends to replace the traditional call in the family parlor as a way of approach between the unmarried, 'the home is endangered,' and all-day Sunday motor trips are a 'threat against the church'; it is in the activities concerned with the home and religion that the automobile occasions the greatest emotional conflicts."[41] For similar reasons, the movies provided cause for alarm. Children and teenagers strayed from the home, and the Muncie families worried about the threat movies posed to family values (by this time, reform discourses on film's effects on children had been widely popularized in the press).[42] Kathy Peiss has shown similar sentiments prevalent among New York City's working-class and immigrant families at the turn of the century, when parents (particularly those of Italian descent) tried to oversee their daughters' activities in the public sphere of commercial entertainment. Moreover, as Peiss demonstrates, this often resulted in family conflicts as daughters found ways to circumvent parental control over leisure pursuits.[43]

The new commercial amusements, then, were thought to disrupt the social dynamics of family life because they eroded distinctions between public and private recreation. Now that leisure was increasingly organized outside the home, traditional modes of family authority broke down. The sexes mingled together in theaters, in the tunnel of love, and in other dark, erotically charged spaces, while young children fell prey to the baser instincts promoted in commercial amusement environments. A moral panic swept the country as middle-class reformers sought to police the new heterosexual commercial pastimes, pressing for codes of decency in nickelodeons and in the films themselves.[44]

For the families of Middletown, as well as others, this skepticism about modern, commercial leisure was tempered by hopes for salvation in the newest type of mechanized amusement—broadcasting. Radio offered what the Lynds called an "intermediate" form of leisure. Rather than taking family members outside the home, it brought the outdoor world inside. As the Lynds suggested, "More than one mother said that her family used to scatter in the evening—but now we all sit around and listen to radio." [45]

Broadcasting to the Home

Although wireless technology was invented in the late nineteenth century, it was not until the 1920s that broadcasting became a national pastime. During the first two decades of the twentieth century, large electrical and wireless companies fought bitter patent disputes in attempts to control the new technology. Radio, during these years, was used primarily by three constituencies: the navy, for purposes of national security and warfare; commercial companies such as United Fruit who used radio to communicate to overseas interests; and radio amateurs (typically men and boys) who envisioned the wireless as a popular form of communication. While the navy and corporate interests used wireless technology in a rational, technocratic fashion—as a system of point-to-point, ship-to-shore communication—amateurs were more romantic, seeing the wireless as a utopian form of communication that would bring the nation closer together in a truly democratic fashion. Their romantic views were accompanied by a spirit of experimentation. Not only did they perfect methods of point-to-point communication, they also devised techniques of mass communication, sending broadcast messages over the air. Despite their interest in radio broadcasting, however, their experiments were limited by their marginal financial and legal standing (in the Radio Act of 1912, Congress gave them only a small spectrum on which to operate), and the popularization of broadcasting did not occur until the 1920s when large corporations began to see it as a commercially viable endeavor.

Hoping to exploit their wireless technology in the boom economy after World War I, the large electrical companies (who now held major shares in the newly created Radio Corporation of America) began to view broadcasting as a viable marketing strategy. Following an early example at a Pittsburgh department store, Westinghouse vice president H. P. Davis concluded that his company would be able to create consumer demand for receivers by advertising sets and broadcasting programs each night so that the public would become accustomed to listening to the radio. In November of 1920, Westinghouse aired a program from its radio station, KDKA in Pittsburgh, the first broadcast in a series of attempts to introduce radio to the public. Over the course of the 1920s, other companies struggled to compete in the new radio market, and the basic characteristics of the broadcasting industry emerged—private ownership, government regulation, networks, commercial sponsorship, and private reception in the home.

The private reception of commercial broadcasting was particularly fostered by the housing boom in the early 1920s, which was facilitated by rising wages, automobile transport, and demographic shifts. Government policies such as the "Own Your Home" campaign, vigorously supported by Herbert Hoover, encouraged consumers to believe that the practical benefits of home ownership would be accompanied by the moral benefits of family life. Moreover, this period saw the formation of the Federal Housing Administration, a government agency that gave support to building starts and mortgages, particularly facilitating the growth of private family housing. Advice manuals and popular magazines also encouraged consumer-family lifestyles in private suburban homes. Experts enthused about close family relationships, presenting a watered-down version of male domesticity where fathers were still advised to partake in family activities, but were largely absolved of arduous household chores.[46] With theories of childhood increasingly stressing the importance of centering the home around the child's needs, men's inclusion in domestic life typically revolved around forms of family play—camping trips, baseball, word games, and so forth.[47] Meanwhile, as labor-reducing technologies became more popular, middle-class women devoted more time to their children, providing stimulating pastimes through which they could grow into moral and healthy adults.

In this context of modern domesticity, with its emphasis on consumer technologies and family leisure, radio was transformed from a technical gadget into a domestic machine that promised to embellish homes across the nation. Still, this transformation did not occur overnight. During the early 1920s, numerous manufacturers marketed radio receivers that were significantly lacking in family appeal. With their faulty reception and crude tuning mechanisms, early receivers required the practical know-how of the radio ham and, thus, were not easily integrated into domestic life. Not surprisingly, the radio craze was at this point mainly enjoyed by men and boys who delighted in the popular science and male camaraderie that had first sparked the interests of radio amateurs in the 1910s. The radio enthusiasts took pleasure in the complex tasks of tuning into distant stations and often built their own receivers out of cheap kits and ordinary household items. Moreover, they envisioned radio as an active sport (in fact, radio was likened to fishing) in which the participant gained a sense of mastery—and increased masculinity—by adjusting the dials and "reeling" in distant signals.[48] Meanwhile, this boy's toy was thought to clash with the more feminine-defined sphere of interior decor. With their exposed technical gizmos, the receivers looked out of place in the home, and since the vacuum set was operated by two batteries, it was often thought to cause problems for the homemaker who might find battery acid on her rug. This, in fact, became a popular theme in magazine stories that showed men devising masterful schemes for sneaking radio sets into the living room.[49]

In addition to disrupting interior decor, the early receivers were not designed for a family audience. They required the use of headphones with wires connecting the listener to a small receiver. Considering the marketing potential of this peculiar setup, one RCA executive even claimed that women thought headphones would spoil their coiffures.[50] More than this, the headphones made it difficult to establish a mode of reception suited to the ideals of family life. A 1922 advertisement in *Life* magazine suggests how hard it was for advertisers to represent the early set in terms of family activities. The ad shows a middle-class domestic setting in which family members (apparently a grandfather, a middle-aged couple, and their grown-up daughter) sit in chairs placed in four corners of the frame and positioned in such a way that no two people appear to acknowledge their mutual presence in the room. Instead, a small radio set, equipped with four separate headphones which run on wires to the ears of each listener, provides a rather odd form of social connection between people in the household. The radio wires dominate, and even seem to tie together, the central space of the composition so that the people in the four corners of the room appear to be caught in a web of electronic transmission and reception. But even if the family members are literally plugged into the same message, their facial expressions register patently different responses ranging from the daughter's ethereal bliss to the mother's look of frustration. Thus, it appears that the experience of listening to radio is one of isolation and fragmentation as family members convene not with each other, but with a distant source of inspiration. We might take this advertisement to represent a significant turn of events in the history of representations of domestic life. The individual in his or her own private home is here depicted as part of a *mass audience* more than as part of a family.[51]

Popular representations of radio also expressed apprehension about the nature of the broadcast message. In the early years, not only the appliance but also the sounds it emitted seemed strange and even disruptive. Not surprisingly in this regard, the 1922 advertisement in *Life* was accompanied by a caption that read, "What are those crazy wires saying?" More generally, the popular press focused on the uncanny and supernatural qualities of the wireless message and even suggested that radio signals were being sent to Earth from Mars.[52] Cartoons showed people frightened by the sounds transmitted by the set, believing so much in the reality of the broadcast that they cried for help when lions roared.

Over the course of the 1920s, radio became a more familiar object and entertainment form. By 1926, there were substantial alterations in receiver design.[53] Technical controls had been simplified down to two knobs (tuning and volume) so that practical know-how was no longer needed, and the cumbersome headphones were replaced with a central loudspeaker that permitted the entire family to enjoy radio together. Meanwhile, radio sets were placed in fine-grained wooden cabinets that blended with interior decor, and since they were now operated by electricity, the unwelcome batteries were eliminated. Now radio could be moved into the living room, where it not only provided family entertainment, but also contributed to the general decorative pleasures of the home. Radio, as both Susan Douglas and Catherine Covert have shown, was increasingly integrated into the woman's sphere of activity, and in the process the nature of radio listening became more and more conceptualized as a "feminine" pastime. Broadcasters further domesticated radio by offering "highbrow" forms such as opera, while advertisers promoted the medium as a means of cultural uplift, displaying elegantly dressed couples listening to radio sets from their stately domestic interiors.[54] Thus, rather than being seen as a boy's sport that offered romantic adventures, radio was now conceptualized as a genteel domestic amusement to be consumed passively by the entire family.

When the Lynds returned to Muncie, Indiana, in 1935 for their second Middletown study, they reported that the community now had its own radio station and that 46 percent of the city's homes had radio sets.[55] Muncie's experience reflected the national situation. While in 1922 only 0.2 percent of American homes had radio, by 1930 that figure had risen to 46 percent. In the next two decades, when smaller receivers became available at reduced prices, ownership continued to climb; by 1940, 81 percent of the nation's households had one or more sets, and by 1950 almost all households—about 95 percent—were equipped with radios.[56] Radio was an extremely popular medium during the Depression and war years, providing the public with entertainment and live on-the-scene news reports from overseas battles. Moreover, program formats had been conventionalized (variety show, news panel discussion, quiz show, soap opera, etc.), so that the public could expect a certain kind of experience when tuning into a specific program type. Radio listening thus became a more familiar and habitual activity, one that seemed more naturally integrated into the rhythms of everyday life.

CHAPTER ONE

Visions of Television

At the same time that radio made its way into the American home, researchers experimented with a new and more elaborate form of broadcasting. American television technology was developed mainly by the large corporations that already controlled radio, and, for this reason, the social agenda for television was largely defined by the corporate mind of the radio interests.[57] During the thirties, RCA and its subsidiary, NBC, imagined that television would be modeled on the radio broadcast system, with private exhibition and network distribution as the key to corporate success. While other parties (including the film industry, advertisers, retailers, the military, and amateurs) were attempting to get in on the ground floor and develop television in ways that suited their own interests, these groups did not have the research labs, manufacturing plants, and distribution networks necessary to compete with the radio interests. Moreover, as researchers perfected the technology, broadcasters gained a further advantage in the business by setting up experimental stations in New York and developing broadcast techniques and public interest in the medium. During the thirties and early forties, NBC, CBS, and DuMont transmitted their rather primitive programs to the homes of upper-class families who thought of their television sets as rich men's toys.[58]

Meanwhile, popular media (including movies, magazines, and newspapers) speculated on the new machine. While the press spoke about television in the 1930s and early 1940s, it exhibited little in the way of utopian optimism, seeing television instead as essentially bound to the commercial interests of the radio industry.[59] Still, industrial fairs and exhibits presented a more wondrous vision of the new medium. As early as 1933, the Hudson-Essex corporation displayed television to the public at the Century of Progress Exhibition, and by September 1938, NBC studios had devised a tour on which visitors were shown miniature television sets and were even given the chance to be televised themselves.[60] The most elaborate—and certainly most remembered—of all these early exhibits took place in 1939 at the New York World's Fair. Here, in the "Land of Tomorrow," visitors strolled into a building that was shaped like a radio tube and marvelled at the images transmitted on the new RCA television receivers. Even for those not lucky enough to convene at the fair, the RCA exhibit was widely publicized. Westinghouse, for example, produced a promotional film that starred the Middletons from Indiana (a fictional family with obvious reference to the Lynds's study), who, among other close encounters with the future, were given their first lesson in becoming television consumers. Under the benevolent gaze of an RCA demonstrator, little Bud Middleton addressed the camera. Not surprisingly, considering the industry's marketing goals, Bud's performance was addressed to a family audience composed of his father who motioned back at him. But even if RCA's exhibit was represented as a breathtaking excursion in family fun, Gallup polls at the time revealed that most Americans did not feel they would install a television set in their own homes.[61]

In that same year, when RCA attempted to get the first national advertising campaign for television off the ground, their efforts were similarly premature. Noting that the National Television System Committee (NTSC) had not yet agreed upon technical standards, the Federal Communications Commission required RCA to delay marketing television sets—a decision that met with disfavor in the popular press. In 1940, NBC kept a file on the press's attacks on FCC policy, a file that included about eighty newspaper and trade journal articles condemning the agency's decision. Typically, critics lashed out at the FCC's undemocratic rule of the airwaves. *The New York Times,* for example, reprimanded the regulators for their "tyrannous restraint" of the ether; the *Toledo Blade* called the incident "another shocking example of New Deal Bureaucracy"; the *Utica Press* called it "highly paternalistic"; and the *New York Sun* condemned the class-based nature of the FCC's decision, claiming that "if a man or woman of low income desires a television receiver in the present stage of development. . . . what power in heaven above or earth beneath or the waters under the earth has commissioned a bureaucrat in Washington to decree that he shall not exercise his own will and his own judgment in the premises?"[62] The populist distrust of government agencies that carried America through the Depression was thus extended to people's private and "natural" rights to consume products (for, as the reporter implies, why should the rich be the only ones to have television sets?). Even at this early stage, the ownership of a television set signified the leveling of class differences that television would come to represent in the postwar era.

Shortly after the controversy, in September 1940, the FCC granted limited commercial operation to broadcast stations. However, with national standards not yet agreed upon, the FCC discouraged the promotion of sets to the public. At this time, the major manufacturers (most aggressively RCA, but also DuMont and Zenith) competed to establish industry standards for receiver technology, a battle that ended in May 1941 when the FCC accepted the NTSC standards established by the Radio Manufacturers Association. However, the mass diffusion of television was delayed once more, this time by the onslaught of World War II.

After the war, in a booming consumer economy, television manufacturers began to promote their receivers. The market opened up in

1946 when DuMont and RCA offered their first black and white sets to the public. At this time, however, television was mainly exhibited in public establishments such as taverns, department stores, and even on buses.[63] But like other manufacturers of household goods, television companies set their sights on the average consumer, hoping to tap into and promote the demand for luxuries that had been denied to the public during wartime shortages. In the five years after World War II, consumer spending rose by 60 percent. By far the most significant rise was in household furnishings and consumer appliances, which increased by 240 percent.[64] In this land of plenty, television would become one of the most sought-after products.

Over the course of the 1950s, television was rapidly installed into American homes. National penetration rates for television rose from .02 percent in 1946 to 9 percent in 1950. After that, penetration rates inclined fairly steadily so that by 1955 about 65 percent of the nation's homes had television.[65] However, in the early fifties, television was not evenly distributed throughout the country. Since the Federal Communications Commission had placed a freeze on station allocation that lasted from 1948 to 1952, many areas in the nation had only one or else no television station. With the most stations to choose from, people in the Northeast installed television sets much more quickly than the rest of the country did. Thus, television was not actually a viable reality for most Americans until 1955, by which time it was installed in a majority of households in *all* areas of the country.[66]

As Americans installed their sets, manufacturers courted consumers with advertisements and promotional gimmicks. By the middle of 1948, television manufacturers were aggressively promoting the sale of receivers in women's magazines, general weeklies, newspapers, and on the airwaves. Television fairs and exhibitions in all parts of the country provided additional opportunities for American consumers to see the new medium.[67] Meanwhile, credit financing and reduced prices helped encourage sales. In mid-1948 the average retail price was $440.00, not including installation, but by 1951 this dropped to $308.00, and by 1954 prices fell to an average of $238.00.[68] Moreover, by 1954 about a third of all television dealers offered bargain prices, especially in large urban centers where discount houses were engaged in fierce competition.[69] Although reduced prices most certainly helped to popularize television, the purchase of a set still required a sizable portion of the family paycheck, and therefore involved a deep commitment to the new medium.

In large part, the public's commitment can be explained by the social circumstances of postwar America, which created a ripe environment for the rapid expansion of television as a cultural form. Television's installation into the American home took place at a time when domesticity was a central preoccupation of the burgeoning middle class. During and after the war, the marriage rate rose to record heights; of those who came of age, 96.4 percent of the female and 94.1 percent of the male populations married—and at younger ages than ever before.[70] The baby boom, which began during the war and lasted through 1964, reversed declining birthrates of previous decades, creating a revitalization of the nuclear family as a basic social construct. This resurgence of the family unit was met with a new model for living—the prefabricated suburban tract home, so affordable that young middle-class couples, and at times lower-middle-class, blue-collar workers, could purchase their piece of the American dream.[71]

The mass-produced suburbs were a response to the severe housing crisis caused by a decline in residential construction that began in the Depression and lasted through World War II. With the rising marriage and birth rates after the war, the demand for already scarce housing became even greater. The Housing Act of 1949, which gave contractors financial incentives to build single-family homes in suburban areas, was intended to alleviate the problem. Government mortgage loans made available through the Federal Housing Administration and the Serviceman's Readjustment Act of 1944 (the GI Bill) made it possible for young families to purchase Cape Cod and ranch-style homes in prefabricated suburban communities. These towns were composed largely of middle-class families, and since the FHA established "redlining" (or zoning) practices designed to maintain property values, black families were literally forced out of the new suburban dream.[72] Thus, in the postwar years, the white middle-class family, living in a suburban tract home, was a government-sanctioned ideal.

Popular media also participated in the cultural revitalization of domesticity, taking the white, middle-class suburban home as their favored model of family bliss. As Betty Friedan suggested in *The Feminine Mystique*, advertisers and women's magazines played a crucial role in convincing women of their familial obligations.[73] In fact, even while married women increasingly took jobs outside the home (by 1962 they comprised about 60 percent of the female work force), popular media typically glorified the American housewife/mother who tended to her family on a full-time basis.[74] Meanwhile, the fact that most female occupations were unchallenging, low-paying, "pink-collar" jobs that the middle class thought of as second incomes gave credence to the popular idea that women would find fulfillment at home rather than at work.

However, postwar domesticity wasn't simply a return to Victorian notions of True Womanhood, and nor was it, as some historians argue, merely an attempt to obliterate the Depression by returning to the family consumerism of the 1920s suburb. Instead, it was an updated version of the family ideal, capable of negotiating traditional ideas about domesticity with the realities of postwar experience. Lillian Gilbreth wrote in her home manual of 1955, "We no longer say, 'Woman's place is in the home,' because many women have their places outside the home. But the home belongs to the family, and it is still true that the family is woman's chief interest, it is even more a privilege and a trust, whether she has an outside job or not." [75] Through such logic, the vast contradictions between modern life and women's traditional roles were smoothed over—but as we shall see, they were never completely resolved.

Thus, even while postwar culture was filled with nostalgia for former visions of family life, it was bent on building a new future responsive to the particular concerns of the present. As Elaine Tyler May has shown, this was a hyperbolic form of "domestic containment," built on the assumptions of cold war logic. All sorts of social problems—from oversexed teens to communist threats—could be contained through private solutions. Of course, as Tyler May has demonstrated through her extensive use of interview data, many people at the time voiced their frustrations with domesticity and the personal sacrifices that it demanded; nevertheless, most people put enormous faith in family life. [76] Indeed, the nuclear family, living in a private suburban home, was a potent utopian fantasy that engaged the imagination of many men and women. While the actual lived experience of domesticity was fraught with problems, the family ideal still promised material benefits and personal stability in a confusing social world.

In the new American dream house, recreation was held at a premium. By the postwar period, the ideology of domestic leisure had evolved from the informal play of the previous decades to an exaggerated obsession with family fun. As early as 1940, Sydnie Greenbie suggested in his book *Leisure for Living* that the home was a "nook for personal living and intimate self-amusement, a kind of miniature clubhouse for a little family group." [77] After the war, the clubhouse concept was adopted with a vengeance. Books with titles such as *The Family Fun Book* and *Planning Your Home For Play* taught postwar Americans how to enjoy the good life, while magazines promised that barbecues, home movies, slide shows, and family vacations would make homes happy.

Most important among the new family activities was television. In magazines, films, newspapers, advertisements, and on the airwaves, this new form of entertainment was constantly considered for both its positive and negative effects on domestic life. In many ways, these popular discussions drew upon ideals for domestic recreation that had been formed and re-formed since the Victorian era. In particular, popular discourses on television were organized around the social hierarchies of family life and the division of spheres that had been the backbone of domestic ideology since the Victorian era. How such notions circulated through the texts of popular culture, and how they helped give meaning to the television set and its place in the home, are the subjects of the following chapters.

Two

Television in the Family Circle

Nicholas Ray's 1955 film, *Rebel without a Cause*, contains a highly melodramatic moment in which family members are unable to patch together the rift among them. The teenage son, Jim, returns home after the famous sequence in which he races his car to the edge of a cliff, only to witness the death of his competitor. Jim looks at his father asleep in front of the television set, and then he lies down on a sofa. From Jim's upside-down point of view on the sofa, the camera cuts to his shrewish mother who appears at the top of the stairwell. In a 180-degree spin, the camera flip-flops on the image of the mother, mimicking the way Jim sees her descending the stairs. This highly stylized shot jolts us out of the illusory realism of the scene, a disruption that continues as the camera reveals a television screen emitting a menacing blue static. As the camera lingers on the TV set, Jim confesses his guilt. Moments later, when his mother demands that he not go to the police, Jim begs his henpecked father to take his side. Finally, with seemingly murderous intentions, Jim chokes him. The camera pans across the TV set, its bluish static heightening the sense of family discord. With its "bad reception," television serves as a rhetorical figure for the loss of communication between family members. In fact, as Jim's father admits early in the scene, he was not even aware of his son's whereabouts during this fateful night, but instead had learned of the incident through an outside authority, the television newscast.

As this classic scene illustrates, in postwar years the television set became a central figure in representations of family relationships. The introduction of the machine into the home meant that family members needed to come to terms with the presence of a communication medium that might transform older modes of family interaction. The popular media published reports and advice from social critics and social scientists who were studying the effects of television on family relationships. The media also published pictorial representations of domestic life that showed people how television might—or might not—fit into the dynamics of their own domestic lives. Most significantly, like the scene from *Rebel without a Cause*, the media discourses were organized around ideas of family harmony and discord.

Indeed, contradictions between unity and division were central to representations of television during the period of its installation. Television was the great family minstrel that promised to bring Mom, Dad, and the kids together; at the same time, it had to be carefully controlled so that it harmonized with the separate gender roles and social functions of individual family members. This meant that the contradiction between unity and division was not a simple binary opposition; it was not a matter of either/or but rather both at once. Television was supposed to bring the family together but still allow for social and sexual divisions in the home. In fact, the attempt to maintain a balance between these two ideals was a central tension at work in popular discourses on television and the family.

The Family United

In 1954, *McCall's* magazine coined the term "togetherness." The appearance of this term between the covers of a woman's magazine is significant not only because it shows the importance attached to family unity during the postwar years, but also because this phrase is symptomatic of discourses aimed at the housewife. Home magazines primarily discussed family life in language organized around spatial imagery of proximity, distance, isolation, and integration. In fact, the spatial organization of the home was presented as a set of scientific laws through which family relationships could be calculated and controlled. Topics ranging from childrearing to sexuality were discussed in spatial terms, and solutions to domestic problems were overwhelmingly spatial: if you are nervous, make yourself a quiet sitting corner far away from the central living area of the home. If your children are cranky, let them play in the yard. If your husband is bored at the office, turn your garage into a workshop where he'll recall the joys of his boyhood. It was primarily within the context of this spatial problem that television was discussed. The central question was, "Where should you put the television set?" This problem was tackled throughout the period, formulated and reformulated, solved and recast. In the process the television set became an integral part of the domestic environment depicted in the magazines.

At the simplest level, there was the question of the proper room for television. In 1949, *Better Homes and Gardens* asked, "Where does the receiver go?" It listed options including the living room, game room, or "some strategic spot where you can see it from the living room, dining room and kitchen." [1] At this point, however, the photographs of model rooms usually did not include television sets as part of the interior decor. On the few occasions when sets did appear, they were placed either in the basement or in the living room. By 1951, the television set traveled more freely through the household spaces depicted in the magazines. It appeared in the basement, living room, bedroom, kitchen, fun room, converted garage, sitting-sleeping room, music room, and even the "TV room." Furthermore, not only the room, but the exact location in the room, had to be considered for its possible use as a TV zone.

As the television set moved into the center of family life, other household fixtures traditionally associated with domestic bliss had to make room for it. Typically, the magazines presented the television set as the new family hearth through which love and affection might be re-kindled.[2] In 1951, when *American Home* first displayed a television set on its cover photograph, it employed the conventionalized iconography of a model living room organized around the fireplace, but this time a television set was built into the mantelpiece. Even more radically, the television was shown to replace the fireplace altogether, as the maga-zines showed readers how television could function as the center of fam-ily attention. So common had this substitution become that by 1954 *House Beautiful* was presenting its readers with "another example of how the TV set is taking the place of the fireplace as the focal point around which to arrange the seating in the room."[3] Perhaps the most extreme example of this kind of substitution is the tradition at some broadcast stations of burning Yule logs on the television screen each Christmas Eve, a practice that originated in the 1950s.

More typically, the television set took the place of the piano.[4] In *American Home*, for instance, the appearance of the television set corre-lates significantly with the vanishing piano. While in 1948 the baby grand piano typically held a dominant place in model living rooms, over the years it gradually receded to the point where it was usually shown to be an upright model located in marginal areas such as basements. Meanwhile, the television set moved into the primary living spaces of model rooms where its stylish cabinets meshed with and enhanced the interior decor. The new "entertainment centers," comprised of a radio, television, and phonograph, often made the piano entirely obsolete. In 1953, *Better Homes and Gardens* suggested as much when it displayed a television set in a "built-in music corner" that "replaces the piano," now moved into the basement.[5] In that same year, in a special issue entitled "Music and Home Entertainment," *House Beautiful* focused on radio, television, and phonographs, asking readers, "Do You Really Need a Piano?"[6] One woman, writing to *TV World* columnist Kathi Norris, an-swered the question in no uncertain terms:

Dear Kathi:

Since we got our television set, we've had to change the ar-rangement of furniture in our living room, and we just can't keep the piano. I need new pictures, but can't afford to buy them with the expense of television, so I was wondering if I

38

might somehow find somebody who would trade me a picture
or two for a perfectly good piano.[7]

This woman and, I suspect, others like her were beginning to think of
television as a replacement for the traditional fixtures of family life.[8]

As the magazines continued to depict the set in the center of family
activity, television seemed to become a natural part of domestic space. By
the early 1950s, floor plans included a space for television in the home's
structural layout, and television sets were increasingly depicted as everyday, commonplace objects that any family might hope to own. Indeed,
the magazines included television as a staple home fixture before most
Americans could even receive a television signal, much less consider purchasing the expensive item. The media discourses did not so much reflect
social reality; instead, they preceded it. The home magazines helped to
construct television as a household object, one that belonged in the family space. More surprisingly, however, in the span of roughly four years,
television itself became *the* central figure in images of the American
home; it became the cultural symbol par excellence of family life.

Television, it was said, would bring the family ever closer, an expression which, in itself a spatial metaphor, was continually repeated in a
wide range of popular media—not only women's magazines, but also
general magazines, men's magazines, and on the airwaves. In its capacity as unifying agent, television fit well with the more general postwar
hopes for a return to family values. It was seen as a kind of household
cement that promised to reassemble the splintered lives of families who
had been separated during the war. It was also meant to reinforce the
new suburban family unit, which had left most of its extended family
and friends behind in the city.

The emergence of the term "family room" in the postwar period is a
perfect example of the importance attached to organizing household
spaces around ideals of family togetherness. First coined in George
Nelson and Henry Wright's *Tomorrow's House: A Complete Guide for the
Home-Builder* (1946), the family room encapsulated a popular ideal
throughout the period. Nelson and Wright, who alternatively called the
family room "the room without a name," suggested the possible social
functions of this new household space:

> Could the room without a name be evidence of a growing de-
> sire to provide a framework within which the members of a
> family will be better equipped to enjoy each other on the basis
> of mutual respect and affection? Might it thus indicate a deep-
> seated urge to reassert the validity of the family by providing a
> better design for living? We should very much like to think so,
> and if there is any truth in this assumption, our search for a
> name is ended—we should simply call it the 'family room.'[9]

39

This notion of domestic cohesion was integral to the design for living put forward in the home magazines that popularized the family room in the years to come. It was also integral to the role of the television set, which was often pictured in the family rooms of the magazines' model homes. In 1950, *Better Homes and Gardens* literally merged television with the family room, telling readers to design a new double-purpose area, the "family-television room."[10]

But one needn't build a new room in order to bring the family together around the television set; kitchens, living rooms, and dining rooms would do just as well. What was needed was a particular attitude, a sense of closeness that permeated the room. Photographs, particularly in advertisements, graphically depicted the idea of the family circle with television viewers grouped around the television set in semicircle patterns.

As Roland Marchand has shown with respect to advertising in the 1920s and 1930s, the family circle was a prominent pictorial strategy for the promotion of household goods. The pictures always suggested that all members of the family were present, and since they were often shot in soft-focus or contained dreamy mists, there was a romantic haze around the family unit. Sometimes artists even drew concentric circles around the family, or else an arc of light evoked the theme. According to Marchand, the visual cliché of the family circle referred back to Victorian notions about domestic havens, implying that the home was secure and stable. The advertisements suggested a democratic model of family life, one in which all members shared in consumer decisions—although, as Marchand suggests, to some extent the father remained a dominant figure in the pictorial composition. In this romanticized imagery, modern fixtures were easily assimilated into the family space:

> The products of modern technology, including radios and
> phonographs, were comfortably accommodated within the
> hallowed circle. Whatever pressures and complexities moder-
> nity might bring, these images implied, the family at home
> would preserve an undaunted harmony and security. In an age
> of anxieties about family relationships and centrifugal social
> forces, this visual cliché was no social mirror; rather, it was a
> reassuring pictorial convention.[11]

Much like the advertisements for radio and the phonograph, advertisements for television made ample use of this reassuring pictorial convention—especially in the years immediately following the war when advertisers were in the midst of their reconversion campaigns, channeling the country back from the wartime pressures of personal sacrifice and domestic upheaval to a peacetime economy based on consumer-

ism and family values. The advertisements suggested that tele
would serve as a catalyst for the return to a world of domestic lo\
affection—a world that must have been quite different from the a
experiences of returning GIs and their new families in the chaotic y
of readjustment to civilian life.

The returning soldiers and their wives experienced an abrupt shift in
social and cultural experiences. Horror stories of shell-shocked men circulated in psychiatric journals. In 1946, social workers at VA hospitals
counseled some 144,000 men, half of whom were treated for neuro-
psychiatric diseases.[12] Even for those lucky enough to escape the scars of
battle, popular media such as film noir showed angst-ridden, sexually unstable men, scarred psychologically and unable to relate to the familial
ideals and bureaucratic realities of postwar life (the tortured male
hero in *Out of the Past* [1946] is a classic example). The more melodramatic social problem films such as *Come Back Little Sheba* (1952) and
A Hatful of Rain (1957) were character studies of emotionally unstable,
often drug-dependent, family men. Such images, moreover, were not
confined to popular fiction. Sociological studies such as William H.
Whyte's *The Organization Man* (1956) presented chilling visions of white-
collar workers who were transformed into powerless conformists as the
country was taken over by nameless, faceless corporations.[13] Even if his
working life was filled with tension, the ideal man still had to be the
breadwinner for a family. Moreover, should he fail to marry and procre-
ate, his "manliness" would be called into question. According to Tyler
May: "Many contemporaries feared that returning veterans would be
unable to resume their positions as responsible family men. They worried that a crisis in masculinity could lead to crime, 'perversion' and
homosexuality. Accordingly, the postwar years witnessed an increasing
suspicion of single men as well as single women, as the authority of men
at home and at work seemed to be threatened."[14] Although the image of
the swinging bachelor also emerged in this period—particularly through
the publication of *Playboy*—we might regard the "swinger" image as a
kind of desperate, if confused, response to the enforcement of heterosexual family lifestyles. In other words, in a heterosexist world, the swinger
image might well have provided single men with a way to deflect popular suspicions about homosexuality directed at bachelors who avoided
marriage.[15]

Meanwhile, women were given a highly constraining solution to the
changing roles of gender and sexual identity. Although middle- and
working-class women had been encouraged by popular media to enter
traditionally male occupations during the war, they were now told to
return to their homes where they could have babies and make color-
coordinated meals.[16] Marynia Farnham and Ferdinand Lundberg's *The*

Modern Woman: The Lost Sex (1947) gave professional, psychological status to this housewife image, claiming that the essential function of women was that of caretaker, mother, and sexual partner. Those women who took paid employment in the outside world would defy the biological order of things and become neurotics.[17] One postwar marriage guidebook even included a "Test of Neurotic Tendencies" on which women lost points for choosing an answer that exhibited their desire for authority at work.[18] The domestic woman needed to save her energy for housekeeping, childrearing, and an active (monogamous) sex life with her husband.[19] The ways in which people interpreted and applied such messages to their own lives is difficult to discern, but their constant repetition in popular media did provide a context in which women could find ample justification for their early marriages, child-centeredness, reluctance to divorce, and tendency to use higher education only as a stepping stone for marriage.[20]

Even if people found the domestic ideal seductive, the housing shortage, coupled with the baby boom, made domestic bliss an expensive and often unattainable luxury. In part, for this reason, the glorification of middle-class family life seems to have had the unplanned, paradoxical effect of sending married women into the labor force in order to obtain the money necessary to live up to the ideal. Whereas before the war single women accounted for the majority of female workers, the number of married women workers skyrocketed during the 1950s.[21] Despite the fact that many women worked for extra spending money, surveys showed that some women found outside employment gave them a sense of personal accomplishment and also helped them enter into social networks outside family life.[22] At the same time, sociological studies such as Whyte's *The Organization Man* and David Reisman's *The Lonely Crowd* (1950) showed that housewives expressed doubts about their personal sacrifices, marital relationships, and everyday lives in alienating suburban neighborhoods. Although most postwar middle-class women were not ready to accept the full-blown attack on patriarchy launched in Simone de Beauvoir's *The Second Sex* (1949; English translation, 1952), they were not simply cultural dupes. Indeed, as the work of feminist historians such as Elaine Tyler May and Rochelle Gatlin suggests, postwar women both negotiated with and rationalized the oppressive aspects of the family ideal.

The transition from wartime to postwar life thus resulted in a set of ideological and social contradictions concerning the construction of gender and the family unit. The image of compassionate families that advertisers offered the public might well have been intended to serve the "therapeutic" function that both Roland Marchand and T. J. Jackson Lears have ascribed to advertising in general. The illustrations of do-

Family members circle around the console in a 1949 RCA advertisement.

mestic bliss and consumer prosperity presented a soothing alternative to the tensions of postwar life.[23] Government building policies and veteran mortgage loans sanctioned the materialization of these advertising images by giving middle-class families a chance to buy into the "good life" of ranch-style cottages and consumer durables. Even so, both the advertising images and the homes themselves were built on the shaky foundations of social upheavals and cultural conflicts that were never completely resolved. The family circle ads, like suburbia itself, were only a temporary consumer solution to a set of complicated political, economic, and social problems.

In the case of television, these kind of advertisements almost always showed the product in the center of the family group. While soft-focus or dreamy mists were sometimes used, the manufacturers' claims for picture clarity and good reception seem to have necessitated the use of sharp focus and high contrast, which better connoted these product attributes. The product-as-center motif not only suggested the familial qualities of the set, but also implied a mode of use: the ads suggested television be watched by a family audience.

A 1951 advertisement for Crosley's "family theatre television" is a particularly striking example. As is typical in these kinds of ads, the copy details the technical qualities of the set, but the accompanying illustration gives familial meanings to the modern technology. The picture in this case is composed as a *mise-en-abyme;* in the center of the page a large drawing of the outer frame of a television screen contains a sharp focus photograph of a family watching television. Family members are dispersed on sofas on three sides of a room, while a little boy, with arms stretched out in the air, sits in the middle of the room. All eyes are glued to the television set, which appears in the center lower portion of the frame, in fact barely visible to the reader. According to the logic of this composition, the central fascination for the reader is not the actual product, which is pictured only in miniscule proportions on the lower margin of the page, but rather its ability to bring the family together around it. The ad's *mise-en-abyme* structure suggests that the Crosley console literally contains the domestic scene, thereby promising not just a television set but an ideal reflection of the family, joined together by the new commodity.[24]

Even families that were not welcomed into the middle-class melting pot of postwar suburbia were promised that the dream of domestic bliss would come true through the purchase of a television set. *Ebony* continually ran advertisements that displayed African-Americans in middle-class living rooms, enjoying an evening of television. Many of these ads were strikingly similar to those used in white consumer magazines—although often the advertisers portrayed black families watching programs that featured black actors.[25] Despite this iconographic substitution, the message was clearly one transmitted by a culture industry catering to the middle-class suburban ideal. Nuclear families living in single-family homes would engage in intensely private social relations through the luxury of television.

Such advertisements appeared in a general climate of postwar expectations about television's ability to draw families closer together. In *The Age of Television* (1956), Leo Bogart summarized a wide range of audience studies on the new medium that showed numerous Americans believed television would revive domestic life. Summarizing the findings, Bogart concluded that social scientific surveys "agree completely that television has had the effect of keeping the family at home more than formerly."[26] One respondent from a Southern California survey boasted that his "family now stays home all the time and watches the same programs. [We] turn it on at 3 P.M. and watch until 10 P.M. We never go anywhere."[27] Moreover, studies indicated that people believed television strengthened family ties. A 1949 survey of an eastern city found that long-term TV owners expressed "an awareness of an enhanced family solidarity."[28] In a 1951 study of Atlanta families, one respondent said, "It keeps us together more," and another commented, "It makes a closer family circle." Some women even saw television as a cure for marital problems. One housewife claimed, "My husband is very restless; now he relaxes at home." Another woman confided, "My husband

and I get along a lot better. We don't argue so much. It's wonderful for couples who have been married ten years or more. . . . Before television, my husband would come in and go to bed. Now we spend some time together." [29] A study of mass-produced suburbs (including Levittown, Long Island, and Park Forest, Illinois) found similar patterns as women expressed their confidence that television was "bringing the romance back." One woman even reported, "Until we got that TV set, I thought my husband had forgotten how to neck." [30]

Typically also, television was considered a remedy for problem children. During the 1950s, juvenile delinquency emerged as a central topic of public debate. Women's magazines and child psychologists such as Dr. Benjamin Spock, whose *Baby and Childcare* had sold a million copies by 1951, gave an endless stream of advice to mothers on ways to prevent their children from becoming antisocial and emotionally impaired. Not only was childrearing literature big business, but the state had taken a special interest in the topic of disturbed youth, using agencies such as the Continuing Committee on the Prevention and Control of Delinquency and the Children's Bureau to monitor juvenile crimes. [31] Against this backdrop, audience research showed that parents believed television would keep their children off the streets. A mother from the Southern California survey claimed, "Our boy was always watching television, so we got him a set just to keep him home." [32] A mother from the Atlanta study stated, "We are closer together. We find our entertainment at home. Donna and her boyfriend sit here instead of going out now." [33] Such sentiments were popularized in a *Better Homes and Gardens* survey in which parents repeatedly mentioned television's ability to unify the family. One parent even suggested a new reason for keeping up with the Joneses. She said, "It [television] keeps the children home. Not that we have had that problem too much, but we could see it coming because nearly everyone had a set before we weakened." [34]

Trouble in Paradise

The ideal of family togetherness that television came to signify was, like all cultural fantasies, accompanied by repressed anxieties that often resurfaced in the popular texts of the period. Even if television was often said to bring the family together in the home, popular media also expressed tensions about its role in domestic affairs. Television's inclusion in the home was dependent upon its ability to rid itself of what *House Beautiful* called its "unfamiliar aspect." [35]

At a time when household modernization was a key concern, women's magazines continually examined the relationship between the family and the machine. The magazines were undecided on this subject, at times accepting, at times rejecting the effects of mechanization. On the one hand, they offered their female readers technological fantasy worlds that promised to reduce the time and energy devoted to household chores. Dream kitchens, which had been displayed by women's magazines since the 1920s, resembled Technicolor spectacles found on the cinema screen, only here the bold primary colors depicted a woman's Shangri-la of electric gizmos and sleek linoleum surfaces. Just in case this pictorial display of technological commodity fetishism was not enough, the magazines didactically reminded their readers of the need to "be up to date." In 1951, *House Beautiful* provided a list of "changes and improvements that arrived [after the war] as predicted." Included were such labor-saving devices as the dishwasher and garbage grinder, but also leisure-enhancing machines, most notably television. In that same year, *House Beautiful* included a quiz entitled "How Contemporary is Your Life?" Most of the fifty-eight questions had to do with the degree to which the home was equipped with "modern" appliances, and the magazine warned its readers that if "you score less than forty . . . you are depriving yourself of too many contemporary advantages." Owning a television set was a must, according to this modernity exam.[36]

Whereas in the prewar and war years a fully mechanized household would have been presented in the popular press as a futuristic fantasy, in the postwar years it appeared that tomorrow had arrived. Moreover, living without an array of machines meant that you were anachronistic, unable to keep pace with tomorrow. Still, this rampant consumerism and its attendant "machine aesthetic" had a dark underside from which the new household technologies and mechanized lifestyles appeared in a much less flattering light.

As numerous cultural historians have shown, since the 1800s American thinkers have exhibited a profound ambivalence toward technology. The idea that people would become prisoners to machines, sacrifice romance for scientific utopias, or trade the beauty of nature for the poisonous fruits of industrialization were central themes for novelists such as Mark Twain, Edward Bellamy, and Henry David Thoreau.[37] With increasing class antagonism and urban strife, this ambivalence grew stronger in the twentieth century, and it was exhibited both in intellectual circles and in popular culture venues. As we saw in chapter 1, such sentiments were not only symptomatic of large-scale political fears about industrialization and the urban milieu: they were also expressed in terms of the micropolitics of everyday life and the increasing mechanization of the middle-class household. Machines provided leisure, comfort, and the possibility of progress, but they also suggested an end to nature and the "natural" order of things both at home and in civic life. By the 1930s, when the American industrial society seemed finally to have collapsed, people were caught between their faith that the wheels of technological progress would transport them out of misery and their bitter resentment toward the mechanized world that had let them down. As Susman has observed, at the same time that Americans were celebrating the technological future in the "Land of Tomorrow" at the 1939 New York World's Fair, the Gallup Poll revealed that most people nevertheless believed technological development caused the unemployment of the Great Depression.[38]

The home magazines of the postwar era adopted this ambivalence toward machines, scrutinizing each step forward in household technology for its possible side effects. *House Beautiful,* the same magazine that tested its readers on their modernity quotients, just as often warned of the dismal future in store for the residents of the mechanized household. In 1951, the magazine asked if the "houses we live in . . . accustom us . . . to feel more at home in surroundings where everything suggests only machines . . . that do as they are told and could never have known either joy or desire." And if so, there is an overwhelming threat that "man is nothing but a machine . . . [who] can be 'conditioned' to do and to want whatever his masters decide."[39] The threat of the "machine man," couched in the rhetoric of behavioralism, gave rise to a host of statements on the relationship between television and the family. Would the television set become the master and the family its willing subject? The adage of the day became, "Don't let the television set dominate you!"

The idea of "technology out of control" was constantly repeated as the language of horror and science fiction invaded discussions of everyday life. The television set was often likened to a monster that threatened to wreak havoc on the family. *Business Week* called television the "New Cyclops," while *American Mercury* referred to it as the "Giant in the Living Room," a kind of supernatural child who might turn against his master at any moment. The essay proclaimed, "The giant . . . has arrived. He was a mere pip-squeak yesterday, and didn't even exist the day before, but like a genie released from a magic bottle in *The Arabian Nights,* he now looms big as life over our heads."[40] As such statements suggest, television posed the intimidating possibility that private citizens in their own homes might be rendered powerless in the face of a new and curious machine.

The threatening aspects of television technology might have been related to its use as a surveillance and reconnaissance weapon during World War II. To some degree, the public was aware of this because television's aircraft and military applications had been discussed in popular literature since the 1930s, and after the war, men's magazines such as *Popular Science* and *Popular Mechanics* continued to present articles on television's wartime uses.[41] Such links between television and World War II sharply contradicted, however, the images of television and domestic bliss that were put forward after the war. It seems plausible that television's military applications created doubts about its ability to enter the home. In fact, television's effect on culture was sometimes discussed in the context of warfare and atomic weaponry. Words such as "invasion" and "battle" were often employed in criticisms of the new medium, and a popular assumption was that television would cause cancer by transmitting waves of radiation. Later in 1961, when FCC Chairman Newton Minow chided the broadcast industry in his famous "vast wasteland" speech, he too used the imagery of atomic warfare to suggest the powerful effects that television might have on the public. Minow claimed:

> Ours has been called the jet age, the atomic age, the space age.
> It is also, I submit, the television age. And just as history will
> decide whether the leaders of today's world employed the
> atom to destroy the world or rebuild it for mankind's benefit,
> so will history decide whether today's broadcasters employed
> their powerful voice to enrich the people or debase them.[42]

Although popular discourses suggested that television technology was out of control, they also provided soothing antidotes to this fear of machines. In 1953, the Zenith Corporation found a way to master the beast, promising consumers, "We keep them [television sets] in a cage until they're right for you." A large photograph at the top of the page showed a zoo cage that contained a Zenith scientist testing the inner components of the receiver. On the bottom of the page was the finely constructed Kensington console model, artfully integrated into a living room setting. As this advertisement so well suggests, the unfamiliar technology could be domesticated by making the set into a piece of glamorous furniture.[43] Stromberg-Carlson advertised its console model with "hand painted Chinese legend on ivory, red, or ebony lacquer," while Sparton television claimed that it was hand crafted by "trained cabinet makers who can turn a fine piece of wood into a masterpiece."[44]

Also typically, the home magazines suggested that television be made to mesh with the room's overall decorative style. As *House Beautiful* told its readers in 1949, "Remember that television can be easily tailored to match the character of your room."[45] Perhaps a testimony to the contradictory character of postwar domesticity, the two most popular styles were Contemporary and Early American design.[46] The constant associations drawn between television and contemporary living, as well as its most basic box-like form, gave the television set a privileged place in the modern style. The home magazines often displayed model rooms composed of simple geometric shapes where the television set seemed to be a natural addition. Conversely, the new machine was often thought to clash with Early American decor. Out of step with the evocation of a colonial past, the set had to be carefully blended into the overall decorative scheme. In 1955, *American Home* placed a receiver on an Early American table that supposedly established a "rapport between Colonial decor and television." In that same year, Zenith advertised its Colonial cabinet by suggesting, "Early American Charm and present day entertainment are a happy blending in this 21 inch console."[47] More typically, however, when it came to colonial decor, the television set was shown to be an unrelenting eyesore. The home magazines often resorted to a kind of "decorative repression" in which the set was placed in a remote corner of the Early American room or else entirely hidden from view.

In fact, this design strategy extended beyond the specific case of Colonial decor. More generally, the decorative attempt to master the machine meant the literal *camouflage* of the set. In 1951, *American Home* suggested that "television needn't change a room" so long as it was made to "retire at your command." Among the suggestions were hinged panels "faced with dummy book backs so that no one would suspect, when they are closed, that this period room lives a double life with TV." In 1953, *House Beautiful* placed a television set into a cocktail table from which it "rises for use or disappears from sight by simply pushing a button." Even the component parts had to be hidden from view. In 1953, *American Home* and *Popular Science* each displayed an indoor antenna fashioned to look like a sailboat.[48]

The attempts to render the television set invisible are especially interesting in the light of critical and popular memory accounts that argue that the television set was a privileged figure of conspicuous consumption and class status for postwar Americans. A basic assumption in the literature on television, this argument can be found in standard histories as well as theoretical accounts like Jean Baudrillard's *For a Critique of the Political Economy of the Sign,* in which he discusses television's value as a sign of class status in lower- and middle-class living rooms.[49] The early attempt to hide the receiver complicates such assumptions because it suggests the visual pleasure of interior decor was at odds with the display of wealth in the home. This popular fascination with hiding the receiver should remind us that the accumulation of commodities in the home might also have had attached to it a degree of shame. The kind of commodity exhibitionism that Thorstein Veblen first identified in 1899 could have been tempered by a contradictory impulse to inhibit the new commodity. Such "commodity inhibitionism" can itself be explained by television's class status during the postwar period. From the point of view of upper-class standards, by the 1950s television might well have been less a status symbol than a sign of "bad taste." Although television had been a rich person's toy in the 1930s and 1940s, its rapid dissemination to the middle and even lower classes after 1948 transformed it into a poor person's luxury. Since middle-class home magazines often reflected upper-class tastes, their decorative suggestions on hiding the television set might have been offered in the context of upper-class prejudices against television.

In addition to offering decorative solutions to the fear of machines, the magazines often associated television with nature. Literally placing the "machine in the garden," popular magazines showed how plants and floral arrangements could transform an ordinary set into a thing of beauty.[50] Anthropomorphism was another popular strategy. In 1951, *House Beautiful* declared that "television has become a member of the family," and *American Home* explained ways to "welcome" television "into the family circle."[51] More generally, the magazines described television as a "newborn baby," a "family friend," a "nurse," a "teacher," and a "family pet" (a symbol that, as we have seen, had previously proven its success when the Victor phonograph company adopted the image of a fox terrier for its corporate logo). As the domesticated animal, television obeyed its master and became a benevolent playmate for children as well as a faithful companion for adults. A 1952 advertisement for Emerson shows a typical scenario. The immanent pet-like quality of the television set emanates from the screen where a child and her poodle are pictured. Meanwhile, the advertising copy conjures up notions of master-servant relations, reminding consumers, again and again, that the set will be a "dependable" machine.[52]

Even if anthropomorphism helped to relieve tensions about television technology, the media continued to express doubts. The idea of "technology out of control" was turned around and reformulated. Now it was viewers who had lost control of themselves. Considering television's negative effects on the family, Bogart claimed in *The Age of Television* that "the bulk of the disadvantages listed by the TV owners reflect their inability to control themselves once the set has been installed in the house."[53] At least at the level of popular discourse, Bogart's suggestions are particularly accurate. The media attributed a wide range of human failures to television, failures that were typically linked to problems of family discord.

Seducing the Innocent

More than any other group, children were singled out as the victims of the new pied piper. Indeed, even while critics praised television as a source of domestic unity and benevolent socialization, they also worried about its harmful effects, particularly its encouragement of passive and addictive behavior. In 1951, *Better Homes and Gardens* complained that the medium's "synthetic entertainment" produced a child who was

"Telebugeye" afflicts the young in this cartoon from a 1950 issue of *Ladies' Home Journal.*

"glued to television."[54] Worse still, the new addiction would reverse good habits of hygiene, nutrition, and decorum, causing physical, mental, and social disorders. A cartoon in a 1950 issue of *Ladies' Home Journal* suggests a typical scenario. The magazine showed a little girl slumped on an ottoman and suffering from a new disease called "telebugeye." According to the caption, the child was a "pale, weak, stupid looking creature" who grew "bugeyed" from sitting and watching television for too long.[55] Perhaps responding to these concerns, some advertisements presented children spectators in scenes that associated television with the "higher arts," and some even implied that children would cultivate artistic talents by watching television. In 1951, General Electric showed a little girl, dressed in a tutu, imitating an on-screen ballerina, while Truetone showed a little boy learning to play the saxophone by watching a professional horn player on television.[56]

As the popular wisdom often suggested, the child's passive addiction to television might itself lead to the opposite effect of increased aggression. These discussions followed in the wake of critical and social scientific theories of the 1930s and 1940s that suggested that mass media injects ideas and behavior into passive individuals. Adopting this "hypodermic model" of media effects, the magazines circulated horror stories about youngsters who imitated television violence. In 1955, *Newsweek* reported on young Frank Stretch, an eleven-year-old from Ventura, California, who had become so entranced by a television western that "with one shot of his trusty BB gun [he] demolished both villain and picture tube."[57] Similar stories circulated about a nine-year-old who proposed killing his teacher with a box of poisoned chocolates, a six-year-old who asked his father for real bullets because his sister didn't die when he shot her with his gun, and a seven-year-old who put ground glass in the family's lamb stew—all, of course, after witnessing murders on television.[58] In reaction to the popular furor, as early as 1950 the Television Broadcasters' Association hired a public relations firm to write pro-television press releases that suggested the more positive types of programming that television had to offer.[59]

Of course, the controversy surrounding television was simply a new skirmish in a much older battle to define what constituted appropriate children's entertainment. Such controversies can be traced back to the turn of the century when reformers, most notably Anthony Comstock, sought to regulate the content of dime novels.[60] Similar battles were waged when middle-class reformers of the early 1900s debated film's impact on American youth, and later these reform discourses were given scientific credence with the publication of the Payne Fund Studies in 1933. Broadcasting became the subject of public scrutiny in that same year when a group of mothers from Scarsdale, New York, began voicing their objections to radio programs that they considered to be harmful to children. The public outcry was taken up in special interest magazines—especially the *Christian Century, Commonweal, New Republic, Outlook, Nation,* and *Saturday Review.*[61] In all cases, childhood was conceived as a time of innocence, and the child a blank slate upon whom might be imprinted the evils of an overly aggressive and sexualized adult culture. In her work on *Peter Pan,* Jacqueline Rose has argued that the image of presexual childhood innocence has less to do with how children actually experience their youth than it does with how adults choose to conceptualize that experience. The figure of the innocent child serves to facilitate a nostalgic adult fantasy of a perfect past in which social, sexual, economic, and political complexities fade into the background.[62]

In the postwar years, the urge to preserve childhood innocence helped to justify and reinforce the nuclear family as a central institution and mode of social experience. Parents were given the delicate job of balancing the dividends and deficits of the ever-expanding consumer culture. On the one hand, they had to supply their youngsters with the fruits of a new commodity society—suburban homes, wondrous toys, new technologies, glamorous vacations, and so forth. Early schooling in the good life would ensure that children continued on a life trajectory of social mobility based on the acquisition of objects. On the other hand, parents had to protect children from the more insidious aspects of the consumer wonderland, making sure that they internalized the ability to tell the difference between authentic culture and synthetic commercial pleasures. According to Helen Muir, editor of the *Miami Herald's* children's books section, there was a difference between the "real needs and desires of children" and "the superimposed synthetic so-called needs which are not needs but cravings."[63] In this context, mass media provided parents with a particularly apt target. More than twenty years before Marie Winn called television "the plug-in drug," Muir and others likened mass media to marijuana and other narcotics that offered children a momentary high rather than the eternal pleasures of real art.

The most vocal critic was psychiatrist Fredric Wertham, whose *Seduction of the Innocent* (1953) became the cornerstone of the 1950s campaign against comic books. For Wertham, the tabula rasa conception of the child was paramount; the visual immediacy of comics, he argued, left children vulnerable to their unsavory content. Although most social scientists and psychologists had a more nuanced approach to mass media than Wertham had, his ideas were popularized in the press and he even served as an expert witness in Estes Kefauver's 1954 Senate Subcommittee hearings on juvenile delinquency.[64] The war that Wertham waged against mass culture struck a chord with the more general fears about juvenile delinquency at the time, and parents were given armor in what popular critics increasingly defined as a battle to protect the young from the onslaught of a hypercommercialized children's culture.[65]

Indeed, discussions about children and mass culture typically invoked military imagery. One woman, who had read Wertham's 1948 article in the *Saturday Review,* wrote a letter that explained how her children had become "drugged" by mass media: "We consider this situation to be as serious as an invasion of the enemy in war time, with as far-reaching consequences as the atom bomb." One year later, anthropologist Margaret Mead expressed similar fears to her colleagues, worrying about children who grew up in a world where "radio and television and comics and the threat of the atomic bomb are every day realities."[66] If in the late 1940s television was seen as just one part of the threatening media environment, over the course of the 1950s it would emerge as a more central problem.

As Ellen Wartella and Sharon Mazzarella have observed, early social scientific studies suggested that children weren't simply using television in place of other media; instead, television was colonizing children's leisure time more than other mass cultural forms had ever done.[67] Social scientists found this "reorganization hypothesis" to be particularly important because it meant that television was changing the nature of children's lives, taking them away from school work, household duties, family conversations, and creative play. This hypothesis was also at the core of early studies conducted by school boards around the country, which showed that television was reducing the amount of time children spent on homework. Researchers and reformers were similarly concerned with television's effects on children's moral and physical welfare. As early as 1949, PTA members voted at their national convention to keep an eye on "unwholesome television programs."[68] Religious organizations also tried to monitor television's unsavory content. In 1950, the National Council of Catholic Women counted violent acts in television programs while Detroit's Common Council (which was composed of religious groups and city officials) drew up a three-prong plan to make the new medium safe for children and teenagers. By 1951, the National Council of Catholic Men had joined the fray, considering a system of program ratings, while Catholic teachers were urging the formation of a Legion of Decency at their annual conference in Washington.[69] Even Wertham, who devoted most of his energy to comic books, included in his book a final chapter on television (appropriately titled "Homicide at Home"), which warned parents that programs such as *Captain Video* and *Superman* would corrupt the potential educational value of the new medium and turn children into violent, sexually "perverse" adults.

Such concerns were given official credence as senators, congressmen, and FCC commissioners considered the problem. Commissioner Frieda Hennock championed educational television, which she believed would better serve children's interests. Thomas J. Lane, representative from Massachusetts, urged Congress to establish government censorship of television programs, claiming that teachers and clergymen "have been fighting a losing battle against the excess of this one-way form of communication," and praising parents who were demanding that the "'juvenile delinquent called television'" be cleaned up "before it ruins itself and debases everybody with whom it has contact."[70] Largely in response to such concerns, the NARTB (following the lead of the film industry and its own experience with radio) staved off watchdog groups and government officials by passing an industry-wide censorship code for television in March 1952, a code that included a whole section on television and children.[71] But the debate persisted and even grew more heated. In that same year, Ezekiel Gathings, representative from Arkansas, spearheaded a House investigation of radio and television programs, which presented studies demonstrating television's negative influence on youth as well as testimony from citizen groups concerned with television's effects on children.[72] By 1954, Estes Kefauver's Senate Subcommittee hearings on juvenile delinquency were investigating television's relationship to the perceived increase in youth crimes, focusing particularly on the "ideas that spring into the living room for the entertainment of the youth of America, which have to do with crime and with horror, sadism, and sex."[73] At the beginning of the next decade, Newton Minow incorporated such concerns into his "vast wasteland" campaign, claiming that children's television was "just as tasteless, just as nourishing as dishwater."[74]

While scholarship has centered around the question of how television affects children, little has been said about the way adults have been taught to limit these effects. What is particularly interesting here is the degree to which discussions about television and children engaged questions concerning parental authority. Summarizing parents' attitudes toward television, Bogart claimed, "There is a feeling, never stated in so many words, that the set has a power of its own to control the destinies and viewing habits of the audience, and that what it 'does' to parents and children alike is somehow beyond the bounds of any individual set-owner's power of control."[75] In this context, popular media offered solace by showing parents how they could reclaim power in their own homes—if not over the medium, then at least over their children. Television opened up a whole array of disciplinary measures that parents might exert over their youngsters.

Indeed, the bulk of discussions about children and television were offered in the context of mastery. If the machine could control the child, then so could the parent. Here, the language of common sense provided some reassurance by reminding parents that it was they, after all, who were in command. As the *New York Times'* television critic Jack Gould wrote in 1949, "It takes a human hand to turn on a television set."[76] But for parents who needed a bit more than just the soothing words of a popular sage, the media ushered in specialists from a wide range of fields; child psychologists, educators, psychiatrists, and broadcasters all recommended ways to keep the problem child in line.

One popular form of advice revolved around program standards. Rather than allowing children to watch violent westerns such as *The Lone Ranger* and escapist science-fiction serials such as *Captain Video,* parents were told to establish a canon of wholesome programs. *Better Homes and Gardens'* readership survey indicated that some parents had already adopted this method of control:

> Forty percent of all the parents answering do not approve of
> some of the programs their children would like to see—chiefly
> crime, violent mystery or horror, western, and 'emotional'
> programs. . . .

About one-fourth of the parents insist on their children viewing special events on TV. In this category they mention parades, childrens shows, educational programs, great artists, and theater productions.[77]

In many ways this canon recalled Victorian notions of ideal family recreation. Overly exciting stimuli threatened to corrupt the child, while educational and morally uplifting programs were socially sanctioned. In response to these concerns, magazines such as *Reader's Digest, Saturday Review,* and *Parents* gave their seal of approval to what they deemed as culturally enriching programs (*Ding Dong School, Romper Room, Shari Lewis, Captain Kangaroo,* and even *Huckleberry Hound*). In all cases, critical judgments were based on adult standards. Indeed, this hierarchy of television programs is symptomatic of the more general efforts to establish an economy of pleasure for children spectators that suited adult concepts about the meaning of childhood.

Moreover, the preoccupation with critical hierarchies reflected a class bias. Summarizing numerous social scientific studies, Bogart claimed that it was mainly the middle class who feared television's influence on children and that while "people of higher social position, income and education are more critical of existing fare in radio, television and the movies . . . those at the lower end of the social scale are more ready to accept what is available." Even if he believed that discriminating taste was a function of class difference, Bogart still internalized the elitist preoccupation with canon formation, lending professional credence to the idea that adults should restrict their children's viewing to what they deemed "respectable" culture. He suggested:

> If television cannot really be blamed for turning children into criminals or neurotics, this does not imply that it is a wholly healthful influence on the growing child. A much more serious charge is that television, in the worst aspects of its content, helps to perpetuate moral, cultural and social values which are not in accord with the highest ideals of an enlightened democracy. The cowboy film, the detective thriller and the soap opera, so often identified by critics as the epitome of American mass culture, probably do not represent the heritage which Americans at large want to transmit to posterity.[78]

Thus, while Bogart noted that working-class parents did not find a need to discriminate between programs, and that the formation of critical standards was mainly a middle-class pursuit, he nevertheless decided that television programs would not please the value systems of "Americans at large." Here as elsewhere, the notion of an enlightened democracy served to justify the hegemony of bourgeois tastes and the imparting of those tastes onto children of all classes.

Meanwhile, for their part, children often seemed to have different ideas. As numerous surveys indicated, youngsters often preferred the programs that parents found unwholesome, especially science-fiction serials and westerns. Surveys also indicated that children often liked to watch programs aimed at adults and that "parents were often reluctant to admit that their children watched adult shows regularly."[79] Milton Berle's *Texaco Star Theater* (which was famous for its inclusion of "off-color" cabaret humor) became so popular with children that Berle adopted the persona of Uncle Miltie, pandering to parents by telling his juvenile audience to obey their elders and go straight to bed when the program ended.[80] Other programs, however, were unable to bridge the generation gap. When, for example, CBS aired the mystery anthology *Suspense,* numerous affiliates across the country received letters from concerned parents who wanted the program taken off the air. Attempting to please its adult constituency, one Oklahoma station was caught in the cross fire between parents and children. When the station announced it would not air "horror story" programs before the bedtime hour of 9:00 P.M., it received a letter with the words "We protest!" signed by twenty-two children.[81]

Perhaps because adult aesthetic hierarchies did not always match children's tastes, popular magazines also concentrated on more forceful methods of ensuring children's proper use of television.[82] Drawing on cognitive and behavioralist theories of childhood that had been popular since the 1920s, and mixing these with the liberal "hands off" approach of Dr. Spock, the experts recommended ways for parents to instill healthy viewing habits in their children. In 1950, *Better Homes and Gardens* wrote, "Because he had seen the results of . . . viewing—facial tics, overstimulation, neglect of practicing, outdoor play . . . homework—Van R. Brokhane, who produces education FM programs for New York City schools, decided to establish a system of control." Brokhane's system was typical; it took the form of a careful management of time and space: "The Brokhanes put their receiver in the downstairs playroom where it could not entice their teen-age daughter away from her homework . . . then they outlined a schedule—their daughter could watch TV before dinner, but not afterward, on school nights."[83] Faced with the bureaucratized institutions of a mass culture that adults found difficult to change, parents could nevertheless exercise their power by disciplining children through a careful system of reward and punishment. Adopting the language of B. F. Skinner's behavioralist techniques, magazines discussed ways to control children's viewing through positive reinforcement. In 1955, *Better Homes and Gardens* reported, "After performing the routine of dressing, tidying up his room . . . Steve knows he can . . . joy of joys—watch his favorite morning TV show. His attitude is now so good he has even volunteered . . . to set the table for breakfast and help his little sister dress."[84] Thus, discipline was conceived not only in the negative sense, but also in the positive "prosocial" terms suggested by behavioralist psychology.

Expert advice also borrowed principles from psychoanalysis to engage in a kind of therapeutic interrogation of family dynamics. Here the television was not so much the cause of aberrant deeds as it was a symptom of deeply rooted problems in the home. As *Better Homes and Gardens* advised in 1950, "If your boy or girl throws a tantrum when you call him away from the set, don't blame television. Tantrums are a sign that tension already exists in a family."[85] In 1951, the magazine called in psychologist Ralph H. Ojemann to verify the claim: "The child who seems permanently enchanted by an electric gadget in the parlor generally gets that way because he has nothing else that challenges him. . . . 'It's unfortunate but true,' Doctor Ojemann says, 'that we're just not too good at building the best environments that the human personality needs for growth.'"[86] For Ojemann the "best environment" was a household that provided stimulating activities beyond television entertainment. Like other experts of the period, he turned the problem of disciplining children spectators into a larger problem of cultivating the home for proper socialization.

The paradox of such expert advice on television and children was that the experts—rather than the parents—took on the authoritative role. To borrow Jacques Donzelot's phrase, this expert advice amounted to a "policing of families" by public institutions.[87] By the turn of the century, American doctors, clergymen, educators, industrialists, architects, and women's groups had all claimed a stake in the management of domestic affairs. One of the central conduits for this was the new mass-circulation women's magazines that functioned in part as a site for reform discourses on the family. During the Progressive era and especially in the 1920s, the public control of domestic life was regularized and refined as outside agencies began to "administer" private life. In the 1920s, Secretary of Commerce Herbert Hoover became a housing crusader. His policies encouraged a proliferation of government agencies and civic centers that disseminated advice on subjects ranging from house building to childrearing. Hoover, in conjunction with private industry and civic groups, thought that outside agencies would help stabilize social and economic turmoil by ensuring a proper home life for all Americans. Women's magazines were closely linked to Hoover's campaigns, most obviously when Mrs. William Brown Meloney, editor of the *Delineator*, asked him to serve as President of Better Homes in America, a voluntary organization that began in 1922 and had 7,279 branches across the nation by 1930. More generally, women's magazines were inundated with advice from professionals and industrialists who saw themselves as the custodians of everyday life.[88]

In the postwar period, television became an ideal vehicle through which to regulate family life. As in the case of Dr. Ojemann's advice, watching television was typically figured as a sign of a larger family problem that needed to be studied and controlled by outside authorities.[89] In this sense, it served to support the social regulation of family life. It made parents more dependent upon knowledge produced by public institutions and thus placed parents in a weakened position.[90]

Perhaps because of their admonishing tones, experts were sometimes unpopular with their audiences. In 1951, an author in *House Beautiful* complained about the loss of parental dominion, claiming:

> It seems that raising a child correctly these days is infinitely more difficult than it was 30 years ago when no one ever heard of Drs. Kinsey and Gessell, and a man named Freud was discussed only in women's beauty parlors. . . .
>
> 20 or 30 years ago when there weren't so many authorities on everything in America, the papas and mamas of the nation had a whole lot easier going with Junior than we have today with the authorities.

The author connected his loss of parental power directly to television, recalling the time when his little boy began to strike the television set with a large stick. Unable to decide for himself how to punish his son, he opted for the lenient approach suggested by the expert, Dr. Spock. Unfortunately, he recounted, "the next day Derek rammed his shovel through the TV screen [and] the set promptly blew up."[91]

In part, anxieties about parental control had to do with the fact that television was heavily promoted to families with children. During the 1950s, manufacturers and retailers discovered that children were a lucrative consumer market for the sale of household commodities. An editor of *Home Furnishings* (the furniture retailer's trade journal) claimed, "The younger generation from one to twenty influences the entire home furnishings industry."[92] As one of the newest household items, television was quickly recognized for its potential appeal to young consumers. Numerous surveys indicated that families with children tended to buy television more than childless couples did. Television manufacturers quickly assimilated the new findings into their sales techniques. As early as 1948, the industry trade journal *Advertising and Selling* reported that the manager of public relations and advertising at the manufacturing company, Stromberg-Carlson, "quoted a survey . . . indicating that children not only exert a tremendous amount of influence in the selection and purchase of television receivers but that they are, in fact, television's most enthusiastic audience."[93] Basing their advertisements on such surveys, manufacturers and retailers formulated strategies by which to pull parents' purse strings—and heart strings as well. In 1950, the American Television Dealers and Manufacturers ran nationwide newspaper advertisements that played on parental guilt. The first ad in the series had a headline that read, "Your daughter won't ever tell you the humiliation she's felt in begging those precious hours of television from a neighbor." Forlorn children were pictured on top of the layout, and parents were shown how television could raise their youngsters' spirits. This particular case is especially interesting because it shows that there are indeed limits to which even advertisers can go before a certain degree of sales resistance takes place. Outraged by the advertisement, parents, educators, and clergymen complained to their newspapers about its manipulative tone. In addition, the Family Service Association of America called it a "cruel pressure to apply against millions of parents" who could not afford television sets.[94] In the midst of this controversy, the American Television Dealers and Manufacturers discontinued the ad campaign. Although this action might have temporarily quelled the more overt fears of adult groups, the popular media of the period continued to raise doubts that often surfaced in hyperbolic predictions of the end of patriarchal family life.

The Trouble with Fathers

Just as advertisements bestowed a new kind of power upon child consumers, television seemed to disrupt conventional power dynamics between child and adult. Popular media complained that the television image had usurped the authority previously held by parents. As television critic John Crosby claimed, "You tell little Oscar to trot off to bed, and you will probably find yourself embroiled in argument. But if Milton Berle tells him to go to bed, off he goes."[95] Here as elsewhere, television particularly threatened to depose the father. Television was depicted as the new patriarch, a threatening machine that had robbed men of their dominion in the home.

Television critics (most of whom were male) lashed out at the appearance of bumbling fathers on the new family sitcoms. In 1953, *TV Guide* asked, "What ever happened to men? . . . Once upon a time (B. TV) a girl thought of her boyfriend or husband as her Prince Charming. Now having watched the antics of Ozzie Nelson and Chester A. Riley, she thinks of her man, and any other man, as a Prime Idiot." One year later, a review in *Time* claimed, "In television's stable of 35 home-life comedies, it is a rare show that treats Father as anything more than the mouse of the house—a bumbling, well-meaning idiot who is putty in the hands of his wife and family."[96]

The henpecked male was, of course, a stock character in previous forms of popular entertainment such as twentieth-century vaudeville and film.[97] The kind of criticism directed at television and its bumbling fathers likewise had its roots in a well-established tradition of mass-culture criticism based on categories of sexual difference. Culture critics have often expressed their disdain for mass media in language that evokes contempt for those qualities that patriarchal societies ascribe to femininity. Thus, mass amusements are typically thought to encourage passivity, and they have frequently been represented in terms of pene-tration, consumption, and escape. As Andreas Huyssen has argued, this analogy between women and mass culture has, since the nineteenth century, served to valorize the dichotomy between "low" and "high" art (or modernism). Mass culture, Huyssen claims, "is somehow asso-ciated with woman while real, authentic culture remains the prerogative of men."[98]

The case of broadcasting is especially interesting in this regard be-cause the threat of feminization was particularly aimed at men. Broad-casting quite literally was shown to disrupt the normative structures of patriarchal (high) culture and to turn "real men" into passive home-bodies. The "feminizing" aspects of broadcast technology were a central concern during radio's installation in the twenties. Radio hams of the early 1910s were popularized in the press and in fiction as virile heroes who saved damsels in distress with the aid of wireless technology (a popular example were the "Radio Boys," Bob and Joe, who used wire-less to track down criminals and save the innocent).[99] But as Catherine Covert has claimed, once radio became a domestic medium, men were no longer represented as active agents. Now they were shown to sit pas-sively, listening to a one-way communication system.[100]

In the early 1940s, the connection between radio technology and emasculation came to a dramatic pitch when Philip Wylie wrote his bitter attack on American women, *Generation of Vipers*. In this widely read book, Wylie maintained that American society was suffering from an ailment which he called "momism." American women, according to Wylie, had become overbearing, domineering mothers who turned their sons and husbands into weak-kneed fools. The book was replete with imagery of apocalypse through technology, imagery which Wylie tied to the figure of the woman. As he saw it, an unholy alliance between women and big business had turned the world into an industrial night-mare. Corporations like Alcoa and General Electric had created a new female "sloth" by supplying the housewife with machines that "de-prived her of her social usefulness." Meanwhile, claimed Wylie, women had become "Cinderellas"—greedy consumers who "raped the men, not sexually, but morally."[101]

In his most bitter chapter, entitled "Common Women," Wylie argued that women had somehow gained control of the airwaves. Women, he suggested, made radio listening into a passive activity that threatened manhood and, in fact, civilization. Wylie wrote, "The radio is mom's final tool, for it stamps everyone who listens to it with the matriarchal brand—its superstitions, prejudices, devotional rules, taboos, musts, and all other qualifications needful to its maintenance. Just as Goebbels has revealed what can be done with such a mass-stamping of the public psyche in his nation, so our land is a living representation of the same fact worked out in matriarchal sentimentality, goo, slop, hidden cruelty, and the foreshadow of national death." [102] In the 1955 annotated edition, Wylie updated these fears, claiming that television would soon take the place of radio and turn men into female-dominated dupes. Women, he wrote, "will not rest until every electronic moment has been bought to sell suds and every bought program censored to the last decibel and syllable according to her self-adulation—along with that (to the degree the mom-indoctrinated pops are permitted access to the dials) of her de-sexed, de-souled, de-cerebrated mate." [103]

The mixture of misogyny and "telephobia" that ran through this passage is clearly hyperbolic; still, the basic idea was repeated in more sober representations of everyday life during the postwar period. Indeed, the paranoid connections that Wylie drew between corporate technocracies, women, and broadcasting continued to be drawn throughout the 1950s as large bureaucracies increasingly controlled the lives of middle-class men. Television was often shown to rob men of their powers and transform them into passive victims of a force they could not control.

A popular theme in the fifties was television's usurpation of the father's parental authority. In 1954, *Fireside Theatre*, a filmed anthology drama, presented this problem in an episode entitled "The Grass is Greener." Based on the simple life of a farm family, the program begins with the purchase of a television set, a purchase that the father, Bruce, adamantly opposes. Going against Bruce's wishes, his wife, Irene, makes use of the local retailer's credit plan and has a television set installed in her home. When Bruce returns home for the evening, he finds himself oddly displaced by the new center of interest. Upon entering the kitchen door, he hears music and gun shots emanating from the den. Curious about the source of the sound, he enters the room where he sees Irene and the children watching a television western. Standing in the den doorway, he is literally off-center in the frame, outside the family group clustered around the television set. When he attempts to get his family's attention, Bruce's status as outsider is further suggested. His son hushes him with a dismissive "Shh," after which the family resumes its fascination with the television program. Bruce then motions to Irene who

Dad interrupts the family during a TV western in this 1954 episode of *Fireside Theatre.*

finally—with a look of condescension—exits the room to join her husband in the kitchen where the couple argue over the set's installation. In her attempt to convince Bruce to keep the set, Irene suggests that the children and even she herself will stray from the family home if he refuses to allow them the pleasure of watching TV. Television thus threatens to undermine the masculine position of power in the home to the extent that the father is disenfranchised from his family, whose gaze is fastened onto an alternate, and more seductive, authority.

The episode goes on to figure this problem of masculinity through an unflattering representation of the male spectator. Bruce first reluctantly agrees to keep the television set on a thirty-day trial basis—so long as it remains in the children's room. But he too soon falls prey to the TV siren; in the next scene we see him alone in his den, slumped in an easy chair, half asleep, watching a western.[104] After Irene discovers him, he appears to be ashamed because he is caught in the act he himself claimed unworthy. Thus, as the narrative logic would have it, the father succumbs to television, and in so doing his power in the home is undermined. Indeed, the act of viewing television is itself shown to be unmanly.

The episode further suggests a waning of masculinity by suggesting

nostalgia for the virile heroes of the Hollywood cinema. When a serviceman installs the television set we learn that Bruce used to be a
screen idol in film westerns. The serviceman looks with awe at the studio portraits of Bruce that are pasted on the den wall. As Irene explains
to the serviceman, Bruce chose to leave the glamor of Hollywood behind for the simple life on their family farm. While Irene boasts about
wholesome virtues, the image track shows the serviceman/fan who appears to be lost in a trance of spectator identification as he ogles the
photographs on the den wall. This excess of male identification, this nostalgic admiration for the ex-movie star, reminds us of Bruce's decreased
authority in the present. As a farmer, Bruce is no longer an idol of spectator admiration; his masculine identity is now at odds with his former
pin-up photos. As this story suggests, the images of masculine prowess
so much a part of the classical Hollywood era (especially in genres like
the western) are now the remnants of a forgotten culture. In place of
these heroes, television gives us pragmatic family types—the bumbling
but well meaning fathers like Ozzie Nelson and Jim Anderson.[105] Indeed,
as audiences must have understood at the time, the larger-than-life cowboy idols of the silver screen were vanishing from the local theater and
reappearing in a debased form on twelve-inch television screens. The
new western heroes were not the John Waynes of classical A-movie
westerns; rather, they were comic book, B-movie heroes who appealed
almost entirely to a male juvenile audience—indeed, Bruce's son is
shown to be an avid fan of TV westerns.

Fireside Theatre's implicit comparison between masculine ideals in
Hollywood and television was more explicitly stated by popular critics
who compared television's family men with Hollywood's virile heroes.
In a 1953 review of *Bonino*, a short-lived situation comedy starring Ezio
Pinza, the *Saturday Review* claimed:

> Philip Morris doesn't know it, but it's sponsoring a crime
> show. . . . The crime is 'Bonino,' starring Ezio Pinza, and the
> victim is an illusion that is slowly being murdered—a beau-
> tiful, vital, and universal illusion, yours and mine. We met it
> first in 'South Pacific' on that enchanted evening when Pinza
> walked into Mary Martin's life. He was romantic, he was cos-
> mopolitan, he was virile. . . .
> And now what have they done to our dream on 'Bonino'?
> They have emasculated, eviscerated, and domesticated it;
> Jurgen has come home to his beer and his bedroom slippers.
> No longer the Phoenix lover, our Pinza is merely a father. . . .
> Where once was assurance and the comforting touch of power,
> now there is only the stereotype of *pater americanus*, well-
> meaning, tenderly stupid, and utterly inadequate in every
> department of his life except his profession. Weep for Adonis![106]

As the review so pointedly suggested, the Golden Age of masculinity was headed for a fall, and importantly, television itself seemed unable to resist commenting on the situation.

The Adventures of Ozzie and Harriet, whose corny, wishy-washy, do-nothing "Pop" was perhaps the prime abuser of the masculine ideal, reflected on the relationship between television and male power in a 1953 episode, "An Evening With Hamlet," which tied the theme of technological emasculation to a more general atrophy of patriarchal culture. The episode opens at the breakfast table as the young son Ricky sadly announces that the television set is broken. As was the case in many postwar households, the father in this home is unable to fix the complicated technology himself. Instead, the family is dependent upon a new cultural hero, the TV repairman, whose schedule is so tight that the Nelsons have to wait patiently for his arrival. Ozzie uses this occasion to assert his parental authority by finding family amusements that compete with television for the boys' attention. His idea of family fun recalls Victorian modes of recreation—specifically, dramatic reading—but his sons are less than pleased. As Ricky says in a subsequent scene, "Hey Mom, that television man didn't get here yet . . . now we're stuck with that darn Shakespeare."

This episode goes on to highlight the competition for cultural authority between fathers and television by objectifying the problem in the form of two supporting characters. While the Nelsons recite *Hamlet,* two men visit the family home. The first is a wandering bard who mysteriously appears at the Nelson door and joins the family recital. The bard, who looks like he is part of an Elizabethan theater troupe, evokes associations of high art and cultural refinement. The second visitor, a television repairman, represents the new electronic mass-produced culture. He is presented as an unrefined blue-collar worker who is good with machines but otherwise inept. A conversation between Ozzie and the repairman succinctly suggests the point:

REPAIRMAN: Oh a play, huh, I used to be interested in dramatics myself.

OZZIE: Oh, an actor!

REPAIRMAN: No, a wrestler.

As this scene so clearly demonstrates, television not only competes with the father at home, but also disturbs the central values of patriarchal culture by replacing the old authorities with a new and degraded art form.

A House Divided

In a home where patriarchal authority was undermined, television threatened to drive a wedge between family members. Social scientists argued that even while families might be brought together around the set, this spatial proximity did not necessarily translate into better family relations. As Eleanor MacCoby observed in her study of families in Cambridge, Massachusetts, "There is very little interaction among family members when they watch TV together, and the amount of time family members spend together exclusive of TV is reduced, so it is doubtful whether TV brings the family together in any psychological sense." [107]

Popular periodicals presented exaggerated versions of family division, often suggesting that television would send family members into separate worlds of pleasure and thus sever family ties, particularly at the dinner table. In 1950, Jack Gould wrote, "Mealtime is an event out of the ordinary for the television parent; for the child it may just be out." In that same year a cartoon in *Better Homes and Gardens* showed parents seated at the dining room table while their children sat in the living room, glued to the television set. Speaking from the point of view of the exasperated mother, the caption read, "All right, that does it! Harry, call up the television store and tell them to send a truck right over!" In 1953, *TV Guide* suggested a humorous solution to the problem in a cartoon that showed a family seated around a dining room table with a large television set built into the middle of it. The caption read, "Your kids won't have to leave the table to watch their favorite programs if you have the Diney model." [108]

Even more alarming than the mealtime problem, television threatened to cause disputes between siblings and between mates. As *House Beautiful* suggested in 1950, "Your wife wants to see *Philco Playhouse* and you don't. So you look too, or are driven from the room." [109] Similarly in 1954, *Popular Science* asked, "Is it hard to balance your checkbook or read while the kids are watching TV? Ever want to see the fights when your wife is chatting with a friend?" [110] Perhaps the most frustrated of all was the well-known critic and radio personality Goodman Ace, who wrote a satiric essay on the subject in 1953, "A Man's TV Set Is His Castle." The irony of this title was quickly apparent as Ace drew a rather unromantic picture of his life with television:

> The big television networks, fighting as they do for the elusive high rating, are little concerned with the crumbling of a man's home. Programs are indiscriminately placed in direct opposition one to the other, regardless of domestic consequence.
> That she [his wife] likes Ann Sothern and I much prefer Wally Cox opposite Miss Sothern is of little import to the executive vice presidents in charge of programming. . . . Perry Como sings for our supper while I wonder where John Cameron Swayze is hopscotching for headlines on the competitive

network. When I should be at ringside for a Wednesday night fight, I'm watching 'This Is Your Life.'

The critic concluded with a tip for the prospective TV consumer: "Don't be misled by advertisements announcing the large 24-inch screens. Buy two 12-inch screens. And don't think of it as losing your eyesight but rather as gaining a wife." [111]

Harmony gave way to a system of differences in which domestic space and family members in domestic space were divided along sexual and social lines. The ideal of family togetherness was achieved through the seemingly contradictory principle of separation; private rooms devoted to individual family members ensured peaceful relationships among residents. Thus, the social division of space was not simply the inverse of family unity; rather, it was a point on a continuum that stressed ideals of domestic cohesion. Even the family room itself was conceived in these terms. In fact, when coining the phrase, Nelson and Wright claimed, "By frankly developing a room which is 'entirely public' . . . privacy is made possible. Because there's an 'extra room,' the other living space can really be enjoyed in peace and quiet." [112]

This ideology of divided space was based on Victorian aesthetics of housing design and corresponding social distinctions entailed by family life. As we saw in chapter 1, the middle-class homes of Victorian America embodied the conflicting urge for family unity and division within their architectural layout. Since the homes were often quite spacious, it was possible to have rooms devoted to intimate family gatherings (such as the back parlor), social occasions (such as the front parlor), as well as rooms wholly given over to separate family members. By the 1950s, the typical four-and-one-half room dwellings of middle-class suburbia were clearly not large enough to support entirely the Victorian ideals of sociospatial hierarchies. Still, popular home manuals of the postwar period placed a premium on keeping these spatial distinctions in order, and they presented their readers with a model of space derived in part from the Victorian experience.

The act of watching television came to be a central concern in the discourse on divided spaces as the magazines showed readers pictures of rambling homes with special rooms designed exclusively for watching television. Sets were placed in children's playrooms or bedrooms, away from the central spaces of the home. In 1951, *House Beautiful* had even more elaborate plans. A fun room built adjacent to the home and equipped with television gave a teenage daughter a "place for her friends." For the parents it meant "peace of mind because teenagers are away from [the] house but still at home." [113]

It seems likely that most readers in their cramped suburban homes did not follow these suggestions. A 1954 national survey showed that 85 percent of the respondents kept their sets in the living room, so that the space for TV was the central, common living area in the home.[114] Perhaps recognizing the practical realities of their readers, the magazines also suggested ways to maintain the aesthetics of divided spaces in the small home. While it might not have been possible to have a room of one's own for television viewing, there were alternate methods by which to approximate the ideal. Rooms could be designed in such a way so that they functioned both as viewing areas and as centers for other activities. In this sense, television fit into a more general functionalist discourse in which household spaces were supposed to be made "multi-purposeful." In 1951, *Better Homes and Gardens* spoke of a "recreation area of the living room" that was "put to good use as the small fry enjoy a television show."[115] At other times such areas were referred to specifically as "television areas." While in many cases the television area was marked off by furniture arrangements or architectural structures such as alcoves, at other times the sign of division was concretized in an object form—the room divider.

In some cases the television receiver was actually built into the room divider so that television literally became a divisive object in the home. In 1953, for example, *Better Homes and Gardens* displayed a "living-dining area divider" that was placed behind a sofa. Extending beyond the sofa, its right end housed a television set. As the illustration showed, this TV/room divider created a private viewing area for children.[116] In 1955, one room-divider company saw the promotional logic in this scenario, showing mothers how Modernfold Doors would keep children spectators at a safe distance. The ad depicts a mother sitting at one end of a room, while her child and television set are separated off by the folding wall. Suggesting itself as an object of dispute, the television set works to support the call for the room divider—here stated as "that tiresome game of 'Who gets the living room.'" Moreover, since room dividers like this one were typically collapsible, they were the perfect negotiation between ideals of unity and division. They allowed parents to be apart from their children, but the "fold-back" walls also provided easy access to family togetherness.[117]

The swiveling television was another popular way to mediate ideals of unity and division. In 1953, *Ladies' Home Journal* described how John and Lucille Bradford solved the viewing problem in their home by placing a large console set on a rotating platform that was hinged to the doorway separating the living room from the play porch. Lucille told the magazine, "The beauty of this idea . . . is that the whole family can watch programs together in the living room, or the children can watch their own special cowboy programs from the play porch without interfering with grownups' conversation." [118]

This sociosexual division of space was also presented in advertisements for television sets. In 1955, General Electric showed how its portable television set could mediate family tensions. On the top of the page a cartoon depicts a family besieged by television as Mother frantically attempts to vacuum up the mess created by her young son who, sitting on his tricycle, changes the channel on the television console. Father, sitting on an easy chair in front of the set, is so perturbed by the goings-on that his pipe flies out of his mouth. The solution to this problem is provided further down on the page where two photographs are juxtaposed. The photograph on the right side of the page depicts Mother and Daughter in the kitchen where they watch a cooking program on a portable TV while the photograph on the left side of the page shows Father watching football on the living room console. This "split-screen" layout was particularly suited to GE's sales message, the purchase of a second television set. The copy reads: "When Dad wants to watch the game . . . Mom and Sis, the cooking show . . . there's too much traffic for one TV to handle." [119]

The depiction of divided families wasn't simply a clever marketing strategy; rather, it was a well-entrenched pictorial convention. Indeed, by 1952, advertisements in the home magazines increasingly depicted family members enjoying television alone or else in subgroups. At least in the case of these ads, it appears that the cultural meanings that were circulated about television changed somewhat over the course of the early years of installation. While television was primarily shown to be an integrating activity in the first few years of diffusion, in the 1950s it came to be equally (or perhaps even more) associated with social differences and segregation among family members. [120]

It is, however, important to remember that the contradiction between family unity and division was just that—a contradiction, a site of ideological tension, and not just a clear-cut set of opposing choices. In this light, we might understand a number of advertisements that attempted to negotiate such tensions by evoking ideas of unity and division at the same time. These ads pictured family members watching television in private, but the image on the television screen contained a kind of surrogate family. A 1953 ad for Sentinel TV shows a husband and wife gently embracing as they watch their brand new television set on Christmas Eve. The pleasure entailed by watching television is associated more with the couple's romantic life than with their parental duties. However, the televised image contains two children, apparently singing Christmas carols. Thus, the advertisement shows that parents can enjoy

In this 1955 advertisement, General Electric promises family harmony through separation. (Courtesy General Electric.)

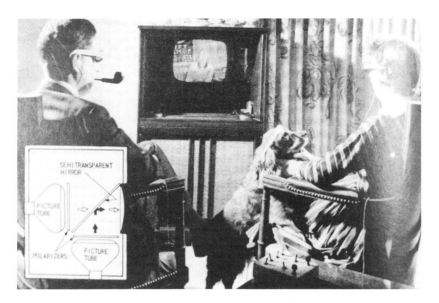

The DuMont Duoscope promotes togetherness through division.

a romantic night of television apart from their own children. But it still sustains the central importance of the family scene because it literally *re-presents* the absent children by making them into an image on the screen. Moreover, the advertisement attaches a certain amount of guilt to the couple's intimate night of television, their use of television as a medium for romantic rather than familial enjoyment. The idea of guilty pleasure is suggested by the inclusion of two "real" children who appear to be voyeurs, clandestinely looking onto the scene of their parents' pleasure. Dressed in pajamas, the youngsters peek out from a corner of the room, apparently sneaking out of bed to take a look at the new television set, while the grownups remain unaware of their presence.[121]

The tensions between opposing ideals of unity and division were also expressed in material form. Manufacturers offered technological "gizmos" that allowed families to be alone and together at the same time. In 1954, *Popular Science* displayed a new device that parents could use to silence the set while their children watched. As the magazine explained, "NOBODY IS BOTHERED if the children want to see a rootin'-tootin' Western when Dad and Mother want to read, write or talk. Earphones let the youngsters hear every shot, but the silence is wonderful."[122] DuMont had an even better idea with its "Duoscope" set. This elaborate construction was composed of two receivers housed in a television cabinet, with two chassis, two control panels, and two picture tubes that were mounted at right angles. Through polarization and the superimposition of two broadcast images, the set allowed two viewers to watch different programs at the same time. Thus, as the article suggested, a husband and wife equipped with polarized glasses were able to watch television together but still retain their private pleasures.[123]

While the Duoscope never caught on, the basic problem of unity and division continued. The attempt to balance ideals of family harmony and social difference often led to bizarre solutions, but it also resulted in everyday viewing patterns that were presented as functional and normal procedures for using television. Popular discourses tried to tame the beast, suggesting ways to maintain traditional modes of family behavior and still allow for social change. They devised intricate plans for resistance and accommodation to the new machine, and in so doing they helped construct a new cultural form.

Three

Women's Work

The Western-Holly Company in 1952 marketed a new design in domestic technology, the TV-stove. The oven included a window through which the housewife could watch her chicken roast. Above the oven window was a TV screen that presented an even more spectacular sight. With the aid of this machine the housewife would be able to prepare her meal, but at the same time she could watch TV. Although it was clearly an odd object, the TV-stove was not simply a historical fluke. Rather, its invention should remind us of the concrete social, economic, and ideological conditions that made this contraption possible. Indeed, the TV-stove was a response to the conflation of labor and leisure time at home. If we now find it strange, this has as much to do with the way in which our society has conceptualized work and leisure as it does with the machine's bizarre technological form.[1]

Since the nineteenth century, middle-class ideals of domesticity had been predicated on divisions of leisure time and work time. The doctrine of two spheres represented human activity in spatial terms: the public world came to be conceived of as a place of productive labor, while the home was seen as a site of rejuvenation and consumption. By the 1920s, the public world was still a sphere of work, but it was also opened up to a host of commercial pleasures such as movies and amusement parks that were incorporated into middle-class life styles. The ideal home, however, remained a place of revitalization and, with the expansion of convenience products that promised to reduce household chores, domesticity was even less associated with production.

As feminists have argued, this separation has justified the exploitation of the housewife whose work at home simply does not count. Along these lines, Nancy Folbre claims that classical economics considers women's work as voluntary labor and therefore outside the realm of exploitation. In addition, she argues, even Marxist critics neglect the issue of domestic exploitation since they assume that the labor theory of value can be applied only to efficiency-oriented production for the market and not to "inefficient" and "idiosyncratic" household chores.[2]

As feminist critics and historians have shown, however, the home is indeed a site of labor. Not only do women do physical chores, but also the basic relations of our economy and society are reproduced at home, including the literal reproduction of workers through childrearing labor. Once the home is considered a workplace, the divisions between public/work and domestic/leisure become less clear. The way in which work and leisure are connected, however, remains a complex question.

Henri Lefebvre's studies of everyday life offer ways to consider the general interrelations between work, leisure, and family life in modern society. In his foreword to the 1958 edition of *Critique de la Vie Quotidienne,* Lefebvre argues:

> Leisure . . . cannot be separated from work. It is the same man
> who, after work, rests or relaxes or does whatever he chooses.
> Every day, at the same time, the worker leaves the factory, and
> the employee, the office. Every week, Saturday and Sunday
> are spent on leisure activities, with the same regularity as that
> of the weekdays' work. Thus we must think in terms of the
> unity 'work-leisure,' because that unity exists, and everyone
> tries to program his own available time according to what his
> work is—and what it is not.[3]

While Lefebvre concentrated on the "working man," the case of the housewife presents an even more pronounced example of the integration of work and leisure in everyday life.

The TV Stove turns cooking into a spectator sport.

In recent years, media scholars have begun to demonstrate the impact that patterns of domestic leisure and labor have on television spectatorship. British ethnographic research has suggested that men and women tend to use television according to their specific position within the distribution of leisure and labor activities inside and outside the home.[4] In the American context, two of the most serious examinations come from Tania Modleski (1983) and Nick Browne (1984), who have both theorized the way TV watching fits into a general pattern of everyday life where work and leisure are intertwined. Modleski has suggested that the soap opera might be understood in terms of the "rhythms of reception," or the way women working at home relate to the text within a specific milieu of distraction—cleaning, cooking, childrearing, and so on.[5] Browne concentrates not on the individual text, but rather on the entire TV schedule, which he claims is ordered according to the logic of the workday of both men and women. "[T]he position of the programs in the television schedule reflects and is determined by the work-structured order of the real social world. The patterns of position and flow imply the question of who is home, and through complicated social relays and temporal mediations, link television to the modes, processes, and scheduling of production characteristic of the general population."[6]

The fluid interconnection between leisure and labor at home presents a context in which to understand representations of the female audience during the postwar years. Above all, women's leisure time was shown to be coterminous with their work time. Representations of television continually addressed women as housewives and presented them with a notion of spectatorship that was inextricably intertwined with their useful labor at home. Certainly, this model of female spectatorship was based on previous notions about radio listeners, and we can assume that women were able to adapt some of their listening habits to television viewing without much difficulty. However, the added impact of visual images ushered in new dilemmas that were the subject of profound concern, both within the broadcast industry and within the popular culture at large.

The Industry's Ideal Viewer

The idea that female spectators were also workers in the home was, by the postwar period, a truism for broadcasting and advertising executives. For some twenty years, radio programmers had grappled with ways to address a group of spectators whose attention wasn't focused primarily on the medium (as in the cinema), but instead moved constantly between radio entertainment and a host of daily chores. As William Boddy has argued, early broadcasters were particularly reluctant to feature daytime radio shows, fearing that women's household work would be fundamentally incompatible with the medium.[7] Overcoming its initial reluctance, the industry successfully developed daytime radio in the 1930s, and by the 1940s housewives constituted a faithful audience for soap operas and advice programs.

During the postwar years, advertisers and networks once more viewed the daytime market with skepticism, fearing that their loyal radio audiences would not be able to make the transition to television. The industry assumed that, unlike radio, television might require the housewife's complete attention and thus disrupt her work in the home.[8] Indeed, while network prime-time schedules were well worked out in 1948, networks and national advertisers were reluctant to feature regular daytime programs. Thus, in the earliest years, morning and afternoon hours were typically left to the discretion of local stations, which filled the time with low budget versions of familiar radio formats and old Hollywood films.

The first network to offer a regular daytime schedule was DuMont, which began operations on its owned and operated station WABD in New York in November of 1948. As a newly formed network which had severe problems competing with CBS and NBC, DuMont entered the daytime market to offset its economic losses in prime time at a time when even the major networks were losing money on television.[9] Explaining the economic strategy behind the move into daytime, one DuMont executive claimed, "WABD is starting daytime programming because it is not economically feasible to do otherwise. Night time programming alone could not support radio, nor can it support television."[10] Increasingly in 1949, DuMont offered daytime programming to its affiliate stations. By December, it was transmitting the first commercially sponsored, daytime network show, *Okay, Mother,* to three affiliates and also airing a two-hour afternoon program on a full network basis. DuMont director Commander Mortimer W. Loewi reasoned that the move into daytime would attract small ticket advertisers who wanted to buy "small segments of time at a low, daytime rate."[11]

DuMont's venture into the daytime market was a thorn in the side of the other networks. While CBS, NBC, and ABC had experimented with individual daytime television programs on their flagship stations, they were reluctant to feature full daytime schedules. With huge investments in daytime radio, they weren't likely to find the prospects of daytime television appealing, especially since they were using their radio profits to offset initial losses in prime-time programming. As *Variety* reported when DuMont began its broadcasts on WABD, the major networks "must protect their AM [radio] investment at all costs—and the infiltration of daytime TV may conceivably cut into daytime radio advertising."[12] In this context, DuMont's competition in the daytime market posed a particularly grave threat to advertising revenues. In response, the other networks gradually began expanding the daytime lineups for their flagship stations.[13]

It was in 1951 that CBS, NBC, and, to a lesser extent, ABC first aggressively attempted to colonize the housewife's workday with regularly scheduled network programs. One of the central reasons for the networks' move into daytime that year was the fact that prime-time hours were fully booked by advertisers and that, by this point, there was more demand for TV advertising in general. As the advertising agency BBDO claimed in a report on daytime TV in the fall of 1950, "To all intents and purposes, the opportunity to purchase good night-time periods of TV is almost a thing of the past and the advertiser hoping to enter television now . . . better start looking at Daytime TV while it is still here to look at."[14] Daytime might have been more risky than prime time, but it had the advantage of being available—and at a cheaper network cost. Confident of its move into daytime, CBS claimed, "We aren't risking our reputation by predicting that daytime television will be a solid sell-out a year from today . . . and that once again there will be some sad advertisers who didn't read the tea leaves right."[15] ABC vice president Alexander Stronach Jr. was just as certain about the daytime market, and having just taken the plunge with the *Frances Langford-Don Ameche Show* (a variety program budgeted at the then steep $40,000 a week), Stronach told *Newsweek*, "It's a good thing electric dishwashers and washing machines were invented. The housewives will need them."[16]

The networks' confidence carried through to advertisers who began to test the waters of the daytime schedule. In September of 1951, the trade journal *Televiser* reported that "47 big advertisers have used daytime network television during the past season or are starting this Fall." Included were such well-known companies as American Home Products, Best Foods, Procter and Gamble, General Foods, Hazel Bishop Lipsticks, Minute Maid, Hotpoint, and the woman's magazine *Ladies' Home Journal*.[17]

Despite these inroads, the early daytime market remained highly unstable, and at least until 1955 the competition for sponsors was fierce.[18] Indeed, even while the aggregate size of the daytime audience rose in the early fifties, sponsors and broadcasters were uncertain about the extent to which housewives actually paid attention to the programs and advertisements. In response to such concerns, the industry aggressively tailored programs to fit the daily habits of the female audience. When it began operations in 1948, DuMont's WABD planned shows that could "be appreciated just as much from listening to them as from watching them."[19] Following this trend in 1950, Detroit's WXYX aired *Pat 'n' Johnny*, a program that solved the housework-TV conflict in less than subtle ways. At the beginning of the three-hour show, host Johnny Slagle instructed housewives, "Don't stop whatever you're doing. When we think we have something interesting I'll blow this whistle or Pat will ring her bell."[20]

The major networks were also intent upon designing programs to suit the content and organization of the housewife's day. The format that has received the most critical attention is the soap opera, which first came to network television in December of 1950. As Robert Allen has demonstrated, early soap opera producers like Irna Philips of *Guiding Light* were skeptical of moving their shows from radio to TV. However, by 1954 the Nielsen Company reported that soaps had a substantial following; *Search For Tomorrow* was the second most popular daytime show while *Guiding Light* was in fourth place. The early soaps, with their minimum of action and visual interest, allowed housewives to listen to dialogue while working in another room. Moreover, their segmented storylines (usually two a day), as well as their repetition and constant explanation of previous plots, allowed women to divide their attention between viewing and household work.[21]

Another popular solution to the daytime dilemma was the segmented variety show that allowed women to enter and exit the text according to its discrete narrative units. One of DuMont's first programs, for example, was a shopping show (alternatively called *At Your Service* and *Shoppers Matinee*) that consisted of twenty-one entertainment segments, all of which revolved around different types of "women's issues." For instance, the "Bite Shop" presented fashion tips while "Kitchen Fare" gave culinary advice. Interspersed with these segments were twelve one-minute "store bulletins" (news and service announcements) that could be replaced at individual stations by local commercials.[22] While DuMont's program was short-lived, the basic principles survived in the daytime shows at the major networks. Programs like *The Garry Moore Show* (CBS), *The Kate Smith Show* (NBC), and *The Arthur Godfrey Show* (CBS) catered to housewife audiences with their segmented variety of entertainment and advice.[23]

Indeed, the networks put enormous amounts of money and effort into variety shows when they first began to compose daytime program schedules. Daytime ratings continually confirmed the importance of the variety format, with hosts like Smith and Godfrey drawing big audiences. Since daytime stars were often taken from nighttime radio shows, the variety programs were immediately marked as being different from

DuMont's *Television Department Stores* lets the housewife shop at home and teach her children how to be good consumers. (DuMont Collection, Archives Center, National Museum of American History, Smithsonian Institution.)

and more spectacular than daytime radio. *Variety* reported in October of 1951:

> The daytime television picture represents a radical departure
> from radio. The application of 'nighttime thinking' into day-
> time TV in regards to big-league variety-slanted programs and
> projection of personalities becomes more and more important.
> If the housewife has a craving for visual soap operas, it is nei-
> ther reflected in the present day Nielsens nor in the ambitious
> programming formulas being blueprinted by the video entre-
> preneurs. . . . The housewife with her multiple chores, it
> would seem, wants her TV distractions on a 'catch as catch
> can' basis, and the single-minded concentration on sight-and-
> sound weepers doesn't jibe with her household schedule. . . .
> [Variety shows] are all geared to the 'take it awhile leave it
> awhile' school of entertainment projection and practically all
> are reaping a bonanza for the networks.[24]

Television thus introduced itself to the housewife not only by repeating tried and true daytime radio formulas, but also by creating a distinct product tailored to what the industry assumed were the television audience's specific needs and desires.

Initially uncertain about the degree to which daytime programs from an audio medium would suit the housewife's routine, many television broadcasters turned their attention to the visual medium of the popular press. Variety shows often modeled themselves on print conventions, particularly borrowing narrative techniques from women's magazines and the women's pages. Much as housewives might flip through the pages of a magazine as they went about their daily chores, they could tune in and out of the magazine program without the kind of disorientation that they might experience when disrupted from a continuous drama. To ensure coherence, such programs included "women's editors" or "femcees" who provided a narrational thread for a series of "departments" on gardening, homemaking, fashion, and the like. These shows often went to extreme lengths to make the connection between print media and television programming foremost in the viewer's mind. *Women's Magazine of the Air,* a local program aired in Chicago on WGN, presented a "potpourri theme with magazine pages being turned to indicate new sections."[25] On its locally owned station, the *Seattle Post* presented *Women's Page,* starring *Post* book and music editor Suzanne Martin. The networks also used the popular press as a model for daytime programs. As early as 1948, CBS's New York station aired *Vanity Fair,* a segmented format that was tied together by "managing editor" Dorothy Dean, an experienced newspaper reporter. By the end of 1949, *Vanity Fair* was boasting a large list of sponsors, and in the fifties it continued to be part of the daytime schedule. Nevertheless, despite its success with *Vanity Fair*, CBS still tended to rely more heavily on well-known radio stars and formats, adapting these to the television medium. Instead, it was NBC that developed the print media model most aggressively in the early fifties.

Faced with daytime ratings that were consistently behind those of CBS and troubled by severe sponsorship problems, NBC saw the variety/magazine format as a particularly apt vehicle for small ticket advertisers who could purchase brief participation spots between program segments for relatively low cost.[26] Under the direction of programming vice president Sylvester "Pat" Weaver (who became NBC president in 1953), the network developed its "magazine concept" of advertising. Unlike the single sponsor series, which was usually produced through the advertising agency, the magazine concept allowed the network to retain control and ownership of programs. Although this form of multiple sponsor participation had become a common daytime practice by the early 1950s, Weaver's scheme differed from other participation plans because it allowed sponsors to purchase segments on a one-shot basis, with no ongoing commitment to the series. Even if this meant greater financial risks at the outset, in the long run a successful program based on spot sales would garner large amounts of revenue for the network.[27]

Weaver applied the magazine concept to two of the most highly successful daytime programs, *Today* and *Home*. Aired between 7:00 and 9:00 A.M., *Today* was NBC's self-proclaimed "television newspaper, covering not only the latest news, weather and time signals, but special features on everything from fashions to the hydrogen bomb."[28] On its premier episode in January 1952, *Today* made the print media connections firm in viewers' minds by showing telephoto machines grinding out pictures and front page facsimiles of the *San Francisco Chronicle*.[29] Aimed at a family audience, the program attempted to lure men, women, and children with discrete program segments that addressed their different interests and meshed with their separate schedules. One NBC confidential report stated that, on the one hand, men rushing off to take a train would not be likely to watch fashion segments. On the other hand, it suggested, "men might be willing to catch the next train" if they included an "almost sexy gal as part of the show." This, the report concluded, would be like "subtle, early morning sex."[30]

Although it was aimed at the entire family, the lion's share of the audience was female. (In 1954, for example, the network calculated that the audience was composed of 52 percent women, 26 percent men, and 22 percent children.)[31] *Today* appealed to housewives with "women's pages" news stories such as Hollywood gossip segments, fashion shows, and humanistic features. In August 1952, NBC's New York outlet inserted "Today's Woman" into the program, a special women's magazine feature that was produced in cooperation with *Look* and *Quick* magazines.[32] Enthused with *Today*'s success, NBC developed *Home* with similar premises in mind, but this time aimed the program specifically at women. First aired in 1954 during the 11:00 A.M. to noon time slot, *Home* borrowed its narrative techniques from women's magazines, featuring segments on topics like gardening, child psychology, food, fashion, health, and interior decor. As *Newsweek* wrote, "The program is planned to do for women on the screen what the women's magazines have long done in print."[33]

In fashioning daytime shows on familiar models of the popular press, television executives and advertisers were guided by the implicit assumption that the female audience had much in common with the typical magazine reader. When promoting *Today* and *Home*, NBC used magazines such as *Ladies' Home Journal, Good Housekeeping,* and *Collier's* (which also had a large female readership) as major venues. When *Home* first appeared it even offered women copies of its own monthly magazine, *How To Do it.*[34] Magazine publishers also must have seen the potential profits in the cross-over audience; the first sponsor for *Today* was Kiplinger's magazine *Changing Times,* and *Life* and Curtis magazines were soon to follow.[35]

The fluid transactions between magazine publishers and daytime producers were based on widely held notions about the demographic composition of the female audience. In 1954, the same year that *Home* premiered, NBC hired W. R. Simmons and Associates to conduct the first nationwide qualitative survey of daytime viewers. In a promotional report based on the survey, Dr. Tom Coffin, manager of NBC research, told advertisers and manufacturers, "In analyzing the findings, we have felt a growing sense of excitement at the qualitative picture emerging: an audience with the *size* of a mass medium but the *quality* of a class medium." When compared to nonviewers, daytime viewers were at the "age of acquisition," with many in the 25 to 34-year-old category; their families were larger with more children under 18; they had higher incomes; and they lived in larger and "better" market areas. In addition, Coffin characterized the average viewer as a "modern active woman" with a kitchen full of "labor-saving devices," an interest in her house, clothes, and "the way she looks." She is "the kind of woman most advertisers are most interested in; she's a good customer."[36] Coffin's focus on the "class vs. mass" audience bears striking resemblance to the readership statistics of middle-class women's magazines. Like the magazine reader, "Mrs. Daytime Consumer" was an upscale, if only moderately affluent, housewife whose daily life consisted not only of chores, but also, and perhaps even more importantly, shopping for her family.

With this picture of the housewife in mind, the media producer had one primary job—teaching her how to buy products. Again, the magazine format was perfect for this because each discrete narrative segment could portray an integrated sales message. Hollywood gossip columns gave way to motion picture endorsements; cooking segments sold sleek new ranges; fashion shows promoted Macy's finest evening wear. By integrating sales messages with advice on housekeeping and luxury lifestyles, the magazine format skillfully suggested to housewives that their time spent viewing television was indeed part of their work time. In other words, the programs promised viewers not just entertainment, but also lessons on how to make consumer choices for their families. One production handbook claimed: "Women's daytime programs have tended toward the practical—providing shopping information, marketing tips, cooking, sewing, interior decoration, etc., with a dash of fashion and beauty hints. . . . The theory is that the housewife will be more likely to take time from her household duties if she feels that her television viewing will make her housekeeping more efficient and help her provide more gracious living for her family."[37] In the case of *Home,* this implicit integration of housework, consumerism, and TV entertainment materialized in the form of a circular stage that the network promoted as a "machine for selling."[38] The stage was equipped with a complete kitchen, a workshop area, and a small garden—all of which functioned as settings for different program segments and, of course, the different sponsor products that accompanied them. Thus, *Home's* magazine format provided a unique arena for the presentation of a series of fragmented consumer fantasies that women might tune into and out of, according to the logic of their daily schedules.

Even if the structure of this narrative format was the ideal vehicle for "Mrs. Daytime Consumer," the content of the consumer fantasies still had to be carefully planned. Like the woman's magazine before it, the magazine show needed to maintain the subtle balance of its "class address." In order to appeal to the average middle-class housewife, it had to make its consumer fantasies fit with the more practical concerns of female viewers. The degree to which network executives attempted to strike this balance is well illustrated in the case of *Home.* After the program's first airing, NBC executive Charles Barry was particularly concerned about the amount of "polish" that it contained. Using "polish" as a euphemism for highbrow tastes, Barry went on to observe the problems with *Home's* class address: "I hope you will keep in mind that the average gal looking at the show is either living in a small suburban house or in an apartment and is not very likely to have heard of Paul McCobb; she is more likely to be at a Macy's buying traditionally." After observing other episodes, Barry had similar complaints: the precocious stage children weren't "average" enough, the furniture segment featured impractical items, and the cooking segment showcased high-class foods such as vichyssoise and pot-de-crème. "Maybe you can improve tastes," Barry conceded, "but gosh would somebody please tell me how to cook corned beef and cabbage without any smell?"[39] The television producer could educate the housewife beyond her means, but only through mixing upper-class fantasy with tropes of averageness.

The figure of the female hostess was also fashioned to strike this delicate balance. In order to appeal to the typical housewife, the hostess would ideally speak on her level. As one producer argued, "Those who give an impression of superiority or 'talking down' to the audience, who treasure the manner of speaking over naturalness and meaningful communication . . . or who are overly formal in attire and manners, do not survive in the broadcasting industry. . . . The personality should fit right into your living room. The super-sophisticate or the squealing life of the party might be all right on occasion, but a daily association with this girl is apt to get a little tiresome."[40] In addition, the ideal hostess was decidedly not a glamour girl, but rather a pleasingly attractive, middle-aged woman—Hollywood's answer to the home economics teacher. When first planning *Home,* one NBC executive considered using the celebrity couple Van and Evie Johnson for hosts, claiming that Evie was "a sensible woman, not a glamor struck movie star's wife, but a wholesome girl from a wholesome background. . . . She works hard at being a housewife and Mother who runs a not elaborate household in Beverly Hills with *no swimming pool.*" Although Evie didn't get the part, her competitor, Arlene Francis, was clearly cut from the same cloth. In a 1957 fanzine, Francis highlighted her ordinariness when she admitted, "My nose is too long and I'm too skinny, but maybe that won't make any difference if I'm fun to be with."[41] Francis was also a calming mother figure who appealed to children. In a fan letter, one mother wrote that her little boy took a magazine to bed with him that had Arlene's picture on the cover.[42] Unlike the "almost sexy" fantasy woman on the *Today* show who was perfect for "morning sex," *Home*'s femcee appealed to less erotic instincts. Francis and other daytime hostesses were designed to provide a role model for ordinary housewives, educating them on the "good life," while still appearing down to earth.

In assuming the role of "consumer educator," the networks went beyond just teaching housewives how to buy advertisers' products. Much more crucially in this early period, the networks attempted to teach women and their families how to consume television itself. Indeed, the whole system pivoted on the singular problem of how to make the daytime audience watch more programming. Since it adapted itself to the family's daily routine, the magazine show was particularly suited for this purpose. When describing the habits of *Today*'s morning audience, Weaver acknowledged that the "show, of course, does not hold the same audience throughout the time period, but actually is a service fitting with the family's own habit pattern in the morning."[43] Importantly, however, NBC continually tried to channel the movements of the audience. Not merely content to fit its programming into the viewer's rhythms of reception, the network aggressively sought to change those rhythms by making the activity of television viewing into a new daily habit. One NBC report made this point quite explicit, suggesting that producers "establish definite show patterns at regular times; do everything you can to capitalize on the great habit of habit listening."[44] Proud of his accomplishments on this front, Weaver bragged about fan mail that demonstrated how *Today* changed viewers' daily routines. According to Weaver, one woman claimed, "My husband said I should put casters on the TV set so I can roll it around and see it from the kitchen." Another admitted, "I used to get all the dishes washed by 8:30—now I don't do a thing until 10 o'clock." Still another confessed, "My husband now dresses in the living room." Weaver boastfully promised, "We will change the habits of millions."[45]

The concept of habitual viewing also governed NBC's scheduling techniques. The network devised promotional strategies designed to maintain systems of flow, as each program ideally would form a "lead in" for the next, tailored to punctuate intervals of the family's daily routine. In 1954, for example, an NBC report on daytime stated that *Today* was perfect for the early morning time slot because it "has a family audience . . . and reaches them just before they go out to shop." With shopping done, mothers might return home to find *Ding Dong School*, "a nursery school on television" that allowed them to do housework while educator Frances Horwich helped raise the pre-schoolers. Daytime dramas were scheduled throughout the day, each lasting only fifteen minutes, probably because the network assumed that drama would require more of the housewife's attention than the segmented variety formats like *Home*. At 5 P.M., when mothers were likely to be preparing dinner, *The Pinky Lee Show* presented a mixed bag of musical acts, dance routines, parlor games, and talk aimed both at women and their children who were now home from school.[46]

NBC aggressively promoted this kind of routinized viewership, buying space in major market newspapers and national periodicals for advertisements that instructed women how to watch television while doing household chores. In 1955, *Ladies' Home Journal* and *Good House-*

keeping carried advertisements for NBC's daytime lineup that suggested
that not only the programs, but also the scheduling of the programs,
would suit the housewife's daily routine. The ads evoked a sense of fragmented leisure time and suggested that television viewing could be conducted in a state of distraction. This was not the kind of critical contem-
plative distraction that Walter Benjamin suggested in his seminal essay,
"The Work of Art in the Age of Mechanical Reproduction." [47] Rather, the
ads implied that the housewife could accomplish her chores in a state of
"utopian forgetfulness" as she moved freely between her work and the
act of watching television.

One advertisement, which is particularly striking in this regard, includes a sketch of a housewife and her little daughter at the top of the
page. Below this, the graphic layout is divided into eight boxes composed of television screens, each representing a different program in
NBC's daytime lineup. The caption functions as the housewife's testimony to her distracted state. She asks, "Where Did the Morning Go?
The house is tidy . . . but it hasn't seemed like a terribly tiring morning. . . . I think I started ironing while I watched the *Sheila Graham
Show*." The housewife goes on to register each detail of the programs,
but she cannot with certainty account for her productive activities in the
home. Furthermore, as the ad's layout suggests, the woman's daily activities are literally fragmented according to the pattern of the daytime television schedule, to the extent that her everyday experiences become
imbricated in a kind of serial narrative. Significantly, her child pictured
at the top of the advertisement appears within the contours of a television screen so that the labor of childrearing is itself made part of the
narrative pleasures offered by the network's daytime lineup. [48]

Negotiating with the Industry's Ideal Viewer

The program types, schedules, and promotional materials devised at the
networks were based upon ideal images of female viewers and, consequently, they were rooted in abstract conceptions about women's lives.
These ideals weren't always commensurate with the heterogeneous experiences and situations of real women and, for this reason, industrial
strategies didn't always form a perfect fit with the audience's needs and
desires. Although it is impossible to reconstruct fully the actual activities
of female viewers at home, we can better understand their concerns and
practices by examining the ways in which their viewing experiences were
explained to them at the time. Popular media, particularly women's
magazines, presented women with opportunities to negotiate with the
modes of spectatorship that the television industry tried to construct. It
is in these texts that we see the gaps and inconsistencies—the unexpected twists and turns—that were not foreseen by networks and adver-

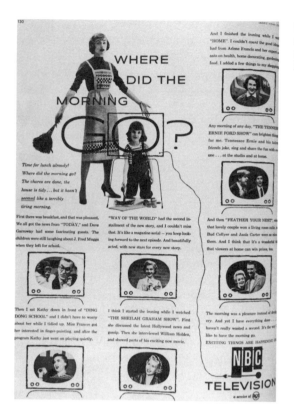

In this 1955 advertisement, NBC shows women how to make housework pleasant.

tisers. Indeed, it is in the magazines, rather than in the highrise buildings of NBC, CBS, and ABC, where female audiences were given the chance to enter into a popular dialogue about their own relations to the medium.

While the networks were busy attempting to tailor daytime programming to the patterns of domestic labor, popular media often completely rejected the idea that television could be compatible with women's work and showed instead how it would threaten the efficient functioning of the household. The TV-addict housewife became a stock character during the period, particularly in texts aimed at a general audience where the mode of address was characterized by an implicit male narrator who clearly blamed women—not television—for the untidy house. In 1950, for example, *The New Yorker* ran a cartoon that showed a slovenly looking woman ironing a shirt while blankly staring at the television screen. Unfortunately, in her state of distraction, the woman burned a hole in the garment.[49] Women's magazines also deliberated upon television's thoroughly negative effect on household chores, but rather than poking fun at the housewife, they offered sympathetic advice, usually suggesting that a careful management of domestic space might solve the problem. In 1950, *House Beautiful* warned of television: "It delivers about five times as much wallop as radio and requires in return five times as much attention. . . . It's impossible to get anything accomplished in the same room while it's on." The magazine offered a spatial solution, telling women "to get the darn thing out of the living room," and into the TV room, cellar, library, "or as a last resort stick it in the dining room." [50]

In *The Honeymooners,* a working-class situation comedy, television's obstruction of household work was related to marital strife. The first episode of the series, "TV or Not TV" (1955), revolves around the purchase of a television set and begins with an establishing shot of the sparsely decorated Kramden kitchen where a clothes basket filled with wet wash sits on the table. Entering from the bedroom in her hausfrau garb, Alice Kramden approaches the kitchen sink and puts a plunger over the drain, apparently attempting to unclog it. As pictured in this opening scene, Alice is, to say the least, a victim of household drudgery. Not surprisingly, Alice begs Ralph for a television set, hoping that it will make her life more pleasant.

In a later scene, after the Kramdens purchase their TV set, this situation changes, but not for the better. Ralph returns home from work while Alice sits before her television set. Here is the exchange between the couple:

RALPH: Would you mind telling me where my supper is?

ALICE: I didn't make it yet. . . . I sat down to watch the four o'clock movie and I got so interested I . . . uh what time is it anyway?

RALPH: I knew this would happen Alice. We've had that set three days now, and I haven't had a hot meal since we got it.

Thus, television is the source of a dispute between the couple, a dispute that arises from the housewife's inability to perform her productive function while enjoying an afternoon program.

A 1955 ad for Drano provided a solution to television's obstruction of household chores. Here the housewife is shown watching her afternoon soap opera, but this unproductive activity is sanctioned only insofar as her servant does the housework. As the maid exclaims, "Shucks, I'll never know if she gets her man 'cause this is the day of the week I put Drano in all the drains!" The Drano Company thus attempted to sell its product by giving women a glamorous vision of themselves enjoying an afternoon of television. But it could do so only by splitting the functions of relaxation and work across two representational figures—the lady of leisure and the domestic servant.[51]

If the domestic servant was a fantasy solution to the conflict between work and television, the women's magazines suggested more practical ways to manage the problem. *Better Homes and Gardens* advised in 1949 that the television set should be placed in an area where it could be viewed, "while you're doing things up in the kitchen." Similarly in 1954, *American Home* told readers to put the TV set in the kitchen so that "Mama sees her pet programs. . . ." Via such spatial remedies, labor would not be affected by the leisure of viewing nor would viewing be denied by household chores.[52] In fact, household labor and television were continually condensed into one space designed to accommodate both activities. In a 1955 issue of *American Home*, this labor-leisure viewing condensation provided the terms of a joke. A cartoon showed a housewife tediously hanging her laundry on the outdoor clothesline. The drudgery of this work is miraculously solved as the housewife brings her laundry into her home and sits before her television set while letting the laundry dry on the television antenna.[53]

The spatial condensation of labor and viewing was part of a well entrenched functionalist discourse. The home had to provide rooms that would allow for a practical orchestration of "modern living activities" that now included watching television. Functionalism was particularly useful for advertisers, who used it to promote not just one household item but an entire product line. In 1952, for example, the Crane Company displayed its kitchen appliance ensemble, complete with ironing, laundering, and cooking facilities. Here the housewife could do multiple tasks at once because all the fixtures were "matched together as a complete chore unit." One particularly attractive component of this "chore unit" was a television set built into the wall above the washer/dryer.[54]

While spatial condensations of labor and leisure helped to soothe tensions about television's obstruction of household chores, other problems still existed. The magazines suggested that television would cause increasing work loads. Considering the cleanliness of the living room, *House Beautiful* told its readers in 1948: "Then the men move in for boxing, wrestling, basketball, hockey. They get excited. Ashes on the floor. Pretzel crumbs. Beer stains." The remedy was again spatial: "Lots of sets after a few months have been moved into dens and recreation rooms."[55] In a slight twist of terms, the activity of eating was said to be moving out of the dining area and into the television-sitting area. Food stains soiling upholstery, floors, and other surfaces meant extra work for women. Vinyl upholstery, linoleum floors, tiling, and other spill-proof surfaces were recommended. Advertisers for all kinds of cleaning products found television especially useful in their sales pitches. In 1953, the Bissell

Carpet Sweeper Company asked housewives, "What do you do when the TV crowd leaves popcorn and crumbs on your rug? You could leave the mess till morning—or drag out the vacuum. But if you're on the beam, you slick it up with a handy Bissell Sweeper."[56] In addition to the mess generated by television, the set itself called for maintenance. In 1955, *House Beautiful* asked if a "misty haze dims your TV screen" and recommended the use of "wipe-on liquids and impregnated wiping cloths to remedy the problem." The Drackett Company, producer of Windex Spray, quickly saw the advantage that television held for its product; in 1948 it advertised the cleaner as a perfect solution for a dirty screen.[57]

Besides the extra cleaning, television also kept housewives busy in the kitchen. The magazines showed women how to be gracious hostesses, always prepared to serve family and friends special TV treats. These snacktime chores created a lucrative market for manufacturers. For example, in 1952 *American Home* presented a special china collection for "Early Tea and Late TV," while other companies promoted TV snack trays and TV tables.[58] The most exaggerated manifestation appeared in 1954. The TV dinner was the perfect remedy for the extra work entailed by television, and it also allowed children to eat their toss-away meals while watching *Hopalong Cassidy.*

While magazines presented readers with a host of television-related tasks, they also suggested ways for housewives to ration their labor. Time-motion studies, which were integral to the discourses of feminism and domestic science since the Progressive era, were rigorously applied to the problem of increasing work loads. All unnecessary human movement that the television set might demand had to be minimized. Again, this called for a careful management of space. The magazines suggested that chairs and sofas be placed so that they need not be moved for watching television. Alternatively, furniture could be made mobile. By placing wheels on a couch, it was possible to exert minimal energy while converting a sitting space into a viewing space. Similarly, casters and lazy Susans could be placed on television sets so that housewives might easily move the screen to face the direction of the viewers.[59] More radically, space between rooms could be made continuous. In 1952, *House Beautiful* suggested a "continuity" of living, dining, and television areas wherein "a curved sofa and a folding screen mark off [the] television corner from the living and dining room." Via this carefully managed spatial continuum, "it takes no more than an extra ten steps or so to serve the TV fans."[60]

Continuous space was also a response to the more general problem of television and family relationships. Women's household work presented a dilemma for the twin ideals of family unity and social divisions, since housewives were ideally meant to perform their distinctive productive functions but, at the same time, take part in the family's leisure-time pursuits. This conflict between female isolation from and integration into the family group was rooted in Victorian domestic ideology with its elaborate social and spatial hierarchies; it became even more pronounced as twentieth-century lifestyles and housing contexts changed in ways that could no longer contain the formalized spatial distinctions of the Victorian ideal.

The problems became particularly significant in the early decades of the century when middle-class women found themselves increasingly isolated in their kitchens due to a radical reduction in the number of domestic servants. As Gwendolyn Wright has observed, women were now cut off from the family group as they worked in kitchens designed to resemble scientific laboratories, far removed from the family activities in the central areas of the home. Architects did little to respond to the problem of isolation, but continued instead to build kitchens fully separated from communal living spaces, suggesting that labor-saving kitchen appliances would solve the servant shortage.[61] In the postwar era when the continuous spaces of ranch-style architecture became a cultural ideal, the small suburban home placed a greater emphasis on interaction between family members. The "open plan" eliminated some of the walls between dining room, living room, and kitchen. However, even in the continuous ranch-style homes, the woman's work area was "zoned off" from the activity area, and the woman's role as homemaker still worked to separate her from the leisure activities of her family.

Women's magazines suggested intricately balanced spatial arrangements that would mediate the tensions between female integration and isolation. Television viewing became a special topic of consideration. In 1951, *House Beautiful* placed a television set in its remodeled kitchen, which combined "such varied functions as cooking, storage, laundry, flower arranging, dining and TV viewing." In this case, as elsewhere, the call for functionalism was related to the woman's ability to work among a group engaged in leisure activities. A graphic showed a television placed in a "special area" devoted to "eating" and "relaxing" which was "not shut off by a partition." In continuous space, "the worker . . . is always part of the group, can share in the conversation and fun while work is in progress."[62]

While this example presents a harmonious solution, often the ideals of integration and isolation resulted in highly contradictory representations of domestic life. Typically, illustrations that depicted continuous spaces showed the housewife to be oddly disconnected from the general flow of activities. In 1951, for example, *American Home* showed a woman in a continuous dining-living area who supposedly is allowed to

91

accomplish her housework among a group of television viewers. However, rather than being integrated into the group, the woman is actually isolated from the television crowd as she sets the dining room table. The TV viewers are depicted in the background while the housewife stands to the extreme front-right border of the composition, far away from her family and friends. In fact, she is literally positioned off-frame, straddling between the photograph and the negative (or unused) space of the layout.[63]

The family circle motif was also riddled with contradictions of this sort. In particular, Sentinel's advertising campaign showed women who were spatially distanced from their families. In 1952, one ad depicted a housewife holding a tray of beverages and standing off to the side of her family, who were clustered around the television set. The following year, another ad showed a housewife cradling her baby in her arms and standing at a window far away from the rest of her family, who were gathered around the Sentinel console.[64] In a 1948 ad for Magnavox Television, the housewife's chores separated her from her circle of friends. The ad was organized around a U-shaped sofa that provided a quite literal manifestation of the semicircle visual cliché. A group of adult couples sat on the sofa watching the new Magnavox set, but the hostess stood at the kitchen door, holding a tray of snacks. Spatially removed from the television viewers, the housewife appeared to be sneaking a look at the set as she went about her hostess chores.[65]

This problem of female spatial isolation gave way to what can be called a "corrective cycle of commodity purchases." A 1949 article in *American Home* about the joys of the electric dishwasher is typical here. A picture of a family gathered around the living room console included the caption, "No martyr banished to kitchen, she never misses television programs. Lunch, dinner dishes are in an electric dishwasher." In 1950, an advertisement for Hotpoint dishwashers used the same discursive strategy. The illustration showed a wall of dishes that separated a housewife in the kitchen from her family, who sat huddled around the television set in the living room. The caption read, "Please . . . Let Your Wife Come Into the Livingroom! Don't let dirty dishes make your wife a kitchen exile! She loses the most precious hours of her life shut off from pleasures of the family circle by the never-ending chore of old-fashioned dishwashing!"[66]

This ideal version of female integration in a unified family space was contested by the competing discourse on divided spaces. Distinctions between work and leisure space remained an important principle of household efficiency. Here, room dividers presented a perfect balance of integration and isolation. In 1952, *Better Homes and Gardens* displayed a room divider that separated a kitchen work area from its dining area.

A 1950 Hotpoint adver-
tisement prescribes a
corrective cycle of com-
modity purchases.
(Courtesy General
Electric.)

The cutoff point was a television set built into the wall just to the right of the room divider. Thus, the room divider separated the woman's work space from the television space, but as a partial wall that still allowed for continuous space, it reached the perfect compromise between the housewife's isolation from and integration into the family. It was in the sense of this compromise that *American Home*'s "discrete" room divider separated a wife's work space from her husband's television space in a house that, nevertheless, was designed for "family living." As the magazine reported in 1954, "Mr. Peterson . . . retired behind his newspaper in the TV end of the living kitchen. Mrs. P. quietly made a great stack of sandwiches for us behind the discrete screen of greens in the efficient kitchen end of the same room." [67]

This bifurcation of sexual roles, of male (leisure) and female (productive) activities, served as an occasion for a full consideration of power dynamics among men and women in the home. Typically, the magazines extended their categories of feminine and masculine viewing practices into representations of the body. For men, television viewing was most often represented in terms of a posture of repose. Men were usually shown to be sprawled out on easy chairs as they watched the set. Remote controls allowed the father to watch in undisturbed passive comfort. In many ways, this representation of the male body was based on Victorian notions of rejuvenation for the working man. Relaxation was condoned for men because it served a revitalizing function, preparing them for the struggles for the workaday world. For women, the passive calm of television viewing was never so simple. As we have seen, even when women were shown watching television, they often appeared as productive workers.

Sometimes, representations of married couples became excessively literal about the gendered patterns of television leisure. In 1954, when the Cleavelander Company advertised its new "T-Vue" chair, it told consumers, "Once you sink into the softness of Cleavelander's cloud-like contours, cares seem to float away." Thus, not only the body, but also the spirit would be revitalized by the TV chair. But while the chair allowed Father "to stretch out with his feet on the ottoman," Mother's TV leisure was nevertheless productive. As the caption states, "Mother likes to gently rock as she sews."[68] Similarly, a 1952 advertisement for Airfoam furniture cushions showed a husband dozing in his foam rubber cushioned chair as he sits before a television set. Meanwhile, his wife clears away his TV snack. The text reads, "Man's pleasure is the body coddling comfort" of the cushioned chair while "Woman's treasure is a home lovely to look at, easy to keep perfectly tidy and neat" with cushioning that "never needs fluffing."[69] In such cases, the man's pleasure in television is associated with passive relaxation. The woman's pleasure, however, is derived from the aesthetics of a well-kept home and labor-saving devices that promise to minimize the extra household work that television brings to domestic space. In addition, the Airfoam ad is typical as it depicts a female body that finds no viewing pleasures of its own but instead functions to assist with the viewing comforts of others.

As numerous feminist film theorists have demonstrated, spectatorship and the pleasures entailed by it are culturally organized according to categories of sexual difference. In her groundbreaking article on the subject of Hollywood film, Laura Mulvey showed how narrative cinema (her examples were Von Sternberg and Hitchcock) is organized around voyeuristic and fetishistic scenarios in which women are the "to-be-looked-at" object of male desire.[70] In such a scheme, it becomes difficult to pinpoint how women can have subjective experiences in a cinema that systematically objectifies them. In the case of television, it seems clear that women's visual pleasure was associated with interior decor and not with viewing programs. In 1948, *House Beautiful* made this explicit when it claimed, "Most men want only an adequate screen. But women alone with the thing in the house all day have to eye it as a piece of furniture."[71] In addition, while these discussions of television were addressed to female readers, the woman's spectatorial pleasure was less associated with her enjoyment of the medium than it was with her own objectification, her desire to be looked at by the gaze of another.

On one level here, television was depicted as a threat to the visual appeal of the female body in domestic space. Specifically, there was something visually unpleasurable about the sight of a woman operating the technology of the receiver. In 1955, Sparton Television proclaimed that "the sight of a woman tuning a TV set with dials near the floor" was "most unattractive." The Sparton TV, with its tuning knob located at the top of the set, promised to maintain the visual appeal of the woman.[72] Beyond this specific case, there was a distinct set of aesthetic conventions formed in these years for male and female viewing postures. A 1953 advertisement for CBS-Columbia Television illustrates this well. Three alternative viewing postures are taken up by family members. A little boy stretches out on the floor, a father slumps in his easy chair, and the lower portion of a mother's outstretched body is gracefully lifted in a sleek modern chair with a seat that tilts upward. Here as elsewhere, masculine viewing is characterized by slovenly body posture. Conversely, feminine viewing posture takes on a certain visual appeal even as the female body passively reclines.[73]

As this advertisement indicates, the graphic representation of the female body viewing television had to be carefully controlled. It had to be made appealing to the eye of the observer, for in a fundamental sense, there was something taboo about the sight of a woman watching television. In fact, the housewife was almost never shown watching television by herself. Instead, she typically lounged on a chair (perhaps reading a book) while the television set remained turned off in the room. In 1952, *Better Homes and Gardens* stated one quite practical reason for the taboo. The article gave suggestions for methods of covering windows that would keep neighbors from peering into the home. It related this interest in privacy to women's work and television: "You should be able to have big, big windows to let in light and view, windows that let you watch the stars on a summer night without feeling exposed and naked. In good conscience, you should be able to leave the dinner dishes on the table while you catch a favorite TV or radio program, without sensing derogatory comments on your housekeeping."[74] Thus, for the housewife, being caught in the act of enjoying a broadcast is ultimately degrading because it threatens to reveal the signs of her slovenly behavior to the observer. More generally, we might say that the magazines showed women that their subjective pleasure in watching television was at odds with their own status as efficient and visually attractive housewives.

Although these representations are compatible with traditional gender roles, subtle reversals of power ran through the magazines as a whole. Even if there was a certain degree of privilege attached to the man's position of total relaxation—his right to rule from the easy chair throne—his power was in no way absolute, nor was it stable. Although such representations held to the standard conception of women as visually pleasing spectacles—as passive objects of male desire—these representations also contradicted such notions by presenting women as active producers in control of domestic affairs. For this reason, it seems that the most striking thing about this gendered representation of the body is that it inverted—or at least complicated—normative conceptions of masculinity and femininity. Whereas Western society associates activity with maleness, representations of television often attributed this trait to the woman. Conversely, the notion of feminine passivity was typically transferred over to the man of the house.[75] It could well be concluded that the cultural ideals that demanded women be shown as productive workers in the home also had the peculiar side effect of "feminizing" the father.

Perhaps for this reason, popular media presented tongue-in-cheek versions of the situation, showing how television had turned men into passive homebodies. In the last scene of *The Honeymooners'* episode "TV or Not TV," for example, the marital dispute between Alice and Ralph is inverted, with Alice apparently the "woman on top."[76] After Ralph scolds Alice about her delinquent housekeeping, Alice's TV addiction is transferred over to her husband and his friend Ed Norton, who quickly become passive viewers. Ralph sits before the television set with a smorgasbord of snacks, which he deliberately places within his reach so that he needn't move a muscle while watching his program. Norton's regressive state becomes the center of the comedic situation as he is turned into a child viewer addicted to a science-fiction serial. Wearing a club-member space helmet, Norton tunes into his favorite television host, Captain Video, and recites the space scout pledge. After arguing over program preferences, Ralph and Norton finally settle down for the *Late, Late, Late Show* and, exhausted, fall asleep in front of the set. Alice then enters the room and, with a look of motherly condescension, covers Ralph and Norton with a blanket, tucking them in for the night.

Men's magazines such as *Esquire* and *Popular Science* also presented wry commentary on male viewers. In 1951, for example, *Esquire* showed the stereotypical husband relaxing with his shoes off and a beer in his hand, smiling idiotically while seated before a television set. Two years later, the same magazine referred to television fans as "televidiots."[77]

Nonetheless, while these magazines provided a humorous look at the man of leisure, they also presented men with alternatives. In very much the same way that Catharine Beecher attempted to elevate the woman by making her the center of domestic affairs, the men's magazines suggested that fathers could regain authority through increased participation in family life.

Indeed, the "masculine domesticity" that Margaret Marsh sees as central to Progressive era lifestyles also pervaded the popular advice disseminated to men in the 1950s. According to Marsh, masculine domesticity has historically provided men with a way to assert their dominion at home. Faced with their shrinking authority in the new corporate world of white-collar desk jobs, the middle-class men of the early 1900s turned inward to the home where their increased participation in and control over the family served to compensate for feelings of powerlessness in the public sphere. Moreover, Marsh argues that masculine domesticity actually undermined women's growing desire for equal rights because it contained that desire within the safe sphere of the home. In other words, while masculine domesticity presented a more "compassionate" model of marriage where men supposedly shared domestic responsibilities with women, it did nothing to encourage women's equal participation in the public sphere.[78]

Given such historical precedents, it is not surprising that the postwar advice to men on this account took on explicitly misogynistic tones. As early as 1940, Sydnie Greenbie called for the reinstitution of manhood in his book, *Leisure For Living*. Greenbie reasoned that the popular figure of the male "boob" could be counteracted if the father cultivated his mechanical skills. As he wrote, "At last man has found something more in keeping with his nature, the workshop, with its lathe and mechanical saws, something he has kept as yet his own against the predacious female. . . . And [it becomes] more natural . . . for the man to be a homemaker as well as the woman."[79]

After the war the reintegration of the father became a popular ideal. As *Esquire* told its male readers, "Your place, Mister, is in the home, too, and if you'll make a few thoughtful improvements to it, you'll build yourself a happier, more comfortable, less back breaking world. . . ."[80] From this perspective, the men's magazines suggested ways for fathers to take an active and productive attitude in relation to television. Even if men were passive spectators, when not watching they could learn to repair the set or else produce television carts, built-ins, and stylish cabinets.[81] Articles with step-by-step instructions circulated in *Popular Science*, and the *Home Craftsman* even had a special "TV: Improve Your Home Show" column featuring a husband and wife, Thelma and Vince, and their adventures in home repairs. *Popular Science* suggested hobbies through which men could use television in an active, productive way. The magazine ran several articles on a new fad—TV photography. Men were shown how to take still pictures off their television sets, and in 1950 the magazine even conducted a readership contest for prize-winning photos that were published in the December issue.[82]

The gendered division of domestic labor and the complex relations of power entailed by it were thus shown to organize the experience of watching television. These popular representations begin to disclose the social construction of television as it was rooted in a mode of thought based on categories of sexual difference. Indeed, sexual difference, and the corresponding dynamics of domestic labor and leisure, framed television's introduction to the public in significant ways. The television industry struggled to produce programming forms that might appeal to what they assumed to be the typical housewife, and in so doing they drew an abstract portrait of "Mrs. Daytime Consumer." By tailoring programs to suit the content and organization of her day, the industry hoped to capture her divided attention. Through developing schedules that mimicked the pattern of her daily activities, network executives aspired to make television a routine habit. This "ideal" female spectator was thus the very foundation of the daytime programs the industry produced. But like all texts, these programs didn't simply turn viewers into ideal spectators; they didn't simply "affect" women. Instead, they were used and interpreted within the context of everyday life at home. It is this everyday context that women's magazines addressed, providing a cultural space through which housewives might negotiate their peculiar relationship to a new media form.

Women's magazines engaged their readers in a dialogue about the concrete problems that television posed for productive labor in the home. They depicted the subtle interplay between labor and leisure at home, and they offered women ways to deal with—or else resist—television in their daily lives. If our culture has systematically relegated domestic leisure to the realm of nonproduction, these discourses remind us of the tenuousness of such notions. Indeed, at least for the housewife, television was not represented as a passive activity; rather, it was incorporated into a pattern of everyday life where work is never done.

Four

The Home Theater

Mr. Public views that television set in his home as a 20th Century electronic monster that can transport him to the ball game, to Washington D.C., to the atomic blast in Nevada—and do it now. The viewer is inclined to accept it as his window to the world, as his reporter on what is happening now—simultaneously. The miracle of television is actually Man's ability to see at a distance while the event is happening.
Gary Simpson, NBC Television Director, 1955[1]

In 1912 the mass periodical, *The Independent*, announced to its readers the imminent arrival of "The Future Home Theater." Acknowledging that utopians like Edward Bellamy had already predicted this future, the magazine promised such dreams would come true through the development and application of two technologies. Sound and image could be transmitted to the public through telephone wires "instantaneously from a central stage" or recorded through a combination of film and disk ("talking pictures"), which in turn might be sent through the telephone wires. In case these elaborate plans seemed excessively strange for the home environment, the magazine promised that the new "electric theater . . . will not seem a mechanical device, but a window or a pair of magic opera glasses through which one will watch the actors or doers." This window would open onto "vistas of reality," illusions far better than the "flat, flickering, black and white [motion] pictures of today," illusions produced through a combination of color, music, and 3-D photography. Best of all, the magazine predicted that these "inventions will become cheap enough to be, like the country telephone, in every home, so that one can go to the theater without leaving the sitting room."[2]

This future home theater of 1912 is now easily recognized as a plan for television, a plan that lacks the sophisticated technology for electronic television in its classical form, but that nevertheless incorporates some of the basic social and cultural meanings that television would have for the public in the 1950s. Indeed, the turning of the home into a theater, a space for looking at "vistas of reality," came to have enormous ideological currency in the postwar years. Popular media instructed the public on how to transform the home into an exhibition space, and just as importantly they demonstrated the unpleasant effects of this transformation, seeking ways to minimize the discomforts entailed by merging the private sphere with the public domain of spectator amusements.

A World within a World

Since the 1950s, television has produced a virtual facsimile community of the air complete with neighborhoods and families that seem to share the same experiences we share, or perhaps to experience social life for us, in place of us. As Daniel Boorstin has argued, after the widespread dissemination of television "the normal way to enjoy a community experience was at home in your living room at your TV set."[3] That this substitute community appeared on television in the postwar era can be better understood in the light of social conditions of the period—in particular, the construction of a new suburbia that contributed to the decline of traditional community life in urban areas among a network of family and friends, which had sometimes included several generations.

The suburban housing boom entailed a massive migration from the city into remote farm lands reconstituted by mass-produced housing that offered, primarily to the young adults of the middle class, a new stake in the ideology of privacy and property rights. Faced with the severe housing crisis in American cities, the middle-class homeless looked to the new prefabricated suburban housing built by corporate speculators such as Levitt and Sons. With the help of the Federal Housing Administration and veteran mortgage loans, postwar consumers, for the first time in history, found it cheaper to buy their own homes than to rent an apartment in the city.[4] One of the prevailing historical descriptions of the ideology that accompanied this move to suburbia emphasizes a generalized sense of isolationism in the postwar years, both at the level of cold war xenophobia and in terms of domestic everyday experience. From this point of view, the home functioned as a kind of fallout shelter from the anxieties and uncertainties of public life. According to this argument, the fifties witnessed a nostalgic return to the Victorian cult of domesticity that was predicated upon the clear division between public and private spheres.[5]

The problem with such an explanation is that it reifies the very ideology of privacy that it attempts to explain—in other words, it begins by assuming that the home was indeed a retreat and that people understood their domestic lives and social lives to be clear cut and distinct entities. Rather, it is likely that the private and public dimensions were experienced in a less distinct fashion. The ideology of privacy was not experienced simply as a retreat from the public sphere; it also gave

people a sense of belonging to the community. By purchasing their detached suburban homes, the young couples of the middle class were
given a new, and flattering, definition of themselves. In newspapers,
magazines, advertisements, and on the airwaves, these young couples
came to be the cultural representatives of the "good life." Furthermore,
the rapid growth of family-based community organizations such as the
PTA suggests that the neo-suburbanites did not barricade their doors,
nor did they simply "drop out." Instead, they secured a position of
meaning in the *public* sphere through their new-found social identities
as *private* land owners.[6] In paradoxical terms, then, privacy was something which could be enjoyed only in the company of others. When describing the landscape of the mass-produced suburbs, a 1953 issue of
Harpers magazine succinctly suggested the new form of social cohesion
that allowed people to be alone and together at the same time. The
magazine described "monotonous" tract houses "where nothing rises
above two stories, and the horizon is an endless picket fence of telephone poles and television aerials."[7] There was an odd sense of connection and disconnection in this new suburbia, an infinite series of
separate but identical homes, strung together like Christmas tree lights
on a tract with one central switch. And that central switch was the
growing communications complex, through which people could keep
their distance from the world but at the same time imagine that their
domestic spheres were connected to a wider social fabric.

The domestic architecture of the period was itself a discourse on the
complex relationship between public and private space. Home magazines, manuals on interior decor, and books on housing design idealized
the flowing, continuous spaces of California ranch-style architecture,
which followed the functionalist design principles of "easy living" by
eliminating walls in the central living spaces of the home.[8] Continuous spaces allowed residents to exert a minimum of energy by reducing
the need to move from room to room. Beyond the "form follows function" aesthetic, however, this emphasis on continuous space suggested a
profound preoccupation with space itself. The rambling domestic interiors appeared not so much as private sanctuaries that excluded the outside world, but rather as infinite expanses that incorporated that world.
Housing "experts" spoke constantly of an *illusion of spaciousness*, recommending ways to make homes appear as if they extended into the public
domain. In *Sunset Homes for Western Living* (1946), the editors of *Sunset*
magazine suggested ways of "bringing the outdoors indoors" in a California ranch-style house.[9] Similarly, in *The American House Today* (1951),
Katherine Morrow Ford and Thomas H. Chreighton claimed that "the
most noticeable innovation in domestic architecture in the past decade
or two has been the increasingly close relationship of indoors to out-

doors." [10] Architectural journals and home magazines illustrated this principle through their elaborate display of structural features and decorative techniques that merged inside and outside spaces. *Architectural Digest* presented exclusive client-built homes that included, for example, a breakfast room whose walls depicted an entire Parisian cafe district and a living room decorated with upholstery and curtain fabric that illustrated a landscape of a country town. [11] Meanwhile, the middle-class home magazines displayed landscape paintings or else wallpaper depicting scenes of nature and foreign cities that welcomed exotic locales into the home.

By far the most central design element used to create an illusion of the outside world was the picture window or "window wall" (what we now call sliding glass doors), which became increasingly popular in the postwar period when mass-produced, large sheets of glass were used not only for commercial structures, but also for housing design. According to Daniel Boorstin, the widespread dissemination of large plate-glass windows "leveled the environment" by encouraging the "removal of the sharp visual division between indoors and outdoors," thus creating an "ambiguity" between public and private space. [12] This kind of spatial ambiguity was a reigning aesthetic in postwar home magazines, which repeatedly suggested that windows and window walls would create a continuity of interior and exterior worlds. As the editors of *Sunset* remarked in 1946, "Of all improved materials, glass made the greatest change in the Western home. To those who found that open porches around the house or . . . even [the] large window did not bring in enough of the outdoors, the answer was glass—the invisible separation between indoors and out." [13]

Given its ability to bring "another world" into the home, it is not surprising that television was often figured as the ultimate expression of progress in utopian statements concerning "man's" ability to conquer and to domesticate space. In 1946, Thomas H. Hutchinson, an early experimenter in television programming, published a popular book designed to introduce television to the general public, *Here is Television, Your Window on the World.* In his opening pages, Hutchinson wrote, "Today we stand poised on the threshold of a future for television that no one can begin to comprehend fully. . . . We do know, however, that the outside world can be brought into the home and thus one of mankind's long-standing ambitions has been achieved." [14] Theorizing the significance of this achievement in *Radio, Television and Society,* Charles Siepmann claimed in 1950 that "television provides a maximum extension of the perceived environment with a minimum of effort. Television is a form of 'going places' without even the expenditure of movement, to say nothing of money. It is bringing the world to people's doorsteps." [15]

As this statement suggests, television meshed perfectly with the aesthetics of modern suburban architecture. It brought to the home a grand illusion of space while also fulfilling the "easy living," minimal motion principles of functionalist housing design.

Indeed, the ideological harmony between utopian dreams for technological solutions to distance and utopian dreams for housing design created a joint leverage for television's rapid growth in the postwar period. Both of these utopias had been on the agenda well before television's arrival in the late forties. As Leo Marx has suggested with reference to nineteenth-century literary utopias, the dream of eradicating distances was central to America's early discourse on technology. In the post-Civil War years, machines of transport (especially the train) were the central rhetorical figure through which this dream was realized in popular discourse and literature.[16] By the end of the nineteenth century, communication technology had supplanted transportation. It was now the telegraph, telephone, radio, and, finally, television that promised to conquer space.

In the years following World War II, this technological utopia was joined with a complementary housing utopia that was, for the first time, mass produced. Although the 1950s witnessed the most extreme preoccupation with the merging of indoor and outdoor space, this ideal had been part of the model for interior design in the suburban houses built in the later nineteenth century. In their widely read book of 1869, *The American Woman's Home,* Catharine Beecher and Harriet Beecher Stowe suggested, for example, that the thrifty Victorian housewife could fashion a "rustic [picture] frame made of branches . . . and garnish the corners with . . . a cluster of acorns," or else copy their illustration of a large window "ornamented with a variety of these rural economical adornings."[17] Also concerned with bringing the outside world into the home were the architects of the late 1870s who began to build bay windows or else smaller windows that were grouped together in order to form a composite view for the residents.[18] In the nineteenth-century imagination, the merging of inside and outside spaces was a response to Victorian domesticity—its separation of private (female) and public (male) spheres. The natural world was associated with the "True Woman" who was to make her home a kind of nature retreat that would counteract the signs of modernity—smokestacks, tenement buildings, crowded streets—found in the urban work centers. As the sharp distinctions between private and public spheres became increasingly unstable at the end of the nineteenth century, the merging of outside and inside space became more important, and its meaning was somewhat altered. By the early decades of the twentieth century, the nature ideal still would have been understood in terms of its association with femininity, but it also began to have the more modern meaning of an erasure between separate spheres of public and private life. The bungalow cottages built across the nation began to merge inside and outside worlds with their large windows and expansive porches upon which residents might sit all day, taking part in neighborhood activities from their own private vantage point.

The most exaggerated effort to erase spatial barriers took place in the modernist architecture movements that emerged in the 1920s in Europe. Architectural modernism, or the "International Style" as it was also called, quickly took root on American soil, and architects working from a number of traditions developed many of the principles of modernist design, not least of all the erasure between public and private domains. House designs ranging from Richard Neutra's classical modernist Lovell house of 1929 (a machine-like futuristic structure) to Richard Keck's glass Crystal Palace of 1934 (displayed at the Century of Progress Exhibition in Chicago) to Cliff May's rambling ranch-style homes of the 1940s emphasized the merging of indoors and outdoors with window walls, continuous living areas, and patios that appeared to extend into interior space. Although these homes of tomorrow were clearly upper-class dreamhouses, too expensive and too "unhomey" for most Americans, the public was at least to some degree familiar with architectural modernism because it was widely publicized through world's fairs, museum exhibitions, department stores, home magazines, and the movies.[19] In the years following World War II, the spatial aesthetics established by the modernists appeared in a watered down, mass-produced version when the Levittowns across the country offered their consumers large picture windows or glass walls and continuous dining-living areas, imitating the principle of merging spaces found in the architectural ideal. That this mass-market realization of utopian dreams for housing was to find its companion in television, the ultimate "space-binding" technology of the twentieth century, is a particularly significant historical meeting.

Indeed, the ideological harmony between technological utopias and housing utopias created a perfect nesting ground for television in the postwar years. Women's home magazines displayed television sets in decorative settings that created the illusion of spatial conquests. The television set was often placed in rooms with panoramic window views, or else installed next to globes and colorful maps.[20] The image of television as a "global village," which media critic Marshall McCluhan spoke of in the 1960s, was already suggested in the popular discourses of the postwar period.

Even the manufacturers seemed to realize the marketing potential of this new global village in a box. Receivers like the Arvin "Williamsburg" and the Sylvania "Hampshire" were named for cities on the map. Advertisers for television typically used the illusion of the outside world as part of their promotional rhetoric. In 1948, DuMont advertised one of its first console models with the slogan, "Your new window on the world."[21] Other advertisers placed TV sets against scenic backgrounds suggestive of the exotic locales that television promised to make domestic. In 1953, Arvin's advertising campaign used the Eiffel Tower and Big Ben as backdrops for its console models.[22] In that same year, Emerson TV went further than Europe. Its television set, with a picture of New York City on its screen, appeared among the planets—and note that the ad also included a smaller TV with a little girl and her poodle, thereby tying domestic meanings to the science-fiction imagery.[23]

The obsession with a view of faraway places was also registered in family sitcoms. Although television critics have often pointed out the claustrophobic aspect of the sitcom's domestic setting, the early programs did provide a privileged opening onto a public sphere. Like the model homes in women's magazines, the TV homes incorporated an illusion of outside spaces that could be seen through large picture windows that often dominated the mise-en-scène. It was not just that these domestic interiors imitated the popular architectural ideal; they also fulfilled expectations about television that were voiced in popular discourses of the time. That is, the depiction of domestic space appears to have been based in part upon those utopian predictions that promised that television would provide for its audiences a view of outside spaces. Thus, the representation of the family's private interior world was often merged with a view of public exteriors, a view that was typically a fantasy depiction of high-priced neighborhoods not readily accessible to television's less affluent audiences. Beginning with its first episode in 1950, *The George Burns and Gracie Allen Show* included numerous windows and glass doors through which appeared a painted backdrop depicting George and Gracie's Beverly Hills yard. In *Make Room for Daddy,* a slightly more realistic window view of New York City dominated the mise-en-scène of the Williamses' luxury penthouse. Margie Albright, the spoiled rich girl character of *My Little Margie,* was typically depicted lounging in her sprawling New York apartment—complete with a terrace view of the city skyline. In 1955, one of the most popular programs, *I Love Lucy,* attempted to give the audience a vicarious vacation by moving its characters to Hollywood for the entire season. The Ricardo's hotel suite contained a wall of windows that opened onto a panoramic view of the Hollywood Hills. The first episode of the Hollywood season, "L.A. at Last," self-consciously directs the audience to the window in the Ricardo suite when Lucy's faithful companion, Ethel Mertz, enters the hotel room, moves toward the window and exclaims, "Oh what a view," in a close-up that registers the dramatic significance of the view for the TV spectator. The travelogue motif was to become conventionalized in the sitcom form when, for example, subsequent seasons saw *Burns and Allen*'s move to New York, *I Love Lucy*'s and *The Honeymooners'* season-long European vacations, *Make Room for Daddy*'s visit to the Grand Canyon, and *Ozzie and Harriet*'s Hawaiian vacation.[24]

This interest in bringing the world into the home can be seen as part of a larger historical process in which the home was designed to incorporate social space. Increasingly in the twentieth century, domestic appliances and other luxury items replaced community facilities. Refrigerators, for example, minimized the extent to which residents had to leave the home in order to purchase fresh foods, while washer-dryers made it unnecessary to visit public laundries. In the postwar years the community activity most affected was spectatorship. According to a 1955 *Fortune* survey, even while Americans were spending a phenomenal "$30 billion for fun" in the prosperous postwar economy, when calculated in terms of disposable income this figure actually reflected about a 2 percent decline since 1947. By far, the greatest slump was in the spectator amusements—most strikingly in movie attendance, but also in baseball, hockey, theater, and concert admissions. The *Fortune* survey concluded that American spectators had moved indoors where high fidelity sound and television promised more and better entertainment than in "the golden age of the box-office."[25]

Fortune's analysis indeed describes what happened to spectator amusements during the early fifties. Even so, its conclusion was also typical of a wider discourse that spoke of television as part of a home entertainment center that promised to privatize and domesticate the experience of spectatorship. As in the case of the *Fortune* survey, it was primarily the theater (and most often the movie theater) that television promised to replace. In 1950, for example, *House Beautiful* announced, "If you're getting so much drama at home, you're not going to seek it out so much in the movie palaces."[26] Advertisements for television variously referred to the "home theater," the "family theater," the "video theater," the "chairside theater," the "living room theater," and so forth. A 1953 Emerson ad went one step further by showing an oversized television set that appears on a movie theater stage as a full house views the enormous video screen. The caption reads, "Now! A TV picture so clear, so sharp . . . you'll think you're at the movies."[27]

Furniture manufacturers and retailers quickly responded to and helped encourage the theatricalization of the home. The retail industry's trade journal, *Home Furnishings,* which served as a principal source of advice for shop owners and display people, emphasized the increased profits to be made from instilling the idea of the home theater in the

Television brings the movie theater home in this 1953 advertisement for Emerson TV. (Courtesy Emerson Radio Corp.)

mind of the consumer. In 1950, the journal reported the predictions of Ross D. Siragusa, the president of Admiral television: "Mr. Siragusa believes the living room in most homes will have to take on the characteristics of a small theater. He is confident that television will greatly expand the furniture market since it brings a return to home entertainment. . . ." In that same year, Maurice Nee, the president of the National Retail Furniture Association, gave this prediction an official stamp when he claimed that television was "the greatest boon" to the furniture industry ever, and that it "stimulates the purchase of all other household goods."[28] Realizing the wisdom of this marketing strategy, furniture companies claimed their sofas and chairs were "perfect for TV viewing."[29] The Kroehler company, a leading manufacturer of movie theater seating, transferred its years of experience to the new home theater, advertising its "Tele-Vue" living room ensembles that were entirely organized around the television set.[30]

The arrangement of the home theater was constantly discussed in women's home magazines, which advised readers on ways to organize seating and ambient lighting so as to achieve a visually appealing effect for the spectator. In these discussions the television set was figured as a focal point in the home, with all points of vision intersecting at the screen. In 1949, *House Beautiful* claimed that "conventional living room groupings need to be slightly altered because televiewers look in the same direction and not at each other."[31] *Good Housekeeping* seconded the motion in 1951, proclaiming that "television is theatre; and to succeed, theatre requires a comfortably placed audience with a clear view of the stage."[32] In his 1953 book, *The House and the Art of Its Design,* Robert Woods Kennedy included a section on "looking" in the home, reminding his readers that "television sets usually focus a limited number of chairs, as in a theater. Rooms where they are used should be planned in such a manner that a bare minimum of change in chair location is required for their use."[33]

Not only did popular media give lessons in managing the resident's gaze at the screen, they also recommended ways to replicate the entire theatrical experience, showing readers how to create a total exhibition environment. In a 1950 issue of *Popular Science,* Richard E. Prentice told male readers how "We Built a Family Theater in Our Living Room" by purchasing numerous home entertainment machines.[34] One year later, *American Home* displayed "A Room that Does Everything," which included a television set, radio, phonograph, movie projector, movie screen, loud speakers, and even a barbecue pit. The magazine said of the proud owners of this total theater, "The Lanzes do all those things in *The Room.*"[35] In fact, the ideal home theater was precisely "the room" that one need never leave, a perfectly controlled environment of mechanized pleasures.

The idea of creating a total entertainment environment was so widespread that it crept into areas of home life not typically associated with entertainment per se. Perhaps the most extreme case is found in the absolute fascination with the electronic regulation of the weather in the home theater, or what the home magazines called "climate control."[36] The control of temperature and air quality was itself a salient topic for discussion in home magazines and advice books during the period. Television proved particularly useful for promoting the use of climate-enhancing products because it increased the amount of time spent in the home environment. Manufacturers of insulation, dehumidifiers, air conditioners, and heating systems all exploited the "home as theater" motif in promotional rhetoric that emphasized bodily comforts for television spectators. In 1952, RCA promoted its diverse product lines by suggesting that consumers not only purchase a new television console, but also " 'Tune in' perfect weather with an RCA Room Air Conditioner."[37] Such advertisements recall the promotional strategies of movie exhibitors in the late teens and twenties, who installed air-conditioning systems and announced this new attraction on their marquees in order to lure passersby on hot summer days. But as the Television Research Institute predicted in 1948, with the new "made-to-order" dreams of television, "it seems likely that the motion-picture-house marquee will no longer cast its shadow over pavements. The millennium in video-movies might be no farther away than 1955, when incidentally, there might also be air conditioning in every home." [38]

Just as machines promised to enrich the physical world of experience in the home theater, decorative motifs promised to heighten the psychological experience of spectatorship. In 1955, the Stockwall Company advertised its mural wallpaper, which depicted a scene designed to enhance the pleasures of spectatorship for the children in the household. The caption reads, "Here's a wonderfully drawn and colored mural of the romantic old west . . . designed particularly for the friendly family room where the youngsters . . . thrill at the hoof beats and pistol shots as they watch their favorite western thriller on television." [39] Such dreams of wall-to-wall narrative pleasure were not merely the stuff advertisements were made of. In 1951, *Time* announced the arrival of "smellies" invented by one Emery Stern, who had just patented a device that could " 'automatically release' various scents from containers built into TV sets." The "odors [were] intended to be appropriate to the type of program—e.g., peach blossom for romance." [40]

Magazines, architectural manuals, advertisers, and retailers thus inundated postwar consumers with an array of spectacle-enhancing devices, demonstrating ways to transform the home into an exhibition space that rivaled the public theater. This new domestic theatricality was hailed as the ultimate communication experience, delivering a dream of spatial transport that had, since the nineteenth century, fascinated the modern imagination. Nonetheless, the realization of this utopian fantasy occasioned a deep sense of cultural and social loss that was also expressed in the postwar media.

Antiseptic Electrical Space

The transformation of the home into a private pleasure dome was never so simple as the promotional and decorative schemes implied. Instead, it entailed a series of problems that called for constant mediation between competing ideals of social life. Indeed, as I suggested at the beginning of this chapter, the centripetal forces that turned Americans toward their homes were always accompanied by the opposite values of social participation in the public sphere. Television was caught in a contradictory movement between public and private worlds, and it often became a rhetorical figure for that contradiction.

CHAPTER FOUR

The postwar period witnessed a significant shift in traditional notions of neighborhood. Mass-produced suburbs replaced previous forms of public space with a newly defined aesthetic of prefabrication. At the center of suburban space was the young, upwardly mobile middle-class family; the suburban community was, in its spatial articulations, designed to correspond with and reproduce patterns of nuclear family life. Playgrounds, yards, and schools provided town centers for community involvement based on discrete stages of family development. People of color, lesbian and gay people, unmarried people, homeless people and senior citizens were simply written out of these spaces, and the zoning practices endorsed by the Federal Housing Administration helped to maintain these exclusions. Suburban space was thus designed to purify communal spaces, to sweep away urban clutter, while at the same time preserving the populist ideal of good neighborliness that carried Americans through the Depression.

Although the attempt to zone out "undesirables" was never totally successful, the antiseptic model of space was the reigning aesthetic at the heart of the postwar suburb. Not coincidentally, it had also been central to utopian ideals for electrical communications since the mid-1800s. As James Carey and John Quirk have shown, American intellectuals of the nineteenth century foresaw an "electrical revolution" in which the grime and noise of industrialization would be purified through electrical power. Electricity, it was assumed, would replace pollution caused by factory machines with a new, cleaner environment. Through their ability to merge remote spaces, electrical communications like the telephone and telegraph would add to such a sanitized environment by allowing people to occupy faraway places while remaining in familiar and safe locales.[41] Ultimately, this new electrical environment was linked to larger concerns about social decadence in the cities. Both in intellectual and popular culture, electricity became a rhetorical figure through which people imagined ways to cleanse urban space of social pollutants; immigrants and class conflict might vanish through the magical powers of electricity. As Carolyn Marvin has suggested, nineteenth-century thinkers imagined that electrical communications would defuse the threat of cultural difference by limiting experiences and placing social encounters into safe, familiar, and predictable contexts. In 1846, for example, *Mercury* published the utopian fantasies of Professor Alonzo Jackman, who imagined a transcontinental telegraph line through which "all the inhabitants of the earth would be brought into one intellectual neighborhood and be at the same time perfectly freed from those contaminations which might under other circumstances be received." Moreover, as Marvin suggests, this xenophobic fantasy extended to the more everyday, local uses of communication technology:

"With long-distance communication, those who were suspect and un-welcome even in one's neighborhood could be banished in the name of progress." Through telecommunications it was possible to make one's family and neighborhood into the "stable center of the universe," elim-inating the need even to consider cultural differences in the outside world.[42]

Although Marvin is writing about nineteenth-century communica-tion technology, the utopian fantasy she describes is also part and parcel of the twentieth-century imagination. The connections made between electricity and the purification of social space continued to be forged by utility companies and electrical manufacturers who hoped to per-suade the public of the link between electricity and a cleaner social en-vironment.[43] In the early 1920s, when radio was first marketed to the public, the dream of filtering social differences through the power of the "ether" was a reigning fantasy in the popular press. According to Susan Douglas, popular critics extolled radio's ability to join the nation to-gether into a homogeneous community where class divisions were blur-red by a unifying voice. Clearly drawing on the logic of cultural purity, one writer told a story of a "dingy house in a dreary street in a little factory town" where a "mother frets through the day to achieve a pass-able cleanliness for her flock." Not only this woman, but hundreds of "illiterate or broken people" like her were saved by a radio that put them "in touch with the world about them." Moreover, according to the pre-dictions of the more optimistic bourgeoisie, this new unifying agent would rid the culture of its "debasing" elements by bringing "all the benefits of high culture to the masses." Importantly, however, these crit-ics also hoped that radio would keep the masses away from them. As Douglas observes, the educated bourgeoisie embraced this new domestic form of entertainment for its ability to "insulate its listeners from hetero-geneous crowds of unknown, different and potentially unrestrained in-dividuals."[44] Thus, radio, like the telegraph and telephone before it, was seen as an instrument of social sanitation.

In the postwar era, the fantasy of antiseptic electrical space was transposed onto television. Numerous commentators claimed that tele-vision allowed people to travel from their homes while remaining un-touched by the actual social contexts to which they imaginatively ventured. As early as 1935, one advertising client for NBC praised an experimental broadcast of a wrestling match that he had seen in the home of a network executive: "The small group of people who saw the broadcast at Mr. Kersta's home felt as though we had actually seen the fight at Ebbetts Field but without all the inconveniences such as parking, elbowing through crowds, etc." By 1949, such sentiments had become more commonplace. As one man stated in a 1949 survey, "The set hasn't prompted me to attend any events in person. Why should I buck the crowds when I can sit here in comfort and see the same thing?"⁴⁵ Thus, according to the popular wisdom, television would allow spectators to participate in the thrills of urban culture, without having to deal with the hustle and bustle of city life.

Television promised more than just practical benefits. Like previous communication technologies, it offered the possibility of an intellectual neighborhood, purified of social unrest and human misunderstanding. As NBC's Pat Weaver declared, television would make the "entire world into a small town, instantly available, with the leading actors on the world stage known on sight or by voice to all within it." Television, in Weaver's view, would create world peace by presenting diverse people with homogeneous knowledge and modes of experience. Television's new electrical towns, he argued, created "a situation new in human history in that children can no longer be raised within a family or group belief that narrows the horizons of the child to any belief pattern. There can no longer be a We-Group, They-Group under this condition. Children cannot be brought up to laugh at strangers, to hate foreigners, to live as man has always lived before." But for Weaver, this democratic utopia was in fact a very small town, a place where different cultural practices were homogenized and channeled through a medium whose messages were truly American. As he continued: "It [is] most important for us in our stewardship of broadcasting to remain within the 'area of American agreement,' with all the implications of that statement, including however some acknowledgement in our programming of the American heritage of dissent." Thus, in Weaver's view, broadcasting would be a cultural filter that purified the essence of an "American" experience, relegating social and ideological differences (what he must have meant by the "American heritage of dissent") to a kind of programming ghetto. Moreover, he went on to say that "those families who do not wish to participate fully in the American area of agreement" would simply have to screen out undesirable messages by overseeing their children's use of television.⁴⁶

The strange mix of democracy and cultural hegemony that ran through Weaver's prose was symptomatic of a more general set of contradictions at the heart of utopian dreams for television's antiseptic electrical space. Some social critics even suggested that television's ability to sanitize social space would be desirable to the very people who were considered dirty and diseased. They applauded television for its ability to enhance the lives of disenfranchised groups by bringing them into contact with the public spaces in which they were typically unwelcome. In a 1951 study of Atlanta viewers, Raymond Stewart found that television "has a very special meaning for invalids, or for Southern Negroes who are similarly barred from public entertainments." One black respondent in the study claimed: "It [television] permits us to see things in an uncompromising manner. Ordinarily to see these things would require that we be segregated and occupy the least desirable seats or vantage point. With television we're on the level with everyone else. Before television, radio provided the little bit of equality we were able to get. We never wanted to see any show or athletic event bad enough to be segregated in attending it."[47]

Rather than blaming the social system that produced this kind of degradation for African-Americans, social scientists such as Stewart celebrated the technological solution. Television, or more specifically, the private form of reception that it offered, was applauded for its ability to dress the wounds of an ailing social system. For example, sociologist David Riesman claimed that "the social worker may feel it is extravagant for a slum family to buy a TV set on time, and fail to appreciate that the set is exactly the compensation for substandard housing the family can best appreciate—and in the case of Negroes or poorly dressed people, or the sick, an escape from being embarrassed in public amusement places."[48] Riesman thus used metaphors of social disease to suggest that disempowered groups willed their own exclusion from the public sphere through the miraculous benefits of television.

Although social critics hailed television's ability to merge public and private spaces, this utopian fantasy of space-binding revealed a dystopian underside. Here, television's antiseptic spaces were themselves subject to pollution as new social diseases spread through the wires and into the citizen's home. Metaphors of disease were continually used to discuss the medium's unwelcome presence in the household. Even before television's innovation in the postwar period, popular media raised the threatening possibility that electrical pollutants might infiltrate the domestic environment and harm, or at least mutate, human life. *Murder by Television*, a decidedly B film of 1935, featured Bela Lugosi in a nightmarish tale about a mad scientist who transmits death rays over the electrical wires. In an early scene, Professor Houghland, the benevolent inventor of television, invites guests to his home to witness a demonstration in which he broadcasts cities from around the globe. As he marvels at the medium's ability to bring faraway spaces into the home, his evil competitor, Dr. Scofield, kills him by sending "radiated waves" through the telephone wires and into Houghland's television camera, so that the professor dies an agonizing death.

In 1951, *American Mercury* asked if television "would make us sick . . . or just what?" Descriptions of broadcast technology went hand in hand with a medical discourse that attributed to television a biological (rather than technological) logic. A 1953 Zenith ad declared, "We test

TV blood pressure so you'll have a better picture." In that same year *American Home* suggested that readers "learn to diagnose and cure common TV troubles," listing symptoms, causes, treatments, and ways to "examine" the set. Thus, the television set was itself represented as a human body, capable of being returned to "health" through proper medical procedures.

Metaphors of pollution and contamination were also commonly used in the rhetoric of censorship debates as people looked for ways to clean up the airwaves. In 1950, when Representative Thomas J. Lane called for the establishment of a Federal Censorship Board, he insisted on the need to "clean up the house of television so that its occupants will not track any more dirt into our homes." Similarly, in 1952, when the House Subcommittee on Interstate and Foreign Commerce held hearings on the subject of television and radio content, ABC broadcaster Paul Harvey voiced his concern about the unwholesome influence that programs broadcast from New York were having on the rest of the country, claiming, "That crowded little island is contaminating an awful lot of fresh air out there somewhere."[49] When questioned by the committee about possible solutions to this problem, Harvey compared the situation to an epidemic: "In the field of medicine we usually try to trace a disease to the source. If there is a nonfilterable virus causing the thing, we try to isolate that virus."[50] Although he did not mention their ethnic roots, Harvey singled out the "New York comedians," who were overwhelmingly Jewish, as the guilty felons of the airwaves. Thus, we might conclude, the disease Harvey particularly feared was the spread of Semitic cultural traditions into the hinterland.

Metaphors of disease were also used to discuss television's effects on its viewers. Dr. Eugene Glynn, for example, claimed that certain types of adult psychoses could be relieved by watching television, but that "those traits that sick adults now satisfy by television can be presumed to be those traits which children, exposed to television from childhood, . . . may be expected to develop."[51] More generally, as discussed in chapter 2, magazine writers worried about the unhealthy psychological and physical effects that television might have on children who, they feared, might become addicted to the new medium. Such worries extended to adults, especially men, who were thought to be particularly susceptible to a modern ailment known as "spectatoritis." In his 1932 book of that title, Jay B. Nash wrote: "This machine age has . . . already supplied an unexampled wealth of leisure and what happens? The average man who has time on his hands turns out to be a spectator, a watcher of somebody else, merely because that is the easiest thing. He becomes a victim of spectatoritis—a blanket description to cover all kinds of passive amusement, an entering into the handiest activity merely to escape boredom."[52] In the television age, the term "spectatoritis" resurfaced to describe a common "male-ady." The powerless fathers and lazy spectators who appeared in magazines, television programs, and Hollywood films all suffered from this illness. Contented and supine, the Ralph Kramdens and Ed Nortons of the nation were bound for a course of inaction that kept them glued to the likes of *Captain Video,* dreaming of the moon as the world passed them by.

Spatial Confusion and the Big Brother Syndrome

Anxieties about television's addicting and contaminating effects were based on a larger set of confusions about the spaces that television brought to the home. Even before television's arrival in the postwar years, film comedies of the thirties and forties contained humorous scenes that depicted confusion over boundaries between electrical and real space. In the farcical *International House* (1933), for example, businessmen from around the globe meet at a Chinese hotel to witness a demonstration of the first fully electronic television set. When Dr. Wong presents his rather primitive contraption to the conventioneers, television is shown to be a two-way communication system that not only features entertainment but can also respond to its audiences. After a spectator (played by W. C. Fields) ridicules the televised performance of crooner Rudy Vallee, Vallee stops singing, looks into the television camera and tells Fields, "Don't interrupt my number. Hold your tongue and sit down." Later, when watching a naval battle on Wong's interactive television set, Fields even shoots down one of the ships in the scene. Similarly, in the popular film comedy serial, *The Naggers,* Mrs. Nagger and her mother-in-law confuse the boundaries between real and electrical space in a scene that works as a humorous speculation about television ("The Naggers Go Ritzy," 1932). After the Naggers move into a new luxury apartment, Mr. Nagger discovers that there is a hole in the wall adjacent to his neighbor's apartment. To camouflage the hole, he places a radio in front of it. When Mrs. Nagger turns on the radio, she peers through the speaker in the receiver, noticing a man in the next apartment. Fooled into thinking that the radio receiver is really a television, she instructs her mother-in-law to look into the set. A commercial for mineral water comes on the air, claiming, "The Cascade Spring Company eliminates the middle-man. You get your water direct from the spring into your home." Meanwhile, Mrs. Nagger and her mother-in-law gaze into the radio speaker hoping to see a televised image. Instead, they find themselves drenched by a stream of water. Since a prior scene in the film shows that the next-door neighbor is actually squirting water at the Naggers through the hole in the adjacent wall, the joke is on the technically illiterate women who can't distinguish between electrical and real space.[53]

By the late 1940s, the confusion between spatial boundaries at the heart of these films was less pronounced. People were learning ways to incorporate television's spectacles within the contours of their homes. By turning one's living room into a theater, it was possible (at least in an ideal sense) to make outside spaces part of a safe and predictable domestic experience. In other words, the theatricalization of the home allowed people to draw a line between the public and the private—or in more theatrical terms—a line between the proscenium space where the spectacle took place and the reception space from which the audience observed the scene.

Indeed, as Lawrence Levine has shown, the construction of that division was central to the formation of twentieth-century theaters.[54] Whereas theater audiences in the early 1800s tended to participate in the show through hissing, singing, and other forms of interaction, by the turn of the century theaters increasingly attempted to keep audiences detached from the performance and from one another. The silent, well-mannered audience became a mandate of "good taste," and people were instructed to behave in this manner in legitimate theaters and, later, in nickelodeons and movie palaces. By making possible the individual contemplation of mass spectacles, theaters helped construct imaginary separations between people. In practice, the bourgeois experiences that theaters encouraged often seem to have had the somewhat contradictory effect of permitting what George Lipsitz (following John Kasson) has described as a kind of "privacy in public."[55] Within the safely controlled environment of the movie house, audiences—especially youth audiences—engaged in illicit flirtation. At a time of huge population increases in urban centers, theaters and other forms of public amusements offered people the fantastic possibility of being alone while in the midst of a crowd. Thus, the middle-class respectability that theaters promoted was always subject to being debased as patrons used theatrical space in unpredictable ways. Still, theater entrepreneurs, prodded by reformers and state licensing boards, attempted to maintain the necessary distance among people in the audience and the events portrayed on the screen.

In the postwar era, this theatrical experience was being reformulated in terms of the television experience. People were shown how to construct an exhibition space that replicated the general design of the theater. However, in this case, the relationship between public/spectacle and private/spectator was inverted. The spectator was now physically isolated from the crowd, and the fantasy was now one of imaginary unity with "absent" others. This inversion entailed a set of contradictions that weren't easily solved. According to the popular wisdom, television had to recreate the sense of social proximity that the public theater offered; it had to make the viewer feel as if he or she was taking part in a public event. At the same time, however, it had to retain the necessary distance between the public sphere and private individual upon which middle-class ideals of reception were based. The impossibility of maintaining these competing ideals gave rise to a series of debates that weighed the ultimate merits of bringing spectacles indoors.

Despite the fact that television was touted as a family medium, to be received within a familiar domestic space, commentators in the popular press worried that the self-enclosed pleasure domes people built might not be so insular after all. In this regard, discussions of television were part of a larger obsession with privacy, an obsession that was typically expressed through the rhetorical figure of the window, the border between inside and outside worlds. Writing for the media trade journal *Variety*, Harry Hershfield complained, "Overnight our homes have taken over the burdens carried by outdoor strolling minstrels, park gatherings and stadiums. Previously, every man's home was supposedly his castle. The lord of the manor decided what and who should enter its sacred precincts." Then, "there was a period of compromise between the outdoor entertainer and your inviolate sanctum. That's when we looked out of the window [at street singers] and bridged the protocols of living. . . . It was an annoying age, but at least there was a line of demarcation in privacies and social standings." With the advent of television, he suggested, this line "has now been battered beyond recognition." [56]

Like Hershfield, critics in women's home magazines were also worried about television's blurring of boundaries between public and private space. Also like Hershfield, they often expressed such concerns by relating them to the larger concern with privacy, and particularly to anxieties about "problem windows." Although the home magazines idealized large picture windows and sliding glass doors for the view of the outside world they provided, they also warned that windows had to be carefully covered with curtains, venetian blinds, or outdoor shrubbery in order to avoid the "fish bowl" effect. In these terms, the view incorporated in domestic space had to be a one-way view. Television would seem to hold an ideal place here because it was a "window on a world" that could never look back. Yet, the magazines treated the television set as if it were a problem window through which residents in the home could be seen. In 1951, *American Home* juxtaposed suggestions for covering "problem" windows with a tip on "how to hide a TV screen." [57] Similarly, in 1954, *Good Housekeeping* inverted the popular conception of television as window on the world by suggesting that the screen be covered with an "old map . . . which, employing a simple window-shade principle, operates on a small spring roller." [58] Here as elsewhere, the attempt to cam-ouflage the technology as a piece of interior decor went hand in hand with the more specific attempt to "screen out" television's visual field, to manage vision in the home so that people could see without being seen. Even the design of the early consoles, with their cabinet doors that cov-ered the screen, suggested the fear of being seen by television.

Perhaps this fear was best stated in 1949 when *The Saturday Evening Post* told its readers, "Be Good! Television's Watching." The article con-tinued, "Comes now another invasion of your privacy . . . TV's prying eye may well record such personal frailties as the errant husband dining with his secretary." [59] The specific fear here was that the television camera might record unsuspecting couples and have devastating effects upon their romantic lives. Billy Wilder's *The Seven Year Itch* (1957) takes up this theme in a film that deals with the comedic escapades of Richard Sherman, a middle-aged husband who finds himself tempted by a glam-orous young television actress (played by Marilyn Monroe) when his wife leaves town for the summer. After flirting with the actress, Richard has a nightmarish vision in which he imagines that she is on television, reporting their illicit affair to the entire television audience—including, of course, his wife.

While *The Seven Year Itch* presented a humorous version of the "pry-ing eye" theme, a highly self-reflexive episode of *Tales of Tomorrow,* one of television's first science-fiction anthologies, gave audiences a more troubling picture. Entitled "The Window," the tale begins as if it were a standard science-fiction drama but is soon "interrupted" when the tele-vision camera picks up an alien image, a completely unrelated view of a window through which we see a markedly lower-class and drunken husband, his wife, and another man (played by Rod Steiger). After a brief glimpse at this domestic scene, we cut back to the studio where a seemingly confused crew attempts to explain the aberrant image, finally suggesting that it is a picture of a real event occurring simultaneously in the city and possibly "being reflected off an ionized cloud right in the middle of our wavelength, like a mirage." As the episode continues to alternate between the studio and the domestic scene, we learn that the wife and her male friend plan to murder the husband, and we see the lovers' passionate embrace. At the end of the episode, after the murder takes place, the wife stares out the window and confesses to her lover that all night she felt as if someone were watching her.

As this so well suggests, the new TV eye threatens to turn back on itself, to penetrate the private window and to monitor the eroticized fan-tasy life of the citizen in his or her home. The fantasy's violent dimension is suggestive of the more sadistic aspects of television technology; tele-vision now becomes an instrument of surveillance. More generally, this fear of being subjected to television's one-way vision was a central figure in science-fiction stories—most notably George Orwell's *1984*, which was first published in 1949. This political nightmare made famous the figure of Big Brother, who kept a close watch on his subjects through television monitors located in citizens' homes. In the years that followed, television's threatening power of surveillance would become a familiar trope in science-fiction films ranging from *War of the Worlds* (1953) to the more contemporary *Blade Runner* (1982).[60]

In the 1950s, television's threatening aspects were represented not only in terms of surveillance per se, but also in terms of a more generalized fear of technologically perfected vision that rivaled human eyesight. This typically took on tones of the Frankenstein myth in which technology becomes an evil force working without human authority—only here, it was figured more precisely as an "evil eye." As *American Mercury* claimed in 1952, television "is almost like a giant eye on life itself." On the one hand, this TV eye might "become the vehicle for masterpieces of a magnitude and power never achieved before in the arts." But on the other hand, "it could also become the worst cultural opiate in history. . . ."[61] Like many other popular media, this magazine was undecided about television's social effects, and like many other popular accounts, it related television's social consequences to its extraordinary ability to bring the outside world into the home.

Screening Sexuality

The link between television, surveillance, and sexuality that the media expressed was clearly the stuff of science-fiction fantasy; however, the more general concern with television's invasive nature, and especially its disruption of the family's sexual life, was widely expressed in the more "down to earth" debates of the time. According to the popular wisdom, once public spectacles were imported into the home, the domestic environment became prone to the eroticized imagery of commercial entertainment. Maintaining a distance between the family and those images thus became a central problem of social sanitation. On the one hand, regulators, citizens groups, educators, psychologists, government officials, and popular critics called for the regulation of the overtly sexual (and violent) dimensions of program content, particularly insofar as children were concerned.[62] On the other hand, when it came to adults, the problem of television's seemingly direct link to the sexual lives of citizens in the home was less obviously addressed. Popular media showed people how television's libidinal imagery, and in particular its invocation of male desire, would disrupt the sexual relationship between husband and wife.

Magazines, advertisements, and television programming often depicted the figure of a man who was so fascinated with the screen image of a woman that his real-life mate remained thoroughly neglected. Close-ups of beautiful women or else scantily dressed bathing beauties emanated from the television screen, presenting themselves to male spectators who watched with undivided attention. Thus, in terms of this exchange of looks, the television set became the "other woman." Even if the screen image was not literally another woman, the man's visual fascination evoked the structural relations of female competition for male attention, a point well illustrated by a cartoon in a 1952 issue of *Esquire* that depicted a newlywed couple in their honeymoon suite. The groom, transfixed by the sight of a TV wrestling match, completely ignores his bride.[63] This sexual scenario was taken up by Kotex, a feminine hygiene company with an obvious stake in female sexuality. The 1949 advertisement shows a woman who, by using the sanitary napkin, is able to distract her man from his television baseball game.[64] Perhaps in these cases the man's fixation on televised sports operated as a kind of conventionally acceptable way to state the more unacceptable possibility that men would find television's images more erotically stimulating than their wives. One cartoon in the trade journal *Broadcasting* suggests as much, showing a man seated before a television set tuned to a baseball game. But rather than looking at the game, the man stares out a large picture window through which he sees his glamorous neighbor, dressed in a bikini and watering her lawn. The man's wife stands in the kitchen doorway, with an angry scowl on her face, apparently begging him to come in for dinner. Speaking in the voice of the husband, the caption reads, "I'll be in to dinner, dear, just as soon as this inning is watered!"[65] Television's window on the world thus turns out to be just a bit too close to the real world where desire roams free.

Perhaps the ultimate expression of female competition with television came in a 1953 episode of *I Love Lucy* entitled "Ricky and Fred Are TV Fans." In the first scene, we see Lucy Ricardo and Ethel Mertz seated in the Ricardo kitchen, discussing the problem of their night's entertainment. With their husbands mesmerized by a TV boxing match, the women are bored and upset. Finally, in a defiant tone, Lucy tells Ethel, "I'm tired of playing second fiddle to a television set. Ricky is my husband and he is going to spend the evening talking to me, or else." The women enter the living room where the first round of the boxing match has just ended, and they stand before the television set during the program's intermission. Covering the TV screen with her full swing skirt, Lucy tells the men, "Ethel and I have decided that you have married us and not a television set. . . . We are sick and tired of sitting around for an hour and a half looking at each other while you look at this silly fight." Suddenly, however, Lucy is cut short, for when the boxing match resumes, Ricky and Fred make violent gestures toward their wives in order to get them away from the set. Frightened, the women return to the kitchen where they agree to go out to the corner drugstore. Once in the drugstore, however, they cannot get the attention of the male soda jerk who is likewise entranced by the television boxing match.

There were also representations in which this sexual/visual competition was figured in ways other than female suffering and objectification, representations that might have appealed to women by offering them ways to use television as a powerful weapon against patriarchal norms. A 1952 Motorola advertisement is one example. The illustration shows a man lounging on a chair and watching a bathing beauty on the television screen. His wife, dressed in an apron, stands in the foreground holding a shovel, and the caption reads, "Let's go, Mr. Dreamer, that television set won't help you shovel the walk." The relationship drawn between the man's fascination with the televised image of another woman and household chores only seems to underscore television's

A woman competes for her husband's attention in this 1949 Kotex advertisement. (Courtesy Kimberly-Clark Corp.)

negative appeal for women; but another aspect of this ad suggests a less "masochistic" inscription of the female consumer. The large window view as well as the landscape painting hung over the set suggests the illusion of the outside world and the incorporation of that world into the home. In this sense, the ad suggests that the threat of sexuality/infidelity in the outside world can be contained in the home through its representation on television. Even while the husband neglects his wife and household chores to gaze at the woman on the television screen, the housewife is in control of his sexuality insofar as his visual pleasure is circumscribed by domestic space. The housewife's gaze at the reader, as well as her forceful posture and cited commentary, further illustrate this position of control.[66]

More generally, television's blurring of private and public space became a powerful tool in the hands of housewives who could use the technology to invert the sexist hierarchies at the heart of the separation of spheres. In this topsy-turvy world, women policed men's access to the public sphere and confined them to the home through the clever manipulation of television technology. An emblematic example is a 1955 advertisement for *TV Guide* that conspires with women by giving them tips on ways to "Keep a Husband Home." As the ad suggests, "You might try drugging his coffee . . . or hiding all his clean shirts. But by far the best persuader since the ball and chain is the TV set . . . and a copy of *TV Guide*." [67]

This inversion of the gendered separation of spheres was repeated in illustrations and advertisements in women's magazines that suggested ways for women to control their husband's sexual desires through television. A 1953 RCA advertisement for a set with "rotomatic tuning" shows a male spectator seated in an easy chair while watching a glamorous woman on the screen. However, the housewife literally controls and sanctions her husband's gaze at the televised woman because she operates the tuning dials.[68] Other advertisements and illustrations depicted women who censored male desire by standing in front of the set, blocking the man's view of the screen.[69] Similarly, a cartoon in a 1949 issue of *The New York Times Magazine* showed how a housewife could dim her husband's view of televised bathing beauties by making him wear sunglasses, while a cartoon in a 1953 issue of *TV Guide* suggested that the same form of censorship could be accomplished by putting window curtains on the screen in order to hide the more erotic parts of the female body.[70] Television, in this regard, was shown to contain men's pleasure by circumscribing it within the confines of domestic space and placing it under the auspices of women. Representations of television thus presented a position for male spectators that can best be described as *passive aggression*. Structures of voyeuristic and fetishistic pleasure common to the Hollywood cinema were still operative, but they were sanitized and neutralized through their incorporation into the home. Now men's libidinal fascination in public spectacles was safely domesticated through their wives' authorization of the image.

If popular media showed women ways to keep their husbands at home with television, they also suggested the unpleasant possibility that television would create further confinement for women. Women's magazines often depicted television as a source of isolation, especially for housewives whose lives were already circumscribed by their labor at home.[71] The new family theaters were typically shown to limit opportunities for social experience that women traditionally had at movie theaters and other forms of public entertainment. In 1951, a cartoon in *Better Homes and Gardens* stated the problem in humorous terms. On his way home from work, a husband imagines a night of TV wrestling while his kitchen-bound wife, taking her fresh baked pie from the oven, dreams of a night out at the movies.[72] Other representations equated television viewing with a lack of male companionship, presenting threatening images of homebodies whose only form of social life took place on the living-room console. A classic example is Douglas Sirk's *All That Heaven Allows* (1955), which tells the story of Carey, an upper-class widow (played by Jane Wyman) who falls in love with a handsome but lower-class and much too young gardener, Ron (played by Rock Hudson). Pressured by her neighbors and children to give up Ron, Carey is left alone and miserable. On Christmas Day, Carey stares out of her window, watching children sing carols in the street. The window serves as a barrier between inside and outside. The camera lingers outside the window, so that Carey appears trapped behind the glass, and the melodramatic violins further suggest the pathos of the scene. Moments later, Carey's son Ned gives his mother her Christmas present—a new table-model television set. In a stunning shot, Carey's face is reflected in the greenish glass of the television screen. Here the television set takes on the figural function of the window, only now the pathos is heightened and the TV/window appears monstrous. The violin music comes to a crescendo while a voice on the sound track adds bitter irony to the image. The television salesman tells Carey, "All you have to do is turn that dial and you have all the company you want right there on the screen— drama, comedy, life's parade at your fingertips." But "life's parade," it appears, is merely Carey's gaze turned back on itself. The final shot of the scene lingers on a close-up of the television screen that contains the image of Carey staring at her own reflection. As this so well suggests, television is not a solution to female isolation from the public sphere. Rather than providing a means of communicating with the world outside, it offers only a projection of one's own subjectivity.

An angry housewife comes between her husband and another woman in this 1953 *Collier's* cartoon.

In this 1951 *Better Homes and Gardens* cartoon, private and public amusements are divided along gender lines. (Courtesy Meredith Corp.)

Similar plots involved young girls whose loneliness was metaphorically represented through their relationship to television. Perhaps most melodramatic in this regard is the film version of *Marty* (1955), which shows the homely Clara who sits with her parents watching Ed Sullivan as she waits longingly for a call from her beau. In 1952, Colgate dental cream used this dilemma as a way to sell its product. An advertisement that ran in *Ladies' Home Journal* showed a young woman sitting at home watching a love scene on her television set, complaining to her sister "All I do is sit and view. You have dates any time you want them, Sis! All I get is what TV has to offer." [73] Of course, after she purchased the Colgate dental cream, she found her handsome dream date. Thus, as the Colgate company so well understood, the surrogate universe that television offered posed its own set of problems. For even if television programs promised to transport women into the outside world, it seems likely that women recognized the discrepancy between the domestic isolation television perpetuated and the imaginary sense of social integration its programming constructed.

In 1955, the working-class comedy, *The Honeymooners*, dramatized this dilemma in the first episode of the series, "TV or Not TV." As described in chapter 4, this program took as its central theme the installation of a television set into the Kramden household. The narrative was structured upon the contradiction between television's utopian promise of increased social life and the dystopian outcome of domestic seclusion. In an early scene, Alice begs her husband to buy a television set:

> I . . . want a television set. Now look around you, Ralph. We don't have any electric appliances. Do you know what our electric bill was last month? Thirty-nine cents! We haven't blown a fuse, Ralph, in ten years. . . . I want a television set and I'm going to get a television set. I have lived in this place for fourteen years without a stick of furniture being changed. Not one. I am sick and tired of this. . . . And what do you care about it? You're out all day long. And at night what are you doing? Spending money playing pool, spending money bowling, or paying dues to that crazy lodge you belong to. And I'm left here to look at that icebox, that stove, that sink and these four walls. Well I don't want to look at that icebox, that stove, that sink and these four walls. I want to look at Liberace!

Significantly, in this exchange, Alice relates her spatial confinement in the home to her more general exclusion from the modern world of electrical technologies (as exemplified by her low utility bills). But her wish to interconnect with television's electrical spaces soon becomes a nightmare because the purchase of the set further engenders her domestic isolation. When her husband Ralph and neighbor Ed Norton chip in for a new TV console, the men agree to place the set in the Kramdens' two-room apartment where Norton is given visitation privileges. Thus, the installation of the set also means the intrusion of a neighbor into the home on a nightly basis, an intrusion that serves to take away rather than to multiply the spaces Alice can occupy. In order to avoid the men, who watch television in the central living space of the apartment, Alice retreats to her bedroom, a prisoner in a house taken over by television.

The anxieties expressed in popular representations were also voiced by women at the time. In an audience study conducted in Southern California, one woman confessed that all her husband "wants to do is to sit and watch television—I would like to go out more often." Another woman complained, "I would like to go for a drive in the evening, but my husband has been out all day and would prefer to watch a wrestling match on television." [74] A nationwide survey suggested that even teen-age girls experienced these problems. As one respondent complained, "Instead of taking us out on date nights, the free-loading fellas park in our homes and stare at the boxing on TV." For reasons such as these, 80 percent of the girls admitted they would rather go to a B movie than stay home and watch TV. [75]

Advertisements in women's home magazines (as well as general audience magazines like *Life* and *Look*) attempted to negotiate the conflict between women's domestic isolation and their integration into social life. Here, television was represented in the context of a night out on the town. In 1955, NBC advertised its evening programs by telling women to "make a date to see the greatest theatre in the world!" [76] Advertisements for television sets particularly evoked this "date" imagery by displaying glamorously dressed partners whose evenings of television took on, for example, the status of a dinner dance. Typical here is a 1955 ad for RCA Victor color television sets that depicts a luxurious living room where a husband, dressed in black tie and jacket, and his wife, in a cocktail dress and evening sandals, appear as if they are about to go to a posh nightclub. Instead, the night's entertainment is provided by the television set from which emanates a musical spectacular. The accompanying ad copy fills in the details of this social tableau with a story told in first person point of view:

> Our guests arrive. One of them notices our handsome new TV set. You turn it on, not saying a word. Then . . . 'Oh, it's Color TV,' someone exclaims.

Thus, according to the ad, television is not a source of domestic confinement, but rather provides a backdrop for enriched social life in the home. [77]

However, even this increased sociability was subject to critical disputes. After all, it directly competed with the ideal of privacy that television also promised. Indeed, the new home theaters threatened to collapse the necessary "distance" between the public sphere and private individual that middle-class modes of theatrical reception had valued for so long. The theatricalization of domestic space always carried with it the unpleasant possibility that the outside world would invade the home, making it vulnerable to unwelcome intrusions. Even if television had sanitized the polluted spaces of urban America, it nevertheless might bring the riff-raff a bit too close for comfort.

The Electronic Neighborhood

Concerns about intrusions from the outside world were especially strong in the early years of innovation when the purchase of a television set quite literally decreased privacy in the home. Numerous social scientific studies revealed that set owners were inundated with guests who came to watch their favorite programs. One early survey suggested:

> Every television set owner soon discovers that he is doing a
> lot more entertaining than formerly and that his bills for food
> and beverages are up sharply. We have been told of cases
> where the 'gang' would all flock to the home of the first person in the group who has a seven-inch set, and then desert
> him for someone with a ten-inch set. If a person wants to
> make friends and climb socially, he should get as big a set as
> possible and tell all his acquaintances about it. But if he wants
> to be left alone, he should either not buy any set or else get a
> small one.[78]

As this observation indicates, neighborly visits were not always seen in a positive light by the families surveyed. As one woman in a Southern California study complained, "Sometimes I get tired of the house being used as a semiprivate theater. I have almost turned the set off when some people visit us."[79] Popular media were also critical of the new "TV parties." In 1953, *Esquire* published a cartoon that highlighted the problem entailed by making one's home into a TV theater. The sketch pictures a living room with chairs lined up in front of a television set and a floor-model ashtray such as might be found in a movie theater lobby. The residents of this home theater, dressed in pajamas and bathrobes with hair uncombed and feet unshod, are taken by surprise when the neighbors drop in—a bit too soon—to watch a TV wrestling match. Speaking in the voice of the intruders, the caption reads, "We decided to come over early and make sure we get good seats for tonight's fight." In that same year, a cartoon in *TV Guide* suggested a remedy for the troublesome neighbors that took the form of a hand-held mechanical device known as "Fritzy." The caption advised, "If your neighbor won't buy his own set, try 'Fritzy.' One squeeze puts your set on the fritz."[80]

Such popular anxieties are better understood when we recognize the changing structure of social relationships encountered by the new suburban middle class. These people often left their families and lifelong friends in the city to find instant neighborhoods in preplanned communities. Blocks composed of total strangers represented friendships only at the abstract level of demographic similarities in age, income, family size, and occupation. This homogeneity quickly became a central cause for anxiety in the suburban nightmares described by sociologists and popular critics, who presented passionate attacks on the increasing loss of ethnic, class, and age differences in the new communities. In addition to being highly homogeneous, the suburbs tended to be insular communities. They were so isolated, in fact, that Herbert Gans, the well-known social scientist and author of *The Levittowners*, argued in an early essay that the new towns were the ideal control group for research and suggested that they "be used as laboratories for the analysis of some urban problems not researchable in the city."[81]

Perhaps because these new towns were relatively identical in demographic composition and also fairly self-contained, the neighborhood ideal was particularly pronounced. In *The Organization Man*, William H. Whyte argued that a sense of community was especially important for newcomers who experienced a feeling of "rootlessness" when they left their old neighborhoods for their new suburban homes. Whyte showed that the developers of the mass-produced suburbs tried to smooth the tensions that arose from this sense of rootlessness by promising increased community life in their advertisements. Park Forest, a Chicago suburb, assured consumers that "Coffeepots bubble all day long in Park Forest. This sign of friendliness tells you how much neighbors enjoy each other's company—feel glad that they can share their daily joys—yes, and troubles, too."[82]

However, when newcomers arrived in their suburban communities, they were likely to find something different from the ideal that the magazines and advertisements suggested. Tiny homes were typically sandwiched together so that, for example, the Smiths' picture window looked not onto rambling green acres, but rather into the Jones's living room—a dilemma commonly referred to as the "goldfish bowl" effect. In addition to this sense of claustrophobia, the neighborhood ideal brought with it an enormous amount of pressure to conform to the group. As Harry Henderson suggested in his early study of the new suburban neighborhoods, the residents were under constant "pressure to 'keep up with the Joneses,'" a situation that led to "a kind of super-conformity" in which everyone desired the same luxury goods and consumer lifestyles.[83] In his humorous critique of the new suburbia, aptly entitled *The Crack in the Picture Window*, John Keats described the life of Mary and John Drone who lived among a mob of equally unappealing neighbors. The pressure to conform in this fictional neighborhood especially took its toll on Mary, who was forced to convene with the neighbors on a daily basis at the "morning lawn day." Keats's fictional housewife is especially interesting because she finds a way to use television subversively, that is, as a weapon against the pressures to conform to the social group. As Keats wrote, "Mary Drone, unwilling and unable to endure the chatter of her neighbors, at first took refuge in her television set. She became aware of Arthur Godfrey. For weeks she watched, fascinated by the rasping chuckles, the strange silences, the peculiar blankness of that pudgy face, the earnest pleadings to buy this or that." But Mary Drone, as Keats's story tells it, finally repented for her antisocial behavior and "emerged in defeat," confessing to neighbor Jane Amiable, "I've been watching TV."[84]

This nightmarish vision of the preplanned community served as an impetus for the arrival of a surrogate community on television. Television provided an illusion of the ideal neighborhood—the way it was supposed to be. Just when people had left their lifelong companions in the city, television sitcoms pictured romanticized versions of neighbor and family bonding. When promoting the early domestic comedy, *Ethel and Albert*, NBC told viewers to tune in to "a delightful situation comedy that is returning this weekend. . . . Yes, this Saturday night, *Ethel and Albert* come into view once again to keep you laughing at the typical foibles of the kind of people who might be living right next door to you."[85] The idea that television families were neighbors was also found in critical commentary. In 1953, *Saturday Review* claimed, "The first thing you notice about these sketches [*The Goldbergs, The Adventures of Ozzie and Harriet, Ethel and Albert,* and the live *Honeymooners* skits] is that they are incidents; they are told as they might be told when neighbors visit (in the Midwest sense of the word) on the front porch or the back fence."[86] Numerous situation comedies and family dramas underscored such notions of traditional neighborhood bonding by dealing with the lives of immigrant and working-class people who lived in urban locales. *The Goldbergs'* quintessential Jewish mother, Molly, always leaned out the window of her Bronxville apartment to greet her neighbor Mrs. Bloom, while *The Honeymooners'* working-class milieu included bosom buddies Ralph Kramden and Ed Norton, who repeatedly displayed the riches of friendship in their otherwise humble surroundings. Since many of these programs had been popular on radio since the Depression (*The Goldbergs, Amos 'n' Andy, Life With Luigi*), they harked

129

back to the populist ideals of "good neighborliness" in hard times, ideals that the more alienating, consumer-oriented suburban culture seemed to brush aside. Indeed, as George Lipsitz has argued, these programs helped legitimate the cultural transitions of the postwar society by linking its consumerist values to nostalgic memories of a more authentic urban and ethnic culture.[87] Significantly in this regard, even the sitcoms that were set in suburban locales reminded viewers of traditional neighborhood networks by including characters who functioned as lifelong friends to the principal characters.[88] According to Madelyn Pugh Davis, a headwriter for *I Love Lucy*, these neighbors were included for storytelling purposes: "In those days all the shows had neighbors. The people had to have somebody to talk to."[89] But the narrative relationships between primary characters and neighbor characters went beyond the functional demands of dramatization and resulted in themes of neighborhood friendship that became standard elements of the family sitcom.

On *I Love Lucy*, the Ricardos and their downstairs landlords, the Mertzes, were constantly together, and the more mature characters, Ethel and Fred Mertz, served a quasi-parental role so that neighbors appeared as a family unit. In 1956, when the Ricardos moved from their New York apartment to an idyllic Connecticut suburb, Lucy and Ricky reenacted the painful separation anxieties that many viewers must have experienced over the previous decade. In an episode entitled "Lucy Wants to Move to the Country," Lucy has misgivings about leaving her best friend, Ethel Mertz, and the Ricardos decide to break their contract on their new home. At the episode's end, however, they realize that the fresh air and beauty of suburban life will compensate for their friendships in the city. After learning their "lesson," the Ricardos are rewarded in a subsequent episode ("Lucy Gets Chummy with the Neighbors") when they meet their new next-door neighbors, Ralph and Betty Ramsy, who were regularly featured in the following programs. While the inclusion of these neighbor characters provided an instant remedy for the painful move to the suburbs, the series went on to present even more potent cures. The next episode, "Lucy Raises Chickens," brings Ethel and Fred back into the fold when the older couple sell their New York apartment to become chicken farmers in the Connecticut suburb—and, of course, the Mertzes rent the house next door to the Ricardos. Thus, according to this fantasy scenario, the move from the city would not be painful because it was possible to maintain traditional friendships in the new suburban world.

Burns and Allen similarly focused on neighborly relations. Every show revolved around the escapades of George, Gracie, and their next door neighbors, Harry and Blanche Morton. The spatial organization of the mise-en-scène allowed for interaction between the couples because the kitchen windows of the two homes looked directly into one another. In fact, the inclusion of these neighbor-characters in the program was a conventionalized part of the narrative structure because the episodes often contained a segment that featured the Mortons alone in their home. *Ozzie and Harriet* also included the regular appearance of "neighbor segments" in scenes between Ozzie and his pal, Thorny, which took place in the adjoining front gardens of Ozzie and Thorny's suburban homes.

The opening credits of fifties sitcoms further encouraged audiences to perceive television's families as neighbors, linked through electrical wires to their own homes.[90] *Father Knows Best*, a domestic comedy-drama, showed an exterior shot of the Anderson family home, a two-story residence that looked like an American landmark, the perfect home in the perfect town. The theme song's dramatic introductory passage underscored the importance of this establishing shot, giving the viewer a sense of awe that one might have had upon setting eyes on the White House. The use of the exterior shot and dramatic music made the viewer aware that the Anderson home was more than just a private haven, more than just a world of interiors and family relations. Instead, the family home was represented as if it were a public spectacle, a monument commemorating the values of the ideal American town. It was only after the initial view of the exterior community that the sequence cut to the interior of the home, where individual family members were introduced to the audience. In fact, these exterior shots were so typically used that they became a narrative convention of the opening sequences in situation comedies. *Ozzie and Harriet* began with a shot of the surrounding suburban neighborhood in which a lamppost sign with the Nelsons' name was pictured close up in the frame. The program then cut to an exterior shot of the Nelsons' home and finally moved into the house where the family members were shown. *Leave It To Beaver* (a sitcom that was first aired in 1957) opened with the Cleaver family exiting their suburban home, while the final credits showed Beaver and Wally Cleaver walking down the tree-lined streets of their beautiful suburban town. In the 1954 season of *Make Room for Daddy*, the opening credits showed the Williams family boarding their new Dodge sedan (a plug for their sponsor), which was parked on the city street of their upper eastside Manhattan neighborhood. The opening credits of *The Goldbergs* showed an exterior shot of the family's Bronxville apartment with Molly leaning out her window, addressing us as if she were our next-door neighbor. In 1954, when Molly and her family moved to Haverville, a fictitious suburban community, the program opened with several scenes of the surrounding neighborhood.

Indeed, these televised neighborhoods seemed to suture the "crack" in the picture window. They helped ease what must have been for many Americans a painful transition from the city to the suburb. But more than simply supplying a tonic for displaced suburbanites, television promised something better. It promised modes of spectator pleasure premised upon the sense of an illusory—rather than a real—community of friends. It held out a new possibility for being alone in the home, away from the troublesome busybody neighbors in the next house. Yet, television also compensated for the guilt feelings attached to this reclusive urge—guilt feelings that made the antisocial Mary Drones join the group against their better wisdom. It did so by maintaining the ideals of community togetherness, but placing them *at a fictional distance*. Television allowed people to enter into an imaginary social life, one that was shared not in the neighborhood networks of bridge clubs and mahjong gatherings, but on the national networks of CBS, NBC, and ABC.

Perhaps this was best suggested by Motorola television in a 1951 advertisement. The sketch at the top of the layout shows a businessman on his way home from work who meets a friend while waiting at a bus stop. Upon hearing that his friend's TV is on the blink, the businessman invites him home for an evening of television on his "dependable" Motorola console. A large photograph further down on the page shows a social scene where two couples, gathered around the living room console, share in the joys of a TV party. Thus, according to the narrative sequence of events, television promises to increase social contacts. What is most significant about this advertisement, however, is that the representation of the TV party suggests something different from the story told by the ad's narrative structure. In fact, the couples in the room do not appear to relate to one another; rather they interact *with and through* the television set. The picture emanating from the screen includes a third couple, the television stars, George Burns and Gracie Allen. The couple on the left of the frame stare at the screen, gesturing towards George and Gracie as if they were involved in conversation with the celebrities. While the husband on the right of the frame stares at the television set, his wife looks at the man gesturing towards George and Gracie. In short, the social relationship between couples in the room appears to depend upon the presence of an illusion. Moreover, the illusion itself seems to come alive insofar as the televised couple, George and Gracie, appear to be interacting with the real couples in the room. Thus, television promises a new kind of social experience, one that replicates the logic of real friendship (as told by the sequence of events in the advertisement's narrative), but which transforms it into an imaginary social relationship shared between the home audience and the broadcast image (as represented in the social scene). In this ad as elsewhere, it is

Television promises a new form of social life. (Courtesy Motorola, Inc.)

the idea of simulated social life that is shown to be the crux of pleasure in television.[91]

Indeed, television at its most ideal promised to bring to audiences not merely an illusion of reality as in the cinema, but a sense of "being there," a kind of *hyperrealism*. Advertisers suggested that their sets would deliver picture and sound quality so real that the illusion would come alive. In 1952, Motorola promised that its "new dimension of realism brings action right into the living room." The "new dimension" was its "standout picture" from which a televised ballerina appeared to pop out of the TV screen.[92] In 1949, Capehart television claimed, "Capehart tone brings television to life." The graphic showed a football player in a television screen with his life-sized replicant to the left of the screen in an apparently real space (i.e., the negative, or unused, space of the layout).[93] Far exceeding the imagination of Capehart's advertising firm were the advertisers for Sparton Television, who produced what might be called the emblematic advertisement of this "come to life" genre. The 1953 advertisement pictured a large, full color photograph of a baseball stadium. On home plate stood a Sparton console model with a picture of a baseball player up at bat on the screen. Out in right field (and in the foreground of the composition), was a modern style easy chair with baseball bats and catcher's mitts placed nearby. In this way, Sparton Television literally transported the living room to the baseball field.[94] The Admiral Company took this sense of hyperrealism right up to the point of purchase with an animated display that promised that the broadcast image would come to life in the showroom. Exhibited at about 800 retail outlets, the display was composed of a cardboard television cabinet with a screen that depicted a clown who blew real bubbles into the store.[95] Admiral thus encouraged shoppers to believe that the television set contained real life, that its illusions would materialize in their presence.

Television producers and executives often took the promise of hyperreality quite seriously, devising schemes by which to merge public and private worlds into a new electrical neighborhood. One of the central architects of the new electrical space was NBC's Pat Weaver, who saw television as an extension of traditional community experiences. Weaver claimed, "In our entertainment, we . . . start with television as a communications medium, not bringing shows into the living rooms of the nation, but taking people from their living rooms to other places—theaters, arenas, ball parks, movie houses, skating rinks, and so forth."[96] Implementing these ideas in 1949, Weaver conceived *The Saturday Night Revue,* a three-hour program designed to "present a panorama of Americans at play on Saturday night." The program took the segmented format of variety acts and film features, but it presented the segments as a community experience shared by people just like the viewers at home. As *Variety* explained, "For a film, the cameras may depict a family going to their neighborhood theatre and dissolve from there into the feature."[97] Thus, television would mediate the cultural transition from public to private entertainment by presenting an imaginary night at the movies.

While Weaver's plan was the most elaborate, the basic idea was employed by various other programs. In 1952, New York's local station, WOR, aired *TV Dinner Date,* a variety program that was designed to give "viewers a solid two-and-a-half hours of a 'night out at home.'"[98] CBS even promised female viewers an imaginary date in its fifteen-minute program, *The Continental.* Sponsored by Cameo Hosiery, the show began by telling women, "And now it's time for your date with the Continental." Host Renza Cesana (whom *Variety* described as "Carl Brisson, Ezio Pinza and Charles Boyer all rolled into one") used a vampire-like Transylvanian accent to court women in the late-night hours. Cesana addressed his romantic dialogue to an off-camera character as he navigated his way through his lushly furnished den, a situation designed to create the illusion that Cesana's date for the night was the home viewer.[99] Meanwhile, during daytime hours, numerous programs were set in public spaces such as hotels or cafes with the direct intention of making women feel as if they were part of the outside world. One of the first successful network shows, *Shoppers Matinee*, used a subjective camera that was intended to take "the place of the woman shopper, making the home viewer feel as if she were in the store in person."[100] In 1952, CBS introduced the daytime show, *Everywhere I Go*, boasting of its "studio without walls" that was designed to "create the illusion of taking viewers to the actual scene" of presentation. One segment, for example, used rear-screen projection to depict hostess Jane Edwards and her nine-year-old daughter against a backdrop of their actual living room.[101] More generally, locally produced "Mr. and Mrs." shows invited viewers into the homes of local celebrities, while network prime-time programs such as Edward R. Murrow's *Person to Person* were, as *Newsweek* claimed, based on "a very simple proposition: that viewers would like to visit people in their homes 'live.'"[102] Television's electrical neighborhood thus allowed viewers to convene imaginatively in familiar family settings with stars that exuded the warmth and intimacy of the people next door.

Again, however, the dreams of a hyperreal social world that television promised its first consumers were tempered by critical voices that were also heard in the popular media. One of the nonbelievers was John Crosby, the well-known New York television critic, who in 1951 wrote a spoof on this notion of hyperrealism, revealing the absurd conflation between the real world and television's imaginary universe. Joking about the way in which he and his wife were beginning to live out TV fantasies in their own lives, he recalled the time when his wife became a bit disoriented while visiting a friend. "She [said] brightly, 'I feel as though I'm sitting right in your living room,'" and "the host snapped back, 'You *are* sitting in my living room.'"[103]

Five

The People in the Theater Next Door

It is the responsibility of television to bear constantly in mind that the audience is primarily a home audience, and consequently that television's relationship to the viewers is that between guest and host.
From Preamble to The Television Code of the National Association of Radio and Television Broadcasters [1]

The radio comedy *Easy Aces* made its television debut on the DuMont network in December 1949. The episode consisted entirely of Goodman Ace and his wife Jane sitting in their living room, watching TV. The interest stemmed solely from the couple's witty commentary on the program they watched. Aside from that, there was no plot. This was television, pure and simple. It was just the sense of being with the Aces, of watching them watch, and of watching TV with them, that gave this show its peculiar appeal. [2]

With its promise to transport viewers to the homes of fictional friends, this program was symptomatic of the domestic sitcoms that proliferated in the early 1950s. [3] Like Jane and Goodman Ace, the families that populated the screen extended a hand of friendship across the border between real life and the parallel universe we now call "TV land." By connecting viewers to a new electronic neighborhood, the genre encouraged audiences to perceive spatial and social relationships in new ways. In addition, it helped naturalize a strange new technology because it conveyed stories about everyday situations that took place in familiar settings. By examining the rise of the family sitcom we can explore the "dialogue" between a communications medium and its wider cultural context. The genre provides us with a set of clues to the question of how television inserted itself into domestic life, how it grew from a curious new contraption to a familiar cultural form.

You Are There: Intimacy, Immediacy, and Spontaneity

Like all genres, the family sitcom is based on a set of common conventions, modes of production, and audience expectations. Today it can typically be expected to include a suburban home, character relationships based on family ties, a setting filled with middle-class luxuries, a story that emphasizes everyday complications, and a narrative structure based on conflicts that resolve in thirty minutes. In 1948, however, the television audience would have had a less concrete sense of what to expect from such a television program. In fact, between 1948 and 1950 the family comedy was a marginal genre. Aside from a few network offerings (which were often short-lived), domestic sketches such as "Ethel and Albert" and "The Honeymooners" appeared as fifteen-minute segments of daytime and prime-time variety programs or else as filler on local stations.[4] Often produced on shoestring budgets, the local programs were particularly primitive by today's video standards. *At Our House,* a fifteen-minute family comedy aired on Chicago's WBKB, attempted to cut corners by minimizing talent costs. *Variety* objected to the fact that the family's "grade school son, Junior, owing to budget restrictions, has yet to materialize on screen, existing meanwhile via script allusions."[5] In such incarnations, the family sitcom was a mere shadow of its radio predecessors, which by the 1940s were often slickly produced in Hollywood studios and featured during network prime-time hours. Indeed, although radio had institutionalized the family series, television did not just adapt these radio programs wholesale. Instead, television's family sitcom would be shaped and reshaped over the course of the early fifties until finally it emerged as one of the networks' staple program types. The development of the form and its rise to popularity has to be seen in relation to the unique problems and aesthetic concerns of the television industry in the early period, which, in turn, responded to cultural expectations for the medium.

In 1948, television programming was a rare commodity. The networks found themselves in a competitive market where stars, writers, camera operators, studio space, and other production facilities were hard to find. The programs that developed during these years were therefore often drawn from other media—radio, burlesque, vaudeville, film, the circus, legitimate theater, and the nightclub all provided source materials for producers. In this respect, early television was varied in style, combining different aesthetic strategies and attempting to tailor them to its own specific demands. Production manuals acknowledged television's use of other media but argued for the development of its own aesthetic properties. As Edward Stasheff claimed in *The Television Program,* "While television derives many of its elements from the theater, the movies, and radio, while it serves as a transmitting medium for sports, news and special events, it is also rapidly developing as a form of entertainment which is unique. That uniqueness is based on immediacy, spontaneity, and intimacy."

Similarly, in *Television Program Production,* NBC producer-director Carroll O'Meara stated, "TV's greatest attributes are its timeliness and intimacy. By timeliness is meant TV's immediacy, its power of delivering direct presence, of transmitting a living scene into the home—NOW, as it happens."[6] Television critics had similar standards.[7] According to Gilbert Seldes, "The essence of television techniques is their contribution to the sense of immediacy . . . they [audiences] feel that what they see and hear is happening in the present." Jack Gould claimed that live television was better than film because it "unites the individual at home with the event afar."[8] Thus, the new medium would ideally give viewers a sense of being in the presence of the performances it transmitted.

The major networks, whose competitive edge lay in their unique ability to transmit live broadcasts to their affiliate stations, drew on conventions of live theatrical entertainment for their big-budget, prime-time programs. With their studios located in New York, CBS and NBC looked particularly to legitimate theater, and they also took a renewed interest in vaudeville as a model for visual spectacle. In all cases, the networks privileged theatricality as a mode of representation, but the theatrical traditions they drew on were quite distinct. The legitimate theater particularly inspired television's live anthology dramas such as *Kraft Television Theater* and *Philco Television Playhouse*, while vaudeville and, to a lesser degree, burlesque and nightclub performances served as models for variety shows such as *Texaco Star Theater* and *Your Show of Shows*.

In all cases, television's turn to the theater was a complicated and muddled affair. By the late forties, theatrical traditions—both legitimate and vaudeville—had already been filtered through radio and film. The public was by now well acquainted with radio's live anthology dramas and filmed versions of theatrical plays. People also had countless opportunities to hear vaudeville stars on radio variety shows and see them in numerous Hollywood "vaudefilms" that featured the comedy turns of teams such as Wheeler and Woolsy or Burns and Allen.[9] Despite the fact that radio stars and programs were often transferred to television, and despite the fact that television imported visual comedy conventions from film, television's debt to these media was typically downplayed by industry executives and television critics. Television, it was constantly argued, would be a better approximation of live entertainment than any previous form of technological reproduction. Its ability to broadcast direct to the home would allow people to feel as if they really were at the theater. Television's capacity for transmitting sight as well as sound would give its programs a sense of credibility that radio lacked, while its intimate privatized address would create a more compelling simulation of reality than film ever could. As Edward Stasheff wrote in his production manual, "If television is to find itself, then, it should accentuate its difference from film. It should make the most of its frequently described power of 'immediacy,' which is its ability to transport the audience to the site of events taking place elsewhere at the same moment." According to such logic, the unique power of the medium was its ability to bind public with private space, and the appeal of the individual television program depended on the degree to which it capitalized on this. As Stasheff said of the variety show, the programs "possibly owe their success not only to their high-powered talent, but to the feeling they give the home viewer of having a front row seat among the members of a theater audience at a Broadway show. That's a good feeling to have in Hinterland, Iowa, or Suburbia, New Jersey." [10] In addition, anthology dramas won critical accolades for their use of naturalistic acting styles, slice-of-life stories, and characterizations that were drawn with psychological depth—all of which were thought to enhance television's unique capabilities by making audiences feel as if they were in the actors' presence, witnessing the events as they happened. [11] According to the popular wisdom, then, television was able to reproduce reality in a way no previous medium could. Whereas film allowed spectators imaginatively to project themselves *into a scene,* television would give people the sense of being *on the scene* of presentation—it would simulate the entire experience of being at the theater.

This aesthetic of "presence" was reinforced by the networks, which promoted television programs in the context of exciting theatrical premieres, inviting critics and celebrities to "opening nights" in their posh new studio theaters. In 1950, for example, when NBC transformed New York's Center Theatre into a television studio, it welcomed its guests to "the biggest theater premiere of all time." New York Mayor Vincent R. Impelleteri, who attended the opening ceremonies, responded in kind, calling television "a vital social force of terrific impact because of its immediacy and intimacy." [12] Similarly, when opening its New York anchor station WJZ, ABC invited industrial and civic figures to New York's Palace Theater to witness a vaudeville program complete with a dog act and soft shoe and comedy routines—shot live, of course, by the television cameras. [13] Television stars and directors (many of whom had worked in the theater) also imagined that they were putting on theatrical plays. Jack Benny observed, "To me, television is an extension of the stage . . . essentially, I picture a theater audience when I plan each program." Delbert Mann, who directed anthology dramas, claimed that "training and experience in the theatre is the most essential background for the director of a television dramatic show." Production handbooks such as *Broadcasting Television and Radio* wrote that "television drama is theater adapted to a new medium. . . . A thorough knowledge of television is less helpful than extensive background in theater." [14] Such interests were more generally reflected in the trade magazine *Theatre Arts,* which regularly printed articles on television production between 1948 and 1953.

Critics were not merely content with programs that imported the theater into the home; instead, they demanded that television perfect and even surpass the theater by offering a privileged vantage point on the action. In 1949, *House Beautiful* compared the televised concert to its performance in the concert hall, claiming that "television not only embodies [the concert performance] it . . . adds a dimension not offered to the concert goer." This dimension was the specialized view that could be had in the home—the "close-up" that permitted "the spectator to look at the orchestra and the conductor from every angle, to peer into the faces of the musicians, to note their physical characteristics, and to watch the play of emotions on their patently exposed faces." [15] Critics in *Variety, The New York Times, Theatre Arts,* as well as other trade and popular magazines, repeatedly disapproved of programs that placed the camera in a static position to film the action on the stage. Instead, they wanted the programs to provide home audiences with a bird's-eye view of the action so that average people sitting in their living rooms could feel as if they were witnessing the production from the best view possible.[16] According to such critics, television was meant to give the home audience not just a view but rather, a *perfect view.*

The emphasis on the perfect view had previously been a central interest in critical commentary on the cinema, which similarly expected film to surpass the theatrical experience by offering ideal angles of sight. However, for a new generation of television critics, this perfect view had specific meanings within the context of broadcasting and home reception. Television was better than the theater because it could give people both a wide view of the action and a sense of intimacy through the close-up—all within the space of one's private living-room theater. In his 1947 book, *The Future of Television,* Orrin E. Dunlap, Jr., wrote that television was "Utopia for the Audience." Appraising an early NBC drama, he claimed, "The view was perfect—no latecomers to disturb the continuity; no heads or bonnets to dodge. . . . In television every seat is in the front row." [17] Perhaps, in this regard, television was meant to democratize what had traditionally been an aristocratic, box-seat view of theatrical spectacle.

In this context of theatrical presentation, live programming became the preferred form.[18] NBC's Pat Weaver was most outspoken about his preference for live origination, claiming, "It is this ability to surpass all expectations in a live performance that will always bring a high degree of excitement to the panoply of forces arrayed when a curtain goes up in the theatre or in television. . . . The unexpected, the spontaneous are always there—the topical, the todayishness, the current and most talked about—these too, are there in live television." [19] East coast television critics such as Gilbert Seldes and Jack Gould also championed live television, particularly the hour-long dramatic series and news programming such as *See it Now.* Even as independent syndicators and Hollywood producers encroached upon the medium with their more economical "telefilm" products, these critics held down the fort for live formats. But by 1955, their critical preferences had little to do with reality; live television was becoming a dinosaur of a bygone "Golden Age" as the networks joined forces with Hollywood film companies to produce the more economically advantageous and highly popular half-hour series. When *I Love Lucy* came to the CBS network in 1951, it was a huge popular success, soaring to number one in the Nielsen ratings. CBS aggressively developed the genre over the course of the early 1950s, and its successes did not go unnoticed by the other networks, which also increasingly turned to sitcoms and other filmed formats. By 1960, there were about twice as many sitcoms as there were variety shows, and the anthology drama (which was now typically shot on film) had almost entirely disappeared.[20]

Given the preference for live television, the half-hour family comedy, which was typically produced on film, would seem to be the black sheep of early television. Indeed, David Swift, a critic for *Variety,* spoke for many when he described the sitcom as the "tasteless pap of triviality."[21] However, other critics (and, ironically, sometimes the same ones that argued for the superiority of live television) often gave these programs good reviews, and many of the shows became widely popular with audiences. Part of the appeal of the shows most certainly had to do with the fact that they assimilated the aesthetics established for live formats. By 1950, the sense of presence that live television was thought to capture had also become part of the critical expectations for the fledgling family comedy form.

Between 1948 and 1950, *Variety* expressed disdain for family comedies that seemed too much like radio or film, searching instead for a more "televisual" aesthetic. ABC's *Wren's Nest,* a fifteen-minute program that depicted the home life of a suburban family, met with critical disfavor because of its "strange combination of radio's soapoperas [sic] and Mr. and Mrs. shows." In addition, *Variety* continued, the premier show "took place entirely in one small corner of the couple's living room and for the most part on a couch. . . . For all the difference it made to viewers, the two could have been standing just as easily around a radio mike." Similarly, when reviewing *Growing Paynes* (a family comedy on DuMont's New York station, WABD), *Variety* said the program was "sewed together into an original design from shreds and patches of familiar radio and screen situations."[22] By 1953, *Variety* was so exasperated with the situation that a front-page story derided the long list of situation comedies imported from radio, claiming that "the basic properties growing out of TV itself, as a medium distinct and apart from radio, are few and far between." [23] Thus, no less than the live formats, the domestic situation comedy was supposed to be tailored to the unique capabilities of the television medium—particularly its ability to convey a sense of presence, to make audiences feel as if they were on the scene of a theatrical performance.

Addressing the Family Audience

Although early television embraced the theater as a model for representation, the suitability of theatrical entertainment for a family environment was often questioned by industry executives, critics, regulators, government officials, and audience members. As J. R. Poppele, president of the Television Broadcasters Association, warned his colleagues, "The theatre has achieved a license which harks back to the middle ages and not a few of the things there to be seen and heard would be difficult to reconcile in a medium which finds its way into the ordinary American home, where standards of purity and decency are still anything but extinct." [24] Some critics even expressed distaste for the use of studio audiences, suggesting that it disrupted the wholesome family environment in which television was received. According to one columnist in *Variety*, "The studio visitors are a motley collection of people on a night out; the audience at home is a family, a group of friends, who are spending a quiet evening by the fireside fiddling around with the television dials in the hopes of being entertained. . . . We're their invited guests, and by golly, they didn't ask us to bring a whole conglomeration of studio guests to interrupt our social visit with laughter." [25] Here, the more general fascination with antiseptic electrical space pervaded ideas about program content as people insisted that the home be kept safe from undesirable elements imported from the public sphere.

The development of family comedy can be seen as a solution to such problems. By merging traditions of live entertainment with stories about wholesome American families, the genre tamed the unrefined elements of the theater, while still maintaining the aesthetics of presence so important in the early period. It did so by integrating two types of theatrical traditions that early television embraced. On the one hand, it drew its conventions from the legitimate stage, incorporating principles of theatrical realism that emphasized story construction and character relationships. On the other hand, it tapped into the culture's renewed interest in vaudeville, a theatrical aesthetic that pulled it toward physical humor that emphasized the immediate impact of performance over and above story development and characterization.

In merging these two theatrical traditions, the family sitcom was in many ways a hybrid of the networks' big-budget, prime-time formats—the live anthology drama and the variety show. While both genres based their appeal on intimacy, immediacy, and spontaneity, they each stressed different aesthetic means to achieve this end. Anthology dramas used conventions of theatrical realism, conventions that had also become the basis for visual representation in the classical Hollywood film. Based on verisimilitude, the anthology drama favored classical story construction, character development, and acting styles that minimized artifice so that audiences might better suspend disbelief and enter into the world of the story. The turn to method acting in early television brought emotional intensity to the small screen as James Dean, Paul Newman, and other actors gave their characters a strong psychological dimension that helped create an aura of authenticity.[26] In addition, like other forms of theatrical realism, the anthology drama erected a wall between audience and actor so that the players never acknowledged the presence of the audience, at least until the curtain call.[27] This "aesthetic distance" was meant to create an illusion of reality so that the story seemed like a world unto itself. In his television production manual, Stasheff likened the anthology drama to cinematic realism, observing that "the motion picture drama must have a certain formality which is necessary even in the theater to maintain 'aesthetic distance' between actor and audience in the interest of successful illusion. An actor never looks into the film camera lens (except in the particular case of subjective shooting) because to do so would make the audience conscious of the camera. This is also true of television drama." The same author noted, however, that, "in all other types of television production . . . the performer most often does look directly into the lens, because that is his connection with the audience at home."[28]

In fact, the early variety show was a perfect example of the "other" kinds of programs to which Stasheff referred. Favoring a vaudeville aesthetic over theatrical realism, the variety comics directly addressed the audience (both the studio and the home audience), highlighting the presentational nature of the show. In the late 1940s, when Milton Berle was "Mr. Television," he was famous for running off the stage into the studio audience, making a mockery out of the "aesthetic distance" so important to theatrical realism. Additionally, the vaudeville aesthetic privileged performance over story, featuring the zany antics of comics and using simple narrative situations—or sketches—primarily as a pretense for gags.

Importantly, the differences between theatrical realism and the vaudeville aesthetic were not just stylistic, but cultural as well. The legitimate theater promised genteel respectability with a polite, quiet audience who sat in sublime contemplation of the story. While twentieth-century vaudeville also presented itself as respectable family entertainment and, in fact, attracted a predominantly middle-class audience, the theaters were attended by all rungs on the social ladder—including working-class people, immigrants, and social elites who enjoyed "slumming with commoners." Although twentieth-century vaudeville incorporated elements of the legitimate theater into its form (numerous stage stars, for example, crossed over to vaudeville palaces), it still retained elements of popular entertainment, often rousing the audience to excitement and directly engaging their participation in the events on stage.[29]

Moreover, as they were developed on television, the two kinds of theater were separated by what television critics perceived as their suitability for the family audience. The anthology drama was the darling of prominent east coast critics who praised the format for its approximation of legitimate theater and its attempt to deal with sophisticated, socially relevant subjects. At times, as broadcast historian Erik Barnouw has observed, the relevancy of these programs deeply grieved sponsors and network executives.[30] Threatened by the McCarthyite sentiments of the period (especially the blacklisting tactics of the anticommunist pressure group Aware, Inc.), and more generally concerned about appealing to the various regional tastes of its broad national audience, the industry often shied away from the controversial subjects that some anthology dramas contained. Less attention has been paid to the variety show, which was also controversial, but for different reasons. Critics, audiences, regulators, and government officials lashed out at the genre's sexual innuendos and wild physical humor, seeking programs that they considered more suitable for a domestic medium. The development of the situation comedy can be seen in part as a compromise between the two types of theatrical aesthetics that were embraced by the early television industry. In merging vaudeville with theatrical realism, the sitcom created a middle-ground aesthetic that satisfied television's overall aim in reaching a family audience. Blending the wild spontaneity of vaudeville performance with the more genteel—and decidedly noncontroversial—aspects of theatrical realism, this genre became the networks' preferred form for reaching a family audience.

Vaudeville's influence on the situation comedy was particularly pronounced in the early period. In the late 1940s, when television variety shows became extremely popular, critics and industry spokespeople continually referred to the rebirth of vaudeville. Shortly after television's introduction, New York's Palace Theater, the key exhibition space for vaudeville shows in the early twentieth century, reopened its doors to the public. In the late 1940s, *Variety* even began to reissue its Palace review columns from the 1920s, claiming that "as vaudeville and video programming . . . have more than a little in common, the tele men find that these reviews often are a key on how bills were booked, why acts were balanced against each other. . . . It's a twist when 25 years after it was written a review of a vaudeville bill is found to be of use to a new branch of show business."[31] Granted, such declarations had conveniently erased the memory of vaudeville's strong presence on radio variety shows (especially in the 1930s) and in numerous anarchistic comedies, revue films, and film shorts. Still, to television producers and critics of the time, it was important to think of themselves as reviving a venerable tradition.[32]

While the television variety shows often contained domestic sketches, their formats depended more on stand-up comedy and sight gags than on storytelling humor.[33] These shows featured the "olio" organization of the vaudeville theater in which a series of separate acts did fifteen-minute sketches that had little relation to the others. So much like vaudeville were these programs that *Variety* continually referred to them as "vaudeo."

Between 1948 and 1950, for example, Milton Berle's *Texaco Star*

Texaco Star Theater featured a stagy vaudeville aesthetic and an outlandish host, Milton Berle (here dressed in drag). (Wisconsin Center for Film and Theater Research.)

Theater was a series of discrete vaudeville turns, including Berle's monologue, short sketches, one or two musical numbers (that often drew on nightclub talent), stand-up comedy performances, and such novelties as impersonators, acrobats, and animal acts. Although Berle was initially an enormous ratings success, the critics were less than pleased with his program. In particular, they disliked the narrative organization of the format, objecting to the lack of continuity between performances. As early as July of 1948, *Variety* claimed that "when broken down into its component parts," *Texaco Star Theater* "came up with some qualitative programming," but lacked "show-wise continuity." Critics reacted in similar ways to other variety formats, calling for better scripting that linked separate acts into a more coherent narrative. DuMont's *School House* lacked a "suitable script" and had "no coherent pattern in the treatment of acts and commercials." Conversely, when Martha Raye hosted NBC's *All Star Revue*, one *Variety* critic liked the "thread of continuity" that made it possible to reduce the number of disparate vaudeville acts.[34]

In other words, what the critics wanted was a story. They wanted the vaudeville format to be more like theatrical realism, with its promise of unity, harmony, and continuous action. As Jack Gould claimed in his favorable review of Ed Wynn's variety format, "The transition from one scene to another . . . is done with the smoothness of the Hollywood films."[35] By the 1952 season, narrative continuity was becoming a conventionalized element of the variety show, which increasingly merged vaudeville performances with the story-centered approach of theatrical realism. After its enormous success with *I Love Lucy* in 1951, the CBS network turned to the filmed half-hour comedy format as a way to compete with NBC's glitzy variety shows. At the same time, the vaudeo programs tried to imitate the sitcom formula, tying together individual acts with a more coherent storyline and theme. In September of that year, *Variety* claimed:

> The Berle craze has subsided as the Lucille Balls and the rival
> CBS-TV situation comedy formula took hold. NBC-TV sta-
> tions, even in single station markets such as Pittsburgh, Kansas
> and Indianapolis, served notice that they weren't picking up
> the Berle show this season. So for the new Berle they dras-
> tically altered the format to embrace situation comedy, in-
> stalled a whole new set of writers, topped by Goodman Ace
> [who was famous for his work on radio's domestic comedy
> *Easy Aces*].

By December 1951, *Variety* reported that the "situation comedy formula has parlayed the Texaco hour into one of the major pleasantries of the season, with Berle becoming the 'new find' of '52."[36]

To be sure, Berle's new look was a product of numerous forces. By the early 1950s, the pressure of producing live television had taken its toll on Berle and other hosts who were checking into hospitals for stress-related ailments. Berle collapsed from overwork; Eddie Cantor suffered a heart attack; Fred Allen fell ill and missed a full season; Ed Sullivan checked into the hospital for ulcers; Red Buttons collapsed from nervous exhaustion; Red Skelton had an operation; Dean Martin, Jerry Lewis, and Donald O'Connor were all told by their doctors to take a break from *The Colgate Comedy Hour;* and Jackie Gleason was "practically . . . making the hospital his 'between shows' home on medic's instructions to keep in trim to offset the hazards of a gruelling assignment." [37] The comics' problems weren't helped by the fact that critics repeatedly disapproved of the dated gags that they recycled in order to meet the schedule demands of live television. Speaking about his trade, Bob Hope told *Variety,* "Milton Berle, Mr. Television himself, has used up so much material he's stealing from himself." [38] Added to this, the extremely high price of variety formats and the problems of finding guest star talent made the shows very difficult to produce. [39] As a remedy to these problems, some shows cut back to a half-hour format or else appeared on a rotating bimonthly schedule. In addition, between 1952 and 1954, comics began emigrating to Hollywood where film techniques and sunny skies promised to reduce the strains of live television. Finally, the programs increasingly turned to storytelling, character-centered comedy that mitigated against repetitive jokes and also helped alleviate the problem of finding big name talent.

Beyond these practical considerations, however, the change in format was also intended to refine television humor for the nationwide family audience. As suggested by the *Variety* article cited above, Berle's transition to situation comedy was in large part related to the fact that his vaudeo humor did not appeal to midwestern audiences who, by 1949, were receiving the show over the coaxial cable. As broadcast historian Arthur Frank Wertheim has shown, Berle's loss of popularity was greatly influenced by the fact that his New York, Yiddish-vaudevillian humor did not appeal to rural midwesterners. [40] More generally, the erasure of ethnic urban roots became an industry prescription for success. Irwin Shane, the publisher of the trade journal *Televiser* and the executive director of New York's Television Workshop, told fellow producers that "a comedy show built entirely upon Broadway humor (or frequent references to the borscht circuit, the Brooklyn Dodgers, the Palace Theatre, or even famous New York Nightclubs) will find an indifferent audience in Kokomo, Indiana, and in the hundreds of Kokomos around the country. To assure an out-of-town audience, the show's content must be broad in its appeal." [41]

In addition to using this nationwide standard, critics found the outlandish behavior, risque jokes, and abrasive personalities of numerous variety clowns unsuitable for a family medium. Again, Berle was the biggest offender. As Jack Gould wrote, "His tricks of whistling, excessively effusive introductions, interruption of other acts and preoccupation with the revival of vaudeville are just tiring and repetitious. A couple of the scenes in the show, what is more, were coarse and unnecessary." [42] Berle's habit of cross-dressing (in one show, for example, he appeared as Carmen Miranda and kissed singer Tony Martin) certainly did not help his image with the critics. Moreover, his personification of a dirty-minded flirt, who regularly chased after glamor girls, clashed with his simultaneous attempts to woo the child audience in the guise of the ultimate family man, "Uncle Miltie." In a survey conducted by the National Council of Catholic Women, one parent expressed disapproval of Berle's "Uncle Miltie" persona, while others called him "valueless," "at time[s] objectionable," "loud," "vulgar," "too insincere," and even "insane." [43] Aware of the negative reactions to Berle, NBC kept close tabs on the program. In 1948, one internal company report claimed, "The Texaco Milton Berle program has included not only slapstick but Berle's very typical humor. On the slapstick we have always checked-double-checked in dress rehearsal such features as the tearing off of a comedian's shirt front, falling pants, etc. As to the gags . . . we are . . . reviewing a confidential advance outline of jokes proposed for use." [44] By the early 1950s, these censorship tactics no longer seemed sufficient to the sponsor and network, who were now concerned with reaching a large nationwide family audience.

When Berle came back in the 1952 season, the vaudeville components of the show were incorporated into a storyline that considerably tamed his brand of humor. Except for sporadic comic asides, Berle no longer addressed the audience directly, and his outrageous parlay with the studio audience was gone. While ethnic Yiddish humor still played a role in the show, it was now incorporated into a story that presented ethnicity, not as a mode of address between a speaker and his constituency, but rather as a running gag that people in the home audience could laugh at. In other words, ethnicity was no longer presented as a shared cultural experience, but rather as the butt of a joke. When, for example, Gertrude Berg (star of *The Goldbergs*) appeared on Berle's revamped format, the program spliced together *The Goldbergs'* family comedy format with Berle's variety show humor. In the first scene, Molly and daughter Rosalie sit in their Bronxville apartment, watching Berle on television, and decide to invite him over to their home. The humor revolves around Yiddish stereotypes, allowing audiences to laugh at the overweight, domineering Jewish mother who plays a matchmaker trying to marry Berle off to his secretary, all the while pushing platters of food in front of him. So popular was this merger of variety humor and situation comedy that NBC even considered making *The Goldbergs* a regular spot on Berle.[45] By the fall of 1953, when the Texaco company withdrew its sponsorship, the network contemplated a new format that would cut the show into two half-hour segments sold to separate sponsors—in other words, the show would be more like a situation comedy.[46]

Berle's repackaging was just one example of a larger industry trend. Starting in the late forties, and especially between 1950 and 1952, watchdog groups and government officials cried out against the "blue" humor of television comics. In 1948, in his capacity as the president of the Television Broadcasters Association, J. R. Poppele (the same man who worried about the importation of theater into the home), claimed that "no form of entertainment lends itself to looseness and questionable material so much as comedy. The point of balance between the clean and the questionable in comedy is so narrow that where any might exist, a blue pencil should be set to work—and quickly."[47]

In 1951, Boston's Archbishop Richard R. Cushing objected to comics who "permit themselves a momentary weakness to cater to the laughter gales of individuals with a perverted sense of humor." One month later, *Variety* reported that "the campaign against below-the-belt humor . . . is gaining momentum on a nationwide scale" and that networks and stations had been told to "watch their step."[48] In that same year, *The New York Times* published letters from concerned parents who also found variety humor less than wholesome. As one man claimed, "With night club performers serving as master of ceremonies on as many variety shows, it will be difficult for them to realize that the things which gain approval in a night club are not the same things which make a 'hit' in the living room." Another letter writer argued, "A good bawdy joke in the right circumstances is swell; in the home with the children and a mother-in-law it is something else again."[49] Similarly, in the 1952 survey conducted by the National Council of Catholic Women, parents voiced their disapproval of the "offcolor" and "vulgar" jokes in such programs as *Your Show of Shows, Toast of the Town, This is Show Business,* and *The Ed Wynn Show.* They also objected to "obscene and suggestive dancing" and particularly disliked displays of female sexuality such as the chorus girls on *Ed Wynn* who "parade under near pneumonia conditions."[50]

Such sentiments reverberated in the nation's capital as government officials became concerned with television content in general, and comedy in particular. Spurred by mounting complaints, FCC chairman Wayne Coy spoke publicly in 1950 about indecency on the airwaves. He especially denounced the "livery stable humor" on television, singling out one "comedian" (generally considered to be Arthur Godfrey) who "gets so big that his network cannot handle him." In 1951, when Representative Thomas J. Lane called for the establishment of a Federal Censorship Board, he alluded to the criticisms of Archbishop Cushing and others concerning "raw jokes" and "poor taste."[51] Even after the industry adopted the NARTB Code on March 1, 1952, watchdog groups and government officials continued to be on the lookout for sordid programming content. As discussed in chapter 4, the debates on censorship at the 1952 House hearings focused on variety show comedy as a special concern. Introduced as a patriot joined in "the fight against Communism and subversive activites," ABC broadcaster Paul Harvey indicted New York comics who were "steeped in Broadway and the bawdy night life of Manhattan."[52] Similarly, when testifying to the Committee, Mrs. Winfield D. Smart of the National Council of Catholic Women claimed that even while there was no popular consensus on the relative worth of television comedians, "we feel that they should abide by a standard of decency. If they overstep that, we feel that, no matter how entertaining they are, they should not be allowed to broadcast."[53] In addition to objections concerning blue humor, the government officials and witnesses disapproved of overly sexualized program content, and variety shows in particular. When describing *You Asked For It* (a half-hour variety format premised on viewers' requests to see various acts), Ezekiel Gathings, representative from Arkansas, claimed that while most of the program was "wholesome . . . something like a vaudeville show," he could not abide one act that featured "a grass-skirted young lady and a thinly clad gentleman dancing the hoochie-coochie. They danced to a very lively tune and shook the shimmy. . . . My children saw that, and I could not get it turned off to save my life."[54] With similar sentiments in mind, Gathings praised the 1952 code for its uplifting influence on the plunging necklines of women's dresses.[55]

The exact influence that these censorship debates had on program development at the networks is difficult to discern. However, as the case of Berle and other variety comics suggests, they did have a chilling effect on the vaudeo format, contributing to its marginalization in the primetime schedule. By 1953, a front page story in *Variety* cited Dick Powell, president of the Television Writers of America, who claimed that the "death of video comedy stars is being caused by censorship. . . . The comedy writer is under much closer line-by-line censorship from agencies and sponsors. . . . If Will Rogers were alive today, he would probably go back to rope-twirling."[56]

In the context of television's growth as a national medium and the increasing climate of censorship, the sitcom format, with its preplanned storylines that mitigated against the comic's spontaneous displays of "adult" humor and ethnic injokes, was a particularly apt vehicle for television. Not surprisingly in this regard, the *Texaco Star Theater's* "sitcomization" in the 1952 season was followed by numerous other such transformations. In 1953, faced with mounting criticism from reviewers and declining ratings, Sid Caesar and Imogene Coca's *Your Show of Shows* revised its variety format, switching from "the dozen or so revue-type spots previously presented to fewer and longer numbers," including a domestic sketch. As in the case of Berle, the change was largely intended to domesticate the stars' humor by "imbu[ing] their work with a low-key note, which has a greater longevity on television." [57] In 1953, Danny Thomas left his variety format on *Saturday Night Revue* for a situation comedy formula that integrated his stand-up shtick and musical numbers. One year later, *The Jackie Gleason Show* extended the length of its situation comedy sketch "The Honeymooners," and in the 1955–56 season entirely dispensed with the live hour-long variety format, producing instead a filmed half-hour version of the comedy sketch. [58] Although the variety show did not entirely fade away (Gleason, for example, returned to the variety format), it had taken a back seat to storytelling comedy. According to a first page story in a 1954 issue of *Variety*, "Today it's the vehicle, not the star that counts." [59]

As the variety show became more like the sitcom, domestic comedies drew on traditions of vaudeville humor, replicating its sense of liveness and spontaneity, but downplaying what was seen as its unsavory content, particularly its explicitly ethnic Yiddish humor and overly suggestive "adult" content. The family comedy merged elements of vaudeville with theatrical realism, integrating the spontaneity and immediacy of live performances—the sense of being at a theater—with seamless storylines. This merger can be seen not only as an aesthetic compromise, but also as a compromise with television's family audiences. These programs allowed people to enjoy the rowdy, ethnic, and often sexually suggestive antics of variety show clowns by packaging their outlandishness in middle-class codes of respectability.

One important difference between variety shows and situation comedies was the fact that the clowns were no longer primarily men. In place of the bad-boy Berles and soda-squirting Skeltons, situation comedies usually put the spotlight on female comics such as Lucille Ball, Joan Davis, and Gracie Allen. Unlike the male variety show comics, the sitcom comediennes were not typically criticized for being abrasive, and they were never called rude or licentious. Even if, like the male clowns, they cross-dressed—Lucy Ricardo disguised as Gary Cooper and Clark Gable in "Harpo Marx" (1955)—and got into compromising positions with the opposite sex—Lucy giving a bare-backed John Wayne a massage in "Lucy and John Wayne" (1955) or Ronald Colman chasing Joan Davis around his apartment in "Joan Sees Stars" (1954)—their antics were not deemed threatening to social mores. This, however, was not because of their "essentially" sweet feminine nature, but rather due to a long history of conventions formed for portraying female comics in ways that did not upset middle-class codes of femininity.

As Shirley Staples has shown in her study of vaudeville, the development of male-female comedy teams provided one way to get women in on the act without causing tension in the audience.[60] In the 1870s, when variety entrepreneurs such as Tony Pastor attempted to attract women into their theaters, the introduction of female comics tempered the rowdy humor of what had previously been a male-dominated amusement venue. By the early decades of the twentieth century, male-female teams, often performing domestic sketches, were regularly featured on vaudeville bills and were among the most popular attractions. But even if vaudeville had introduced women in order to appeal to family audiences, the representation of the female comic was accompanied by a series of taboos that, in turn, developed into a set of conventions by which women's humor was deemed more respectable. It was permissible for women who were considered unattractive to tell bawdy tales and play shrews who browbeat their henpecked husbands, but the humor was constructed in such a way that they were the "butt" of the joke. While audiences and critics enjoyed laughing at these overly aggressive "mannish" women, they were offended when pretty, more dainty women took these roles. To ease this situation, conventionally attractive women adopted grotesque disguises, or else played unthreatening characters such as little children (known as "kid" acts) and "Dumb Dora" roles in which an attractive woman's humor is tempered by her exaggerated lack of wits. In the 1930s, these roles for female comics were incorporated into radio comedy and also featured in numerous films and film shorts that based their plots around domestic situations.[61]

In the postwar period, the situation comedy drew on and developed these stock characterizations for comediennes. As in the case of vaudeville, the introduction of female stars into domestic sketches was thought to appeal to television's family audience, particularly the housewife. Jack Gould claimed: "Women comics, however brilliant, have always been outnumbered by the male of the species on the stage and screen. One of television's accomplishments has been to bring the distaff clowns into virtually equal prominence with the males. The rise of the comedienne in TV may be attributed to the nature of the medium itself. Since the TV audience is the family at home, the domestic comedy, revolving about the woman of the house, is a natural formula."[62] Still, as with their vaudeville predecessors, the representation of the female comic

Lucy and Ethel disguise their femininity in this 1952 episode of *I Love Lucy.* (Wisconsin Center for Film and Theater Research.)

had to be carefully controlled. The few variety show comediennes that existed were either the conventionally unattractive type such as "big mouth" Martha Raye or else the more waifish Imogene Coca, who used excessive mugging and grotesque costuming to distort her femininity. Situation comedy comediennes such as Gracie Allen and Jane Ace played Dumb Dora roles, while Lucille Ball, Joan Davis, and Gale Storm distorted their femininity with grotesque disguises. The list of Lucy's masquerades as something other than a woman is in fact almost as long as the series itself, including episodes in which she appeared as a Martian ("Lucy Is Envious," 1954), a cowboy ("Home Movies," 1954) and even Superman ("Lucy and Superman," 1957).

The situation comedy smoothed the female comics' abrasive edges by embedding their wild physical humor in domestic scenarios. Here, the comediennes' zany antics were always tamed by the fact that they were also depicted as loving daughters (*My Little Margie*'s Gale Storm); charming housewives (*I Love Lucy*'s Lucille Ball, *Burns and Allen*'s Gracie Allen, *My Favorite Husband*'s Joan Caulfield, *I Married Joan*'s Joan Davis); or, in the working-girl formula, devoted teachers (*Our Miss Brooks'* Eve Arden) and faithful secretaries (*My Friend Irma*'s Marie Wilson and *Private Secretary*'s Ann Sothern). Thus, even while the female comics mugged for the camera, donned unfeminine disguises, and generally created havoc, this was always recuperated by stories and characterizations that assured viewers of their essentially female nature. Jack Gould encapsulated the situation perfectly in an article on female comics that described Lucille Ball as a "vastly amusing exaggeration of a wife's most needed quality—patience," and Joan Caulfield as "appropriately kittenish and skittinish, and yet always becomingly female."[63] Importantly, however, the comedienne's femininity was not erotically charged. Instead, the domestic comedies featured zany clowns such as Lucy Ricardo; perfectly groomed, straight-laced, middle-aged housewives such as Margaret Anderson and Harriet Nelson; or else, in the ethnic comedies, matronly types such as the Jewish mother Molly Goldberg and the careworn Katherine Hansen (*Mama*).[64] For those who found the plunging necklines and suggestive sexuality of female stars inappropriate for a family medium, such characters must have seemed like a welcome alternative.

In addition to presenting nonthreatening women, the situation comedy also domesticated men. Like the new toned-down Berle and low-key Caesar, male stars were fashioned as family types. Good-natured—if sometimes short-tempered—husbands populated the early series with characters like Ricky Ricardo, Danny Williams (*Make Room For Daddy*), Ozzie Nelson, Charlie Ruggles (*The Ruggles*), and George Burns, all putting their faith in marriage. The domestic narrative thus worked to contain the overly aggressive, and often adolescent, masculinity of the variety show, while also placing men such as Cuban Desi Arnaz and Lebanese Danny Thomas into safely middle-class settings where their ethnicity was just one more running gag. Even if critics railed against the "emasculation" of the American man, these bumbling fathers were ultimately less controversial than the overindulgent clowns. The situation comedy, with its domesticated humor and broad-based appeal, would become one of television's preferred modes for addressing the nation's families.

Livening Things Up: Vaudeville or Folksy Realism?

While the domestic sitcom worked to defuse the more threatening elements of variety comedy, it nevertheless maintained elements of kinetic vaudeville humor, evoking the sense of presence so important in early television. By emphasizing the immediacy of performance, the programs created an aura of theatricality, encouraging viewers to feel as if they were on the scene of presentation, watching a live show.

As was typical in radio, some early family comedies used studio audiences in order to provide the sense of spontaneity that spectators enjoy at the theater. "We put on the show as if we were putting on a theatrical show," recalls director Ralph Levy about the first two seasons of *The Burns and Allen Show*, which were shot live in the studio.[65] By 1952, *Burns and Allen* and other comedies like it were increasingly shot on film, a method that allowed producers to edit out mistakes, consolidate production schedules, and, most importantly, reap additional profits in reruns. Even as the networks turned to filmed formats, however, the programs themselves retained their theatrical sensibility as producers found ways to replicate the sense of presence that had been so important in live shows. Desilu, the production company that created *I Love Lucy*, developed a multiple camera system that allowed the program to be shot in continuous takes in front of a live studio audience. The retention of the studio audience, Desilu assumed, would make the comedy appear more spontaneous to home viewers.[66] Although many of *Lucy's* successors dispensed with studio audiences in order to cut production costs, they still created a sense of theatrical presence and spontaneous group reaction by using canned laughter.[67]

Early situation comedies also produced an aura of liveness by integrating the performance principles of the variety show format into domestic narratives. Much like previous radio programs such as *The Burns and Allen Show* and *The Phil Harris-Alice Faye Show*, television series merged comic and musical performances with character comedy. Programs such as *I Married Joan* and *Heavens to Betsy* were typically comprised of two or three domestic sketches (only loosely joined by a narrative thread) that highlighted the comic performances of the stars. *I Love Lucy* was also originally premised on the idea of merging vaudeville acts with stories about family life. In 1949, singing star Desi Arnaz planned to produce a variety show featuring his Cuban band, and one year later he and wife Lucille Ball took to the road where they performed a vaudevillian variety show together. That show provided the impetus for the *I Love Lucy* pilot, which was based on the premise of integrating Desi's nightclub performances and guest stars into a domestic husband and wife show.

Perhaps the most extreme case was *Burns and Allen*. In its 1940s radio format, the program integrated vaudevillian domestic sketches with guest star performances. When it made the transition to television in 1950, the series created an even stronger sense of theatricality by including variety ensembles that performed song and dance numbers between acts of the sitcom story. Midway into the premier episode, for example, the domestic plot was interrupted as if for an intermission when George Burns introduced viewers to the Skylarks, a singing group that performed on a stage in front of the domestic setting.

The merger of performance with storytelling elements is clearly evident in a 1950 episode ("Tax Auditor") when George utters the ultimate metacriticism of his program's narrative strategy. After the first act of the night's episode, the curtains close on the domestic setting and George introduces us to singer Helen Hanley. Following the song, George directly addresses the audience, saying, "Well now I think it's time to put a little plot in the show. And we try to strike a happy medium. We have more plot than a variety show and not as much as a wrestling match." The curtains then rise to reveal the Burns's living room where Gracie confesses she has dented the car fender (a plot device that was repeated in many of the episodes). The camera cuts back to the stage where George admits to the audience, "Yeah, that's it. That's the plot. What'd you expect, Shakespeare? I'll tell you something about plot, but don't tell this to Ed Sullivan or Eddie Cantor. It's cheaper than guest stars." Indeed, as the industry would learn throughout the early 1950s, sitcoms were more economical to produce than the hour-long variety shows. One of the reasons for this was already known to radio comedians of the thirties and forties who found that comedy series such as *Amos 'n' Andy* saved money by basing their appeal on continuing characters rather than on high-priced star properties. George Burns and Gracie Allen applied this rule to television at an early stage in television production when the star-studded variety comedies seemed to be the popular choice.

Aside from the economic factor, however, George's monologue reveals significant assumptions about the nature of storytelling comedy for television. According to the logic of his monologue, it was necessary to strike a happy medium between variety comedy and comedy structured around a story. In the early episodes of the series, this happy medium was achieved through presenting a kind of comedy that was the inverse of the variety shows. By organizing its episodes around loose plot lines that were interspersed with variety acts on the stage, the early episodes of *Burns and Allen* presented the flip side of the variety show's narrative structure. This, however, was a primitive strategy, for as the sitcom developed it would smooth over the discontinuous breaks between story and performance. The history of the sitcom can be seen precisely as movement toward narrative equilibrium between the "situation" and the "comedy."

In fact, the programs were continually judged on their ability to merge the two. Just as the critics were wary of variety shows that lacked proper continuity and integration, they also disliked family comedies that emphasized broad physical humor over story development and character integration. This was particularly true of critical commentary in *Variety,* which consistently called for more of a balance between well-scripted, realistic plots and the stars' performances. When reviewing

Heavens to Betsy, a sustaining program on NBC, *Variety* claimed: "The plot, if you could call it that, is highly familiar; the enactment has a burlesque air, unreal and artificial. And the opener was not enhanced by the insertion of a clown act. If more reality could be injected into the story, the stanza would be immeasurably better." Similarly, when reviewing the premier episode of the ABC comedy *The Ruggles,* one *Variety* critic claimed that the show had "only the sketchiest of plots," and relied too much on "slapsticky" situations.[68] While generally approving of some of the traditions associated with vaudeville—particularly spontaneous, kinetic performances that gave viewers a sense of being on the scene—the critics did not like shows that failed to integrate these performances into a realistic story.

Indeed, in quite contradictory ways, the ideal sitcom was expected to highlight both the experience of theatricality and the naturalism of domestic life. At the same time that family comedies encouraged audiences to feel as if they were in a theater watching a play, they also asked viewers to believe in the reality of the families presented on the screen. Like Jane and Goodman Ace, these television families created an aura of intimacy by giving audiences the impression that they were lifelong companions. Indeed, as seen in chapter 4, the programs emphasized the importance of neighborliness, and since many had previously been on radio, the characters must have seemed like familiar friends. When radio comedies made the transition to the television medium, critics judged the degree to which the addition of sight to sound enhanced the characters' credibility and the programs' overall sense of intimacy. As *Variety* noted in its review of *The Goldbergs'* first televised episode, "There's no basic change in the familiar characterizations, but it's as though a new dimension has been added to bring them to life via the new medium."[69]

Moreover, *The Goldbergs* and other ethnic family comedies were particularly praised for their warmth and sentimentality, qualities that added to their aura of believability. One *Variety* critic claimed that Molly Goldberg's "Yiddishisms, the background and her impossible malaprops only savor the story and character and bring it closer to credibility," while another critic liked *Mama's* depiction of a turn-of-the-century Norwegian family, claiming its presentation of "Ups and Downs [of] family life crystalized into personal identification."[70] Even the more middle-class family comedies were judged on their ability to create warmth and sentimentality. *Variety* praised *Ethel and Albert* for its "charm and simplicity," *My Son Jeep* for its "believable and warm family group," *Marge and Jeff* for its "relaxed performances, with characters registering realistically."[71] Such sentiments also filled the pages of general readership magazines, creating a popular hierarchy that favored a naturalistic portrayal of everyday life. *Time* liked the "real recognizable domesticity" of *My Favorite Husband* and the "homey" quality of *Easy Aces*, while *Saturday Review* praised the unstrained dialogue in *Ethel and Albert* that "rises out of and reflects the natural rubbing-along-together" of the characters.[72]

These programs also produced a sense of intimacy and authenticity by encouraging viewers to believe that the characters were real families who just happened to live their lives on television. "TV couples" such as Jane and Goodman Ace, Ozzie and Harriet, Burns and Allen, and Lucy and Desi were an ambiguous blend of fiction and reality. By appealing to viewers' "extratextual" knowledge (their familiarity with television celebrities through fan magazines and other publicity materials), these programs collapsed distinctions between real life and television. When Lucille Ball became pregnant in 1952, the program replicated the event in a season of episodes that revolved around Lucy's pregnancy and the eventual delivery of her son. In the January 19, 1953, episode, which scored an all time high rating of 68.8 on the Trendex scale, Little Ricky (the fictional baby) materialized immediately after the real Desi, Jr., was born, so that audiences could imagine they had witnessed the birth of the real child.[73] As *Newsweek* claimed in its cover story on the blessed event, "All this may come under the heading of how duplicated in life and television *can* you get."[74] Advertising and product tie-ins further encouraged audiences to confuse the boundaries between reality and fiction by allowing people to purchase elements of the story. Lucy and Desi smoking gowns, comic books, Little Ricky dolls, nursery furniture, and even replicas of the fashionable waterproof bags in which Lucy carried her baby bottles gave the fictional world a material status.[75] Most explicitly here, a 1953 advertisement for Lucy and Desi bedroom suites told consumers to "Live Like Lucy!" and even included a tie-in advertisement for Lucy and Desi matching pajamas so that couples could completely simulate the bedroom life of the stars.

Television critics fostered this materialization of the fictional world by judging such sitcoms on the degree to which they depicted a naturalistic picture of the stars' "real" family life. Here, naturalistic performance meant a sense of ordinariness and familiarity. Reviewing one of the earliest of these comedies, "Mary and Johnny Kay" (1949), a critic for *Variety* claimed it "allegedly parallel[ed] the actual experiences of its stars" and thus "had an unforced quality of naturalness which is the greatest asset."[76] Critics for popular magazines also praised the naturalistic feel of comedies such as *The Adventures of Ozzie and Harriet*, which were based on dialogue and character interaction. In 1952, a critic for *Newsweek* detailed the everyday adventures of the real Nelson family, telling readers, "Ricky kicks his shoes off during the filming, just as he does at home, and both boys work in front of the cameras in their regular clothes. In fact, says Harriet, they don't even know the cameras are there."[77] And in 1953, a reviewer for *Time* wrote, "The Nelson children apparently accept their double life as completely natural." In that same year, the *Saturday Review* commented, "The Nelsons are apparently living their lives in weekly installments on the air. . . ." Indeed, this unobstructed, unmediated view of the Nelson family was the essence of television theater that critical discourses described. Even the comedies that did not include real-life families were publicized in this fashion. *Make Room For Daddy*, starring Danny Thomas, was a case in point. In 1954, *Newsweek* assured its readers that Danny was a "Two Family Man," and that "Danny's TV family acts like . . . Danny's Own Family." The reviewer even went on to suggest that Danny Williams (the character) resembled Danny Thomas (the star) more than Gracie Allen resembled herself on *The Burns and Allen Show.*[78]

With its emphasis on theatrical/studio performance on the one hand, and domestic normality on the other, the family comedy was a site of contradictions and tensions. It seemed to be undecided about how to depict domestic life, and perhaps for this reason it often tended to break the rules of unity and balance found in the classical novel and film.[79] A strange mix of naturalism and theatricality, the family comedy was a virtual "theater of the everyday" that presented reality in a heightened, exaggerated fashion.

The Theater of Everyday Life: Self-Reflexivity and Artifice

Torn as it was between theatricality and naturalism, the family comedy seemed unable to resist reflecting back on the paradox of its own form. Self-reflexivity was indeed a hallmark of the genre between 1950 and 1955, the years in which it became one of the most popular and widely used program types. Quite contrary to the popular assumption that genres become more self-reflexive as they mature, self-reflexivity was in fact integral to the rise of this form. As demonstrated throughout this book, family comedies included plots that revolved around television's effects on the household. Television's first families were, above all else, families that owned television sets and thought quite a bit about the medium's place in their daily lives. Equally important, many of these programs self-consciously acknowledged the theatrical artifice involved in representing a naturalistic picture of domesticity.

By far the most self-reflexive was *The Burns and Allen Show*, whose entire premise revolved around a real-life couple (George Burns and Gracie Allen) who played themselves playing themselves as real-life performers who had a television show based on their lives as television stars. If this is a bit confusing, it should be because the entire show was based on the paradox involved in transforming everyday life into a play for television. Designed to be the television version of *Our Town*, the program featured George Burns as part-time narrator/part-time character, who continually stepped out of his role in the family scene, reflecting on the stage business and the plot. A 1952 episode took this to the extreme, basing its plot on a TV party that George and Gracie held for the producers of their show. While Gracie scuttled around the house "performing" her hostess chores, George sat with his network cronies, somehow miraculously watching himself on his own live television program. In the final scene, George turns to the home audience and smirks into the camera, calling attention to the plot's absurd premise.

Although *Burns and Allen* was an extreme example, its self-reflexivity was symptomatic of a general trend. Numerous series included episodes that revolved around characters going on television programs, restaging their domestic lives for the camera. *I Love Lucy*, which told the story of an average housewife and her celebrity husband, made ample use of this device, producing twelve "TV" episodes between 1951 and 1955.[80] In "Mr and Mrs. TV Show" (1954), the Ricardos are invited to host their own morning television program for Phipp's Department store, broadcast live from their breakfast table. In "The Ricardos Are Interviewed" (1955), Lucy, Ricky, and their friends the Mertzes appear on *Face to Face*, a *Person to Person* type talk show in which television cameras film the private lives of the stars.[81] And in "Ricky's Hawaiian Vacation" (1954), Lucy and Ricky try their luck on Freddie Fillmore's game show *Be a Good Neighbor*, a plot that was also used in a 1955 episode of *The Goldbergs*, a 1952 episode of *Burns and Allen*, and a 1954 "Honeymooners" sketch on *The Jackie Gleason Show*.[82] Similarly, such family comedies as *I Married Joan*, *Make Room for Daddy*, and *The Honeymooners* depicted characters who performed on television panel shows, variety shows, or commercials.[83]

The Ruggles, a suburban family comedy aired between 1949 and 1955, is a particularly good example of how the programs self-consciously reflected on the artifice involved in representing a naturalistic picture of family life. Although shot live in the studio, the program was similar to its better-known filmed successor, *Father Knows Best*. The father, played by Hollywood character actor Stuart Erwin, dealt with the everyday problems of his wife Margaret and his four children. In many ways a "mirror" of family life, the show nevertheless reflected back on its own conventionality.

An episode entitled "Charlie's Lucky Day" (1950), for example, begins in the living room of the Ruggles's suburban home. Wife Margaret and daughter Sharon work at the sewing table in the adjoining dining room, while the other children sit in the living room doing homework and playing games. Charlie Ruggles roams around the room, humming tunes and interrupting his children who politely ask him to quiet down. The scene thus presents a picture of a tranquil, uneventful night at home, punctuated only by Charlie's attempt to liven up the scene. Suddenly, however, these domestic doldrums are interrupted as a camera crew from the local newspaper invades the home and begins taking pictures of the family. The confused Ruggles spend the rest of the evening attempting to figure out why they are celebrities. Finally, Sharon suggests that they have probably won a contest on the radio show *Surprise Me* and that radio crews have hidden wires in their home in order to broadcast the family to the rest of the nation. Alarmed by the prospect, Mr. Ruggles objects, "Now wait a minute, this is my home, they're not going to wire anybody for sound here," after which his family begins a frantic search for the radio equipment. Moments later, the Ruggles find that their search is in vain as a television crew invades the home, sets up cameras, and informs the Ruggles that they are on the *Tender Delicious Raspberry Show* to receive a case of the sponsor's product and a check for $1,000. The flustered Mrs. Ruggles protests the invasion, shouting, "Now listen to me, you are not going to televise my home." Nevertheless, the show goes on.

This rather bizarre plot serves to highlight the fact that despite their protestations, the Ruggles are indeed a television family. The naturalistic portrait of the American family in the opening scene turns out to be nothing other than an act for mass media—first for the newspaper, then for radio, and finally for television. The final scene self-consciously acknowledges this paradox when the narrative returns to the domestic doldrums of the opening scene. By this point, however, the naturalistic picture of family life has a very different meaning since it seems only to highlight the artifice entailed in staging domesticity. Rather than looking like a slice of life, this scene now seems blatantly theatrical, with the "actors" back in place as if nothing happened. The final exchange between Mr. and Mrs. Ruggles reflects back on this situation. Wandering around the room, bored and restless, Charlie finally asks Margaret if he can invite the neighbors over to liven things up. With a twinkle in her eye and a tone of irony in her voice, Margaret replies, "That's the trouble with our modern life nowadays. Too sedentary. Nothing ever happens." Thus, as the dialogue so wistfully suggests, the attempt to sketch a realistic portrait of everyday life is always "mediated" by technological reproduction that recasts ordinary experience into a dramatic play.

More than just a witty commentary on its own medium, the family comedy was part of a much larger history of ideas about and representations of the family. Links between theatricality and domesticity can be traced back to the Victorians' fascination with display and ritual, their elaborate staging of social relations, and penchant for exhibiting household finery. In fact, at midcentury, bourgeois Victorians were so fascinated with theatricality that they literally turned their parlors into theaters, staging plays with friends and family members in their homes. As Karen Halttunen has observed, these "parlor theatricals" were sold in books that people purchased and adapted for their own use at parties. Using their front parlor as a proscenium space and their back parlor as a backstage area, Victorians constructed theatrical spaces, even adorning entrance and exit ways in the home with curtains and other decorations.

The plays themselves were often extremely self-reflexive in nature, including dialogue and actions that self-consciously referred to the artifice of everyday life. According to Halttunen, "the parlor theatrical was itself a play within a play, an explicit theatrical performance taking place within the larger, implicit theatrical performance that was middle-class gentility." Moreover, she argues, "Parlor players often emphasized the connection between the parlor theatrical and the larger genteel performance of which it was a part by freely crossing the invisible boundary between stage and audience and by dropping briefly out of their stage characters to reveal themselves in their private characters. In other words, they delighted in subverting the play by revealing its theatricality." Describing one of the most popular plays, "Irresistibly Impudent," Halttunen shows how the promptor (or what we might call a narrator) directly addressed the audience, emerging from backstage "to argue with a player who had forgotten his lines, and then appealed to the audience for vindication," and even stepped out of character, asking the audience how they thought the play should end. Through such techniques as these, Halttunen suggests, "the parlor theatrical continually emphasized the fact that players were all performers, and repeatedly drew the audience on stage as well, thus suggesting that all the world was a stage and all men and women merely players. Many popular private theatricals succeeded in collapsing the distinction between the overt theatricality of the play and the implicit theatricality of all parlor social conduct. The message of parlor theatricals was simply this: middle-class social life was itself a charade."[84]

The plays that Halttunen describes sound like a prototype for the television comedies of the early 1950s, which often played with the boundaries between fiction and reality, between theatricality and everyday life. Like the nineteenth-century cast of "Irresistibly Impudent," television personalities often left their roles as characters or narrators to speak directly to the audience. Ozzie and Harriet Nelson often stepped out of the story to invite viewers to tune in next week or enter a sponsor's contest (in fact, at the beginning of the episode, Ozzie sometimes appeared on a theatrical stage, greeting the home audience). At the end of *I Love Lucy*, Lucy and Ricky Ricardo returned to their star personae of

Lucille Ball and Desi Arnaz, inviting viewers to smoke Philip Morris cigarettes. And of course, George Burns, the most exemplary case, literally stepped out of his role as husband in the domestic setting and onto a stage where he directly addressed viewers, inviting them to consider Gracie's madcap logic. By 1957, George even installed a "magic television set" in his house through which he would literally rewind the narrative, reflecting on plot events and possible outcomes. Indeed, like the play within a play structure of the parlor theatrical, family comedies presented an intensely self-referential world where the distinction between fiction and reality was constantly thrown into question.

Given this, Halttunen's sociological interpretation of the parlor theatrical can be usefully applied to the family comedy. Although the television comedy appeared in a different historical context from its nineteenth-century predecessor, its self-conscious acknowledgment of its own artifice was similarly directed to a more general, implicit self-reflection on middle-class life. If in the nineteenth century this self-reflection was aimed at codes of Victorian gentility, in the context of the 1950s it was directed toward the artifice of postwar consumer culture, its prefabricated, hypercommercialized ideals of middle-class family life.

Such an interpretation is more convincing when we consider the links between domesticity and theatricality throughout modern culture, and particularly in the postwar era. Although the grandeur and scope of the Victorian home gave way to increased comfort, family life was still represented in terms of spectacle and theatricalization. Consumer magazines and advertisements of the 1920s devised elaborate ways to depict the home as a showcase for glamorous commodity lifestyles, while discourses of architecture and interior decor adopted metaphors of theatricality when speaking about domestic space. In 1940, Louise Pinkey Sooy and Virginia Woodbridge's *Plan Your Own Home* began by asking female readers, "If all the world's a stage, what drama is being presented within your four walls? For what parts are the members of your family cast? As the director of production, are you, the homemaker, creating a backdrop against which the story of your family life may be sympathetically and beautifully portrayed?"[85] Thus, even before the 1950s, theatricality was a potent metaphor for modern domesticity.

Postwar Americans—particularly those being inducted into the ranks of middle-class home ownership—must, to some degree, have been aware of the theatrical, artificial nature of family life. For people who had lived through the Depression and the hardships of World War II, the new consumer dreams must have seemed somewhat synthetic or, at least, unorthodox. Leaving ethnic and working-class areas for mass-produced suburbs, these people must have been cognizant of the new roles they were asked to play in a prefabricated social setting.

This perception is suggested by sociologists of the era, whose studies showed that people were sensitive to the theatrical quality of everyday life.

The strongest case was made in 1955 by sociologist Nelson Foote. In his article "Family Living as Play," Foote claimed that "family living in a residential suburb has come to consist almost entirely of play." While he admitted that the "popular recognition of this *fait accompli* is only partial," he went on to detail how "the family home may be most aptly described as a theater." The members of the family, he argued, were all performers: "The husband may be an audience to the wife, or the wife to the husband, or the older child to both." Acknowledging the relation between this form of family play and the impact of television's domestic stagings, Foote observed that "by no means is this conception [of the home as a theater] to be reduced to watching television. . . . The ration of time spent by family members as an audience for the performance of each other as against time spent in watching commercial portrayals may signify how well the home rates as a theater in their own eyes."[86]

If Foote saw theatricality as a metaphor for family relations, other sociologists concentrated on the wider drama of social relations, showing how families transformed their homes into showcases for their neighbors. In his study of the mass-produced suburbs, Harry Henderson suggested that "constant attention to external appearance 'counts for a lot' and wins high praise from neighbors." While residents decorated their homes in distinctive ways, none strayed far from the predictable standards exhibited in middle-class magazines—in fact, Henderson argued that "what many [new home owners] sought in their furniture was a kind of 'approval insurance.'"[87] Sociologist William H. Whyte claimed that furniture store owners had noticed that people who moved to the suburbs quickly acquired new, more refined tastes, turning away from the "purplest purples and pinkest pinks" toward "something plainer."[88] Moreover, if people were unable to live up to the standards of middle-class tastes, problems ensued. Whyte told of one woman who was "so ashamed of the emptiness of her living room that she smeared the picture window with Bon Ami; not until a dinette set arrived did she wipe it off."[89] Lacking the props with which to display her social prestige, the woman simply inverted the terms of conspicuous consumption, literally making her poverty inconspicuous to her neighbors.

Home manuals, magazines, and advertisements extended this emphasis on the home as showcase, recommending ways to create glamorous backgrounds on which to enact spectacular scenes. In *The House and the Art of Its Design*, Robert Woods Kennedy claimed that the housewife needed "an effective and glamorous background for her as a sexual being, commensurate with the amount of energy she expends on clothes, make-up, and society."[90] Home magazines and their advertisements continually suggested this idea in illustrations that depicted housewives who were visually integrated into domestic backgrounds by color, shape, and size. In 1949, one upper-crust, planned community in Great Neck, New York (the Kings Point Estates) took the house-as-showcase aesthetic to its logical extreme, basing the entire suburb around principles of theatrical design. Built by Homer Harmon, who had formerly been director of advertising and publicity at the Roxy Theater, the community was engineered by a production team that included Charles Burton (designer of Paramount Theaters), Herbert Coe (who had once been on the executive staff of Columbia Pictures), and Arthur Knorr (the executive producer at the Roxy Theater). According to the Home section of *The New York Times*, the architects incorporated "many of the unusual features of the homes of Hollywood stars . . . in a colony of theatrical and ranch style residences."[91]

Given the emphasis on social performance and spectacle display in postwar culture, it seems reasonable to assume that the genre of family comedy, with its self-conscious reflections on the theatricality of everyday life, might well have struck a familiar chord with audiences at the time. Like the nineteenth-century parlor theatrical, these television shows allowed people to laugh at their own social conventions by pointing to the artifice entailed in middle-class domesticity.

Of course, by the 1950s, this form of domestic theater had become an extremely mediated affair, as the television industry, rather than the public itself, staged the theatrical scenes. As spectators rather than players, people were now divorced from the sphere of dramatic action. Nevertheless, the genre compensated for this lack of participation by offering viewers a chance to imaginatively venture onto the scene of theatrical presentation—where, of course, they would find people just like themselves playing the roles of average American families. Quite paradoxically in this regard, the early family comedy invited audiences to visit the people in the theater next door. They welcomed viewers into a simulated neighborhood where everyone was putting on a show.

All the Home's a Stage: Domestic and Theatrical Space

The self-reflexive strategies of early television worked in two, seemingly opposite, directions. On the one hand, self-reflexivity provided viewers with critical distance from everyday life—the ability to laugh at the stagy artifice of domesticity. On the other hand, it encouraged viewers to feel closer to the scene of action, as if they had an intimate connection to the scene. By acknowledging its own artifice and theatricality, the family comedy encouraged viewers to feel as if they had been let in on a joke, while at the same time allowing them to take that joke seriously.

This situation was most clear in the case of *Burns and Allen*, which used self-reflexivity not simply to reveal its own artifice, but also to give audiences a sense of being at the theater. As in the parlor theatricals that Halttunen describes, this program's fundamental principle was a mise-en-abyme structure, an endless stage within a stage, a bottomless pit of representation. Gracie Allen's style of humor was also a kind of bottomless pit in which audiences were caught in an endless quagmire of metarealities. In formal construction, the program repeated the mise-en-abyme structure because it continually "reframed" the action in two separate, but intricately linked spaces—a stage space and a domestic space. The juxtaposition of these two spaces encouraged audiences to feel as if they were witnessing a live theatrical production.

There were a variety of ways in which this was achieved. In the most simple form, the stage was shown as a proscenium space with drawn curtains, behind which the domestic setting was contained. After the initial commercial, the scene shifted to the stage, the curtains opened,

The realistic mise-en-scène of *Burns and Allen's* backyard creates a sense of neighborhood intimacy, even as their comic banter recalls the artifice of vaudeville theater. (Wisconsin Center for Film and Theater Research.)

the domestic setting was revealed, and the evening's story unfolded. It wasn't simply the image of the stage on the television screen that gave the illusion of being at the live theater; rather it was the alternation between the stage space and the domestic space that produced a sense of "being there." Through this alternation, viewers experienced a kind of layered realism in which the stage appeared to contain the domestic space, and thus, the stage seemed spatially closer—or more real—than the domestic space.

The heightened sense of realism was further suggested by the shifting forms of address as the program moved from the domestic to the stage space. At various intervals during the program, the plot was momentarily frozen as George left his role in the story and walked onto the stage where he delivered a monologue in direct address to the audience (ambiguously the studio audience and the home audience). For example, in a 1952 episode, George literally walks out of his role as a character in the story, moves upstage to reveal the entire domestic setting, takes his place in front of the curtain on the right side of the stage, and delivers a monologue. After this, George walks back across the stage to reveal once more the domestic setting behind him. He arrives at the front porch, knocks on the door, Gracie answers, and George walks into his living room—literally returning to his place in the story. Obviously, in this example the domestic space is rendered with a high degree of artifice; in fact, there is no attempt to sustain the illusion that it is a real space at all. Instead, it is the stage space that is represented through realist conventions. The stage is depicted as a unified real space, never subject to the kind of spatial disorientation that occurs in the domestic space, and actions on the stage always appear to unfold in real time, that is, in the time that it takes the home audience to watch the program. Thus, the stage appears more real than the domestic space—and the home audience is given the sense of watching a live play in the theater.

Such play-within-a-play devices also served to create a program environment conducive to the display of sponsors' products. In a number of episodes, the program presented a literal mise-en-abyme when George and Gracie appeared within the logo of one of their sponsors, Goodrich Rubber. The couple was pictured in the cutout circle of the Goodrich tire from which they waved goodbye to the home audience. A similar graphic strategy was used in *Ozzie and Harriet*, which sometimes depicted the Nelson family within the Hotpoint logo (a sign spelling out the company name). Ozzie and Harriet appeared within the letters "O" and "P" of the Hotpoint sign while Ricky and David sat on top of the first and last letters, where they threw a football back and forth at one another. Such framing devices had the effect of showing viewers that the advertiser was responsible for the night's entertainment because the stars were literally contained within the company logo. At the same time, they also underscored the artifice involved in representing domesticity because these "real life" families were transformed into ideal advertising types—transformed into graphic spectacles of consumption.

In a 1952 episode of *I Love Lucy* ("Lucy Does a Commercial"), the sponsor's product literally served as the stage of representation for the narrative. In the opening sequence, we see a cartoon drawing of an oversized box of Philip Morris cigarettes. The cigarette box turns into a stage when two cartoon figures that represent the real-life stars, Lucille Ball and Desi Arnaz, approach the box. They peel up the cigarette box wrapper (which now looks like a curtain) to reveal a narrative space in which the lead character, Lucy Ricardo, appears sitting on her living room sofa. The camera then zooms into this narrative space and the sitcom story begins. At the end of the story, an animated sketch representing a theater stage appears, and the two cartoon drawings of the stars draw the curtains over the domestic setting of the Ricardo home. Subsequently, the real-life Lucille Ball and Desi Arnaz appear in a heart-shaped frame and deliver a commercial for their sponsor. Not only did this framing structure work as a graphic reminder that the story had been brought to our homes through the courtesy of the sponsor, it also served to make the advertiser's pitch appear to be in a world closer to the viewer's real life since the commercial message was conveyed by stars who came out of their roles in the story to directly address the viewer at home.

This scheme is most pronounced in *The Goldbergs*. At the start of each episode Molly Goldberg (but also, ambiguously, the star, Gertrude Berg) leaned out of her window and delivered her sponsor's commercial directly into the camera. This served to give the home audience a sense of being Molly's next-door neighbor, and the advertising pitch seemed more like interpersonal communication than mass marketing. The intimacy of the commercial message was further constructed through the transition into the domestic space where the story unfolded. In a 1952 episode, for example, the transition from the window frame to the domestic space served to produce an illusion of moving from a level of pure discourse to the level of story, of moving from a kind of unmediated communication to a narrative space where a fiction took place.[92]

The episode begins with Molly leaning out her window, advertising RCA television sets in her motherly, Yiddish accent. This leads to another mise-en-abyme structure when Molly introduces us to an RCA representative who demonstrates "true tone" television sets that all picture Molly Goldberg at her window. At the end of this demonstrational narrative we cut back to the window where Molly continues the commercial with her neighborly advice. The commercial ends as Molly turns

Molly Goldberg leans out her window to greet neighbor Mrs. Cohen in *The Goldbergs.* (Wisconsin Center for Film and Theater Research.)

away from the window frame (as well as the frame of the television image) to enter the Goldberg living room, where she now takes her place in the story. The transition from commercial to story is made absolutely explicit in the program because Molly literally *turns her back* on the advertisement's enunciative system and *takes her position* in the tale as she walks into the living room where her daughter, Rosalie, now addresses Molly as a character in the story. In this way, Molly's turn from commercial to fiction dramatizes the separation of the advertisement from the program, thus giving the ad a nonfictional status. However, the transition from ad to story also alerts the viewer to the artifice of the domestic setting, thus making us more aware of the fictional status of the story itself.

The world onto which Molly Goldberg's window opened was, as in all television, an alternate view, an endlessly self-referential world as opposed to a document. The domestic spaces contained within the frame of these stages were also often represented as stagelike, as prosceniums rather than real spaces. In some ways, this had to do with technological conditions and in-studio shooting practices. On the ten- and twelve-inch television screen, it was typically difficult to show depth of field, and the even, high-key lighting used for live and live-on-film television gave the picture a kind of flattened-out quality. In addition, because many of these sitcoms were broadcast live, or else filmed live in real time, it was impossible to shoot reverse fields. Even the use of multiple cameras for filmed programs created a sense of proscenium space. Since the camera setups were designed to capture continuous action, the multiple camera strategy allowed for less variation in angle, distance, and lighting than it was possible to achieve in the cinema. Finally, although technicians were experimenting with sound techniques during the period, sound booms were often rooted in one place at the front of the stage so that the principal dialogue usually took place in a frontal, proscenium position.[93]

However, the theatrical quality of these programs wasn't only determined by technological and practical circumstances. Instead, the programs consistently drew on and developed themes that brought to the forefront the theatrical nature of domestic life, presenting the home as if it were a stage for performance. In *Burns and Allen*, for example, domestic spaces actually took on the functions of the stage space. After the early episodes, which featured such variety acts as the Skylarks on the stage, the series began to incorporate performances into the domestic setting. Here, rather than simply interrupting the story, performances were motivated by narrative elements. For example, in "The Teenage Visit" (1951), two teenagers visit George and Gracie's home. The teenage characters turn out to be professional jitterbuggers who dance, not on the stage, but in the Burns's living room; that is, the performance takes place within the narrative space. This in turn has the effect of making the domestic space appear stage-like, for even while the performance is motivated by the story, the dance segment is represented as if it were a variety act being performed on a theatrical stage. George and Gracie clear the furniture from their living room/set so that the domestic details of the mise-en-scène vanish. The camera remains in a frontal and static position, thus depicting a flattened-out proscenium space. In this way, the program was able to create a smooth continuous transition from story to performance but still evoke the sense of live theater so important to early television. *Burns and Allen* found a way in which to mediate the demands of theatrical realism with the sense of presence that television promised to its public.

In presenting the home as a theatrical space, television programs such as *Burns and Allen* were no doubt drawing on previously established conventions of the Hollywood cinema. In her analysis of *Meet Me in St. Louis* (Vincente Minnelli, 1944), Serafina Bathrick demonstrates how the Hollywood musical mixed performance and storytelling conventions within the domestic setting.[94] Although early domestic comedies imported these kinds of representational strategies from the cinema, they developed them in relation to their own broadcast context. The inclusion of theatrical performance fulfilled the popular expectation that television should approximate the experience of going to a live theater.

Indeed, numerous sitcoms presented the home as if it were a venue for theatrical performance. In *The Ruggles* ("Charlie's Lucky Day"), the domestic setting is turned into a stage as numerous comedians, who play highly stereotyped roles reminiscent of stock characters in vaudeville sketches (a policeman, an inventor, and an insurance agent), knock on the door, enter the living room, and begin performing short sketches full of comic banter and broad physical humor. Similarly, in *The Honeymooners* the Kramden apartment was often turned into a theatrical arena where the stars exhibited their talents to viewers. When, for example, Alice Kramden invites all of her neighbors to take mambo lessons in her home, the domestic space becomes a stage for a hilarious burlesque-type performance as a Latin lover teachers the working-class housewives how to dance ("Mama Loves Mambo," 1956). Another episode depicts Ralph Kramden and his pal Ed Norton playing piano in the Kramden home, rehearsing for their appearance on a television program ("The $99,000 Answer," 1956). Even in the more folksy comedy of *Ozzie and Harriet*, the interior space of the Nelson home was often rendered in a highly theatrical fashion, particularly in the early seasons. In the opening sequence of "The New Chairs" (1952), the foyer in the Nelson home served as a proscenium in which the events took place. A round white rug, which covered the center of the foyer floor, functioned as a spotlight for the action as Ricky and David humorously performed a game of football. Architectural elements of the home, such as doorways and partitions between rooms, served to frame the stage direction of the actors as they entered and exited the frame. In other episodes, when Ozzie and his best friend Thorny met in their front yards, the camera was placed in a frontal, static position, thus giving the comic banter between the characters a stagy feel and transforming elements of the domestic setting into a proscenium space where performance took place. Similarly in *Burns and Allen*, windows, doorways, and passageways between rooms were used to frame performance segments. Sometimes the couple performed a vaudeville sketch on their front porch at the end of the show, with the porch serving as a stage for the action. Often these kinds of "framing segments" appeared to take place within the story itself. For example, in a 1953 episode (untitled), Gracie embarks on one of her famous comedic double-talk routines as she talks to her neighbor Blanche Morton in her backyard. While speaking, the women stand behind a white picket fence, and since the camera remains in a frontal position, the scene resembles a puppet show. The fence frames Gracie's comic routine and thus showcases the performative aspects of the tale.

Other programs featured the theatrical nature of domestic life by using conventions of the backstage musical. In these cases, the narratives were structured around characters who were constantly in the process of putting on a show (and it should be noted that while they were based on real-life celebrities, both *Burns and Allen* and *Ozzie and Harriet* did not typically include plots about show business). One of the first such programs, *The Truex Family*, dealt with the family life of thespians Ernest Truex and his wife Sylvia Field. Broadcast on New York's local station WPIX in 1949, the first episode detailed Truex's attempt to win a part in a play by impressing a wealthy producer whom he invited over to dinner. As in many backstage musicals, the performances were motivated by rehearsals—only here the rehearsals took place in Mr. Truex's home as he read the script to his family. Eager to get in on the act, the entire family began pitching their talents to the producer who, in a case of mistaken identity, turned out to be an insurance salesman.[95] In this and other "showbiz" family comedies, theatricality seemed to be a natural condition of domestic life.

Two of the most popular and critically acclaimed programs, *Make Room for Daddy* and *I Love Lucy*, are perfect examples of this theatrical narrative strategy. Like *Burns and Allen*, both were based upon the alternations between a stage space and a domestic space. Unlike *Burns and Allen*, there was no formal division between the action on the stage and the events that took place in the domestic sketches. Instead, these programs seamlessly joined the premises of family drama with those of variety-show entertainment through storylines that focused on the domestic lives of "showbiz" families. The male heroes (Danny Williams and Ricky Ricardo) were entertainers who regularly performed on their nightclub stages. However, these performance segments were just as often incorporated into the domestic space where they were integrated with the story. Danny Williams often sang in his apartment, and the Ricardos typically performed at home. For example, in "Rusty's Report Card" (1953), Danny is shown rehearsing at his living room piano, while Ricky takes his entire band home with him for a shindig in "Breaking the Lease" (1953). In addition, these family comedies often welcomed guest stars into their homes so that the attractions of variety comedy were cleverly interwoven into the sitcom form. *I Love Lucy* first used this strategy in 1954 when Tennessee Ernie Ford played a displaced hillbilly camping out in the Ricardo living room. More typically, however, guest stars simply appeared as themselves. During the season in which Lucy and Ricky moved to Hollywood (1954–55), the inclusion of movie stars was narratively motivated by the fact that the Ricardos were living the lives of film actors, with Ricky under contract to a major Hollywood studio. In *Make Room For Daddy*, such celebrities as Dinah

Shore and Jack Benny were introduced as friends of the family and did routines both on the nightclub stage and in the Williamses' apartment.

The showbiz narrative was thus a perfect vehicle for the integration of story and performance. The comic gags and musical numbers of the variety show were now contained within a realistic story that created an aura of sentimentality. As one critic wrote in *Saturday Review:* "Mr. Thomas is in his idiom. When he cracks a joke at home it's habit and we believe it. When he says to his daughter, 'let's play horsey,' he makes a floor-show gag out of her response. . . . The family values are authentic, and the professional behavior rings true. The expert blending of the two in the opening programs promises the most consistently amusing life-with-father show on the air."[96] A *Variety* critic similarly praised *Lucy* for its ability to merge performance spectacles into a well-crafted story about domestic life: "Lucy's emergence as refreshing and bigtime video . . . . cannot help but strengthen the growing belief that video programming, to save face and sponsors, must of necessity detour into such avenues where the writing and the material, the human equations and comedy formulas inherent in well-produced situation comedies, will take TV out of its present rut of overproduced spectacles."[97]

This is not to argue that *I Love Lucy* and *Make Room For Daddy* were "realistic." Lucy's slapstick clowning, trick costumes, and wild antics made for highly unrealistic depictions of domesticity (and, in fact, many critics disapproved of the show for that reason). However, I would suggest that while these programs included hyperbolic and theatrical renditions of everyday life, they presented a classical solution to the elements that subvert verisimilitude. Although these showbiz family sitcoms highlighted the talents of famous stars, the performances were never as radically detached from the story as were those in the early episodes of *Burns and Allen*. The inclusion of a fictional audience (either in the form of nightclub patrons or family members) helped created a bridge between performance and story, and since the alternation between the nightclub and domestic settings was motivated by narrative events, the programs established a continuity between performances on the stage and those that took place in the domestic arena. In the showbiz narrative there seemed to be a direct causal link between the theatrical depiction of the stage space and the theatrical representation of the domestic space.

Even so, these showbiz family narratives constantly reflected back on the artifice of middle-class family ideals and presented what can be called a kind of "fractured domesticity." While seamlessly integrating story and performance, showbiz narratives nevertheless disrupted the naturalistic portrayal of everyday life by turning the home into a stage where spectacles took place. In particular, through this fracturing of the domestic situation, these programs dramatized the artifice of gender roles in postwar life.

Backstage Mothers

With their merger of domestic and theatrical worlds, sitcoms turned housekeeping into a literal performance. In both *I Love Lucy* and *Make Room For Daddy*, the heroine was able to traverse the two spheres (at times literally, at other times figuratively) by exhibiting her talents in two arenas. In these programs domestic space served as a backdrop for the housewife/star's performance. Everyday activities were often intertwined with comedy routines so that mundane jobs such as cleaning the living room became an occasion for the display of star talents contained within the average housewife character. But in the showbiz family narrative, the inclusion of the literal stage/nightclub setting repeatedly served to reflect back on the spectacle of housekeeping. As Patricia Mellencamp has argued, Lucy's performances were a form of rebellion against the domestic ideal as Lucy attempted to get out of the kitchen and into the act.[98] Even while these performances were contained within narratives that were resolved in conservative ways, and even while they usually resulted in making a comic spectacle out of the woman, they nevertheless expressed anxieties about postwar notions of domesticity.

Typically, the programs alternated between the domestic and nightclub settings. In *Make Room for Daddy* ("Margaret's Career," 1953), Danny Williams appears on the nightclub floor as his wife Margaret watches from the audience. In the middle of his act, Danny introduces Margaret to the audience and, as it turns out, Margaret gets a round of applause for her ad-libbed performance. The following scene takes place in the Williamses' apartment where a theatrical agent attempts to convince Margaret to star in her own one-woman show. Upon hearing this, Danny becomes outraged at the thought of Margaret working for a living, but Margaret, defying her husband, decides to accept the agent's offer. In the next scene, the arena of performance is shifted from the nightclub to the domestic space where Margaret, dressed in a formal evening gown, now sings a somewhat off-key rendition of "All of Me" while her black maid plays the piano. The audience for this "act" is composed of Margaret's two little children, Rusty and Terry. Although Margaret eventually "learns her lesson" and agrees to stay out of show business, her performance at home works to collapse the boundaries between domesticity and theatricality.

Similar situations occurred in *I Love Lucy*. In "The Audition" (1951), Lucy learns that television talent scouts are planning to visit Ricky's nightclub. Sitting before her bathroom mirror, Lucy begs her husband to let her into the act, telling Ricky, "You need a pretty girl in your act to advertise the sponsor's product." Unable to convince him with words, Lucy launches into a series of performances, dancing through her home with a lamp shade on her head and singing "A Pretty Girl is Like a Melody."[99] The next scene takes place in the Tropicana Nightclub where Ricky rehearses his show for the night. This scene works much like a backstage musical in which performances are framed by the "story of the show." In this particular case, Buffo the clown falls off his trick bicycle while practicing his act and, following Ricky's suggestion, Buffo goes to the Ricardo apartment in order to recuperate. As usual, Lucy is able to connive her way into the act, this time by convincing Buffo to let her take his place in the show. The final scene takes place in the Tropicana where Ricky now entertains the television executives singing his famous "Babalu" number. Running onto the stage in an oversized tuxedo and carrying a large cello, Lucy masquerades as Buffo. Lucy effectively upstages Ricky as she plays the cello, impersonates a seal, and rides Buffo's trick bicycle.

As in this episode, many of the programs employed self-reflexive strategies to dramatize the unequal distribution of power between the sexes. Numerous plots revolved around women who saw television as a channel of access to power in the marketplace. In a *Make Room For Daddy* episode ("The Opera Singer," 1953), the Williamses promote the career of a young singer, Maria, whose uncle does not want her to leave home. Maria's access to the public sphere is gained through a television performance, which becomes the crux of dramatic conflict. Her uncle begs her to give up her dreams of a show business career, telling her not to perform on a television variety show. Maria, however, sees the television engagement as an exciting alternative to her domestic role as caretaker for her uncle. Although television serves as a narrative figure for family discord, it nevertheless functions to restore harmony at the end of the episode. Thinking that Maria is performing live on television, her uncle switches on his set. However, to his delight, he discovers that he is watching a delayed broadcast and that Maria is actually back home with him. Thus, television technology helps Maria to balance the competing desires for a career and a family life by allowing her to be in two places at once.

Lucy Ricardo also attempted to launch a career by performing on television. In "The Million-Dollar Idea" (1954), she and Ethel decide to start their own salad-dressing business by purchasing advertising time on a local television station. This, in turn, provides the motivation for a female version of the vaudevillian traveling salesman skit in which Lucy plays a little old lady, "Aunt Jenny," who pitches her product to the television audience. Similarly, in "Lucy Does a Commercial," Lucy begs

Ricky to let her advertise the sponsor's product in his television variety show. Attempting to prove her salesgirl abilities, she scoops out the inside of her television set, climbs inside and, dressed as the Philip Morris Boy, auditions for the part. After Ricky refuses to let her in on the act, she connives her way onto the show behind his back, where she appears as a spokeperson for "Vitameatavegamin," a pick-me-up tonic that is 23 percent alcohol. This now classic scene provides a stage for the comic talents of Lucille Ball, whose character Lucy Ricardo becomes increasingly inebriated on the tonic as she rehearses the commercial. When the show goes on, a thoroughly intoxicated Lucy misses her cue for the commercial, interrupts Ricky's musical performance, and waves hello to her friends at home. Ricky then literally drags Lucy off the stage, reeling her back to her housewife role as Lucy Ricardo.

I Married Joan, famous for being *I Love Lucy*'s clone, presented similar scenarios. While the program was not a showbiz family comedy per se, it was based on the premise that Joan Stevens gave up her aspirations for stardom to become a housewife. Not surprisingly in this regard, Joan often fantasized about having a glamorous career, and her fantasies typically provided the motivation for vaudevillian performances that fractured the domestic scene. In a 1952 episode, the scene opens on Judge Brad Stevens (Joan's husband) who counsels a couple arguing over the wife's desire to get a job. The next scene is motivated by Brad's flashback as he recalls the time when Joan wanted a career of her own. The flashback also involves an extended slapstick comedy routine. In a humorous skit, Joan mops her kitchen floors, becomes exasperated with her homemaker role, and tries to break into show business. After landing a job as an actress in a television commercial for a new heavy-duty kitchen mop, Joan is given ample time to perform another slapstick routine. Cast as an old hausfrau, Joan mops the floor the "old fashioned way" in a gag that finds Joan covered in household grime from head to toe. This section of the narrative is motivated not so much by the story of Joan Stevens's career, but rather by the comedic performance of the star Joan Davis who upstages the domestic story altogether. In 1957, this plot was repeated almost verbatim on *Make Room for Daddy* (now retitled *The Danny Thomas Show*) when wife Kathy longs to become the spokesperson for a floor cleaner.

In all of these cases, the programs had struck a compromise between competing ways of addressing family audiences. Retaining the aesthetics of spontaneous live performance, they featured comediennes, and in some cases vocalists, who used the backdrop of domesticity as a stage for their unique talents. Embedding these performances in seamless storylines and domestic settings, the programs toned down the more threatening elements of variety comedy, even as they maintained, through

Joan's leading role in a TV commercial turns out to be less than glamorous in this 1952 episode of *I Married Joan*. (Wisconsin Center for Film and Theater Research.)

their self-reflexive theatricality, an implicit critique on gender roles in middle-class society.

From Gender to Generation

By 1955, the move to realism in family comedies had become more pronounced as the genre increasingly emphasized storytelling over and above zany vaudeville performance or revue-type fare. *Ozzie and Harriet's* appearance in 1952 marked the transition to a more naturalistic type of comedy where good, clean family normality was the reigning aesthetic. Like *I Love Lucy*, the program featured a well-known celebrity couple who sometimes performed on the show. In an episode entitled "Tutti-Frutti Ice Cream" (1957), for example, an elaborate dream sequence shows the Nelson family in a musical-comedy revue number, singing and dancing the Charleston in an old-fashioned soda fountain. Unlike *Lucy*, this program typically downplayed the talents of the celebrity couple, centering most of its plots around the rather mundane "adventures" of the group—episodes in which, for example, Ozzie goes on a diet ("The

177

Pills," 1952) and the Nelsons don't like their pancakes ("The Pancake Mix," 1953). Aired until 1966, the program was the epitome of wholesome TV fun designed for a family audience. In the words of one *Variety* critic who reviewed the series' premier episode, "It's a socko family show, built mainly around the talents of the young Nelson offspring."[100]

As Mary Beth Haralovich has shown, the realist suburban family sitcom flourished at the end of the 1950s, with programs such as *Father Knows Best, Leave It To Beaver,* and *The Donna Reed Show* drawing on codes of verisimilitude to present portraits of everyday life in the white middle-class suburbs.[101] De-emphasizing the theatricality of performance and becoming less self-conscious about their own artifice, these programs worked to "naturalize" family life, to make it appear as if this living arrangement were in fact the only one possible. Except for occasional episodes, the unhappy housewife character was gone. Dealing with generational rather than gender conflicts, they based their dramatic appeal on sibling rivalries and the dilemmas of childrearing. *Father Knows Best* focused on the problems of young Bud's failed attempt to become a newspaper boy, little Kathy's preteen angst about being a tomboy, or daughter Betty's lessons in becoming a woman when she chooses between a "male" career as an engineer or dating her boss. Similarly, *The Donna Reed Show* presented the troubles of young Jeff Stone, who felt neglected when his father refused to take him camping, or else it focused on Donna and Alex's parental dilemma when their daughter Mary fell for an older man who took her to an Ingmar Bergman movie.

Not surprisingly in this regard, not only stories but also performances typically centered around the children. Ricky Nelson's singing career was launched by his parents in a 1957 episode ("Ricky the Drummer"), in which he performed with his father's big-band friends, and later his singing numbers became a regular feature of the show. Likewise, Shelley Fabares and Paul Peterson of *The Donna Reed Show* both performed their hit singles in episodes of the program. Presented as slick pop songs addressed to a new generation of middle-class teens, these performances were fundamentally different from the antics of vaudeville clowns whose wild physical humor disrupted the domestic doldrums of family life. Rather than fracturing domesticity, these teen idols seemed to repair it by bringing the new youth culture, with its threatening Elvis Presleys and Little Richards, into a domestic world where children sang the latest hits under the watchful gaze of their parents. In fact, when Ricky first played with his father's band in "Ricky the Drummer," Ozzie, Harriet, and big brother David were watching and eventually even joined him on stage to sing a family quartet. Similarly, in 1962 when Shelley Fabares/Mary Stone stood in her yard and sang "Johnny Angel,"

The Nelson family bridges the generation gap by incorporating teen idol Ricky Nelson into a family quartet. (Wisconsin Center for Film and Theater Research.)

mother Donna looked tenderly at Mary through her bedroom window. Just in case the message of parent-child bonding wasn't clear enough, another episode featured Paul Peterson/Jeff Stone singing the top ten single "My Dad." [102] The new "teen-vid" strategy was so popular that in the 1955–56 season *Burns and Allen* incorporated their son Ronnie into the act, hoping to capitalize on the new storytelling trend of heartwarming teenage troubles over and above the vaudevillian tradition of male-female comedy routines. In 1959, *The Danny Thomas Show* went one step further, featuring teen idol Annette Funicello in numerous episodes where she appeared as Gina, an Italian exchange student who lived with the Williamses. Although the vaudevillian sitcoms still existed, the family comedy, at least for a little while, embraced a more realistic style of presentation, portraying an ideal picture of contented suburbanites. [103]

Still, in its earliest manifestations, the family comedy provided television viewers with more than just an idealistic picture of themselves at home. A refraction rather than a reflection of family life, the domestic sitcom appealed to viewers' experiences in postwar America and, above all, their fascination with the new television medium. The self-reflexive genre wedded everyday life to theatricality, revealing the artifice entailed in staging domesticity for television cameras. In the process, it offered viewers a sense of imaginary transport, promising to carry them into the homes of familiar television neighbors, who lived in a new electronic landscape where the borders between fiction and reality were easily crossed.

Epilogue

Question: When did the home theater concept first come about?

Answer: I believe this was in the mid 1980's, with the increase in the popularity of rental videotapes.

Interview conducted by Electronic Industries Association with Roger Dressler, Technical Director, Licensing Group, Dolby Laboratories[1]

In September 1989, the *Chicago Tribune* printed a story about Levittown, Pennsylvania, assuring readers that "the community has aged with a grace that would surprise many of its early critics." In place of the "ticky-tacky boxes" were distinct houses that "took on the character lines of middle age," and instead of the muddy acreage and barren lots, there were now tall trees lining Lavender Lane. Hal Lefcourt, a resident for thirty-seven years, claimed that "Bill Levitt . . . opened our horizons to stuff we didn't know existed. It was the land of milk and honey with things like community swimming pools and shopping centers." Selma Golub, one of the first to move to the community in the 1950s, said, "I grew up in the 40s and 50s, when you went to the movies a lot, and that was the culture you saw. You grew up with certain things in mind: to get married, have a family, own a car and own a house. For me to own a home in my 20s—I thought that was the greatest thing."[2] These memories of suburban relocation give closure to lives lived in the midst of the cultural transitions that marked the postwar world. For such people and, no doubt, for other members of the white middle class, the migration to suburbia is remembered as a time of joyful acquisition. However, the article suggests, this first generation of suburbanites shares little in common with its present-day neighbors. Now Levittown is populated by senior citizens and "dual career, two-income households," with many residents commuting to jobs in Manhattan, eighty miles away. The suburban wilderness of postwar America is now the epitome of American civilization, a sign of tradition in a culture built on shifting ground as the dream of nuclear familialism gives way to new ideals and new social constraints.

Not surprisingly, in the contemporary cultural landscape, discourses on communication technologies continue to proliferate, promising utopian possibilities and tempering fears about technology out of control.

Cable television, satellites, video technology, high definition television, and digital sound systems offer consumers an electronic cornucopia that promises to solve social problems and replace the doldrums of everyday life with thrilling, all-encompassing entertainment spectacles. Consumer magazines are full of articles and advertisements that promote these new technologies—often through the same rhetorical strategies that were used in the 1950s. This is not to argue that history repeats itself, but rather that the discursive conventions for thinking about communication technologies are very much the same. Indeed, as the case of Levittown suggests, the actual historical conditions of contemporary society are quite different from those of the 1950s, as the nuclear family gives way to a new social formation. Rising divorce rates and falling birthrates, as well as significant increases in the number of young married women holding jobs, are among the changes that inflect contemporary notions of family life. Between 1970 and 1980, the number of households with married parents and one or more children under eighteen had declined by 13 percent.[3]

Still, our culture speaks about new communication technologies in remarkably familiar ways. The "home theater," a salient concept since at least the turn of the century—and certainly a central fascination in the discourse on television—is now being touted as the distinct result of new electronic technologies. In a 1989 press release, the Electronic Industries Association promised that video, digital sound, laser disks, and other new developments would transform the home into a total exhibition environment. Richard Noakes, sales manager for the stereophonic systems corporation Harmon-Kardon/JBL, explained:

> People should be aware that they are not only recreating music in the home theater. For example, when you hear a thunderclap, you should feel it and sense it, not just hear it. A home theater system should be quiet enough so that when you're supposed to be experiencing the sound of winter in a forest, you can hear the trees cracking in the wind without hearing background hiss. The system should also recreate the sound of birds and other natural sounds. The experience should always come forward. . . . You're trying to recreate nature with electronics.[4]

Typically here, the discursive categories for thinking about new technologies and implementing them for everyday use hark back to familiar themes. Through their ability to bring the outside world into the home, electronics promise to domesticate nature, giving the private citizen the chance to travel imaginatively into the outside world while remaining in the comforts of the home. Not only will this home theater simulate the natural environment, it will, like television before it, replicate experiences in social settings. As the press release continued, "The marriage of large screen televisions and sophisticated sound processors with videodisc players and VCRs have enabled individuals and families to approximate the experience they might have in a movie theater." Moreover, new technologies promise to strengthen family ties, for the "home theater is enjoying great popularity due to the family enjoying each other's company while watching movies together." And, finally, as in the case of television, these social benefits are said to be truly democratic, for as the press release assures us, there "is nothing exotic about the technology," it is eminently "affordable" and "almost everyone already has some of the components that make up a home theater system."[5] Similarly, an article in *American Home* tells readers that "you may be pleasantly surprised to learn there's a 'home theater' to match just about any budget."[6] Thus, notions of democratic accessibility—a domestic ideal enjoyed by all—still serve to structure predictions about new communication technologies, predictions that promise utopian alternatives through a consensual model of social progress.

Despite the "democratic" impulse of such speculations, the new electronic home theaters are in fact represented in terms of privileged lifestyles. Upscale consumer magazines such as *Audio/Video Interiors* and *Sound & Image* depict new technologies in elaborate domestic interiors, promising readers the ultimate luxury of having lavish public theaters in their private homes. As the title of one article claims, having a home theater is just like "Puttin' on the Ritz." Here as elsewhere, the retro style of art deco and other fashions from the pre-World War II period are particularly valued. In this home theater, "authentic 1930s [movie] seats," a large lobby poster of *All I Desire,* a candy concession complete with an original Coke machine, and even a copy of the 10-inch-wide frieze in Radio City's ladies room are all used to transform the domestic interior into a virtual replica of a lost public culture based on cinematic spectacles.[7] Advertisements in these magazines take up similar themes, promising consumers the ultimate luxury of bringing the world to their doorsteps. Shure's "theater technology for the home" promotes its sound system by offering consumers a peek at three people watching television, who are pictured inside a large window frame. Since the window is completely filled with an image of the moon landing, it appears as if the television viewers are actually on the moon while simultaneously inside the home. Moreover, just as in the 1950s, magazines find ways of negotiating luxury dream houses with the consumer's less affluent middle-class lifestyle. Yamaha, for instance, promotes its Digital Soundfield Processor by telling the story of Ralph, who "actually lives in a one bedroom condo." With the aid of the new machine Ralph and other people like him can turn their small apartments into "opera houses, stadiums, jazz clubs, concert halls, movie theaters, discos, cathedrals and amphitheaters."[8] In a country where the middle-class dream of home ownership has given way to condo-aesthetics, new technology promises to bring outside spaces into even the smallest interiors.

Such themes of technological utopia are, however, disrupted by traces of a more troubled relation to high-tech gadgets. As in the 1950s, interior and product designers place particular emphasis on "integrating" new technologies into the domestic environment. Concealment of technology through the use of push-button screens, wall murals, tapestries, and other familiar devices is a central fascination. As a spokesperson for Sharp electronics claims, "Your living room can be your living room when you want it to be, and it can turn into a home theater when you want it to."[9] One sound-systems company is even selling outdoor speakers that are fashioned like large rocks so that they'll fit in perfectly with the naturalistic feel of a poolside environment.[10]

More generally, new technologies remain a central fascination in the popular culture. Films such as *Poltergeist* (1982), *Videodrome* (1983), and *Terrorvision* (1986) present images of people being tortured by such items as remote controls, large screens, VCRs, and satellite dishes. Meanwhile, more mundane stories about marital spats over channel "grazing" with remote controls proliferate, while new "picture in picture" sets promise to ease these disagreements with a contemporary answer to the DuMont Duoscope. A computerized television system called "Smart TV," which records and catalogues programs for the viewer, promises to alleviate the continuing anxieties about television's effects on children by monitoring their viewing and allowing parents to choose a "menu" of wholesome programs for their youngsters. And just as in the 1950's, the control of children's viewing seems to be related to wider fears about parental dominion over the medium, their families, and even themselves. When discussing "Smart TV," the popular science program *Beyond Tomorrow* (1989) told viewers that the system "has the capacity to record almost 200 hours [of TV] a week. Let's face it, if you watch more than that you don't need a Smart TV, you need a life."

In addition, like television before them, new technologies threaten to destabilize gender dynamics in the home. Popular media continue to display male boobs who are seduced by the TV siren and a host of video toys. In *The Simpsons*, Homer Simpson, the classic "male boob" of the 1990s, runs home to television after a hard day at the nuclear reactor, and in one episode he even fights ruthlessly (and unsuccessfully) with son Bart to win a video game. New technology is also shown to render unstable the power of vision that traditionally entitled men to look voyeuristically at images of women. In 1989, in an issue entitled "The Future and You," *Life* considered the new electronic space that the home

184

laser holographic movie might offer in the twenty-first century. Not coincidentally, this holographic space was defined by male desire. As Marilyn Monroe emerged from the screen in her costume from *The Seven Year Itch*, a male spectator, with remote control in hand, watched her materialize in the room. Importantly, the man's dominion over the female image is thrown into question because he is depicted as a lackluster homebody, relaxed and supine in his futuristic La-Z-Boy Lounger. Although the scene was clearly coded as a science-fiction fantasy, this form of home entertainment was just the latest version of the older wish to control and purify public space. Sexual desire, transported to the home from the Hollywood cinema, was made possible by transfiguring the celluloid image into an electrical space where aggressive, voyeuristic forms of cinematic pleasure were now sanitized and made into "passive" home entertainment. The aggression entailed in watching Monroe was clearly marked as passive aggression, as a form of desire that could be contained within domestic space. But just in case the desire for this electronic fantasy woman could not be properly contained, the article warned readers to "fasten the seatbelt on your La-Z-Boy."[11]

The holograph is just one example of an increasing interest in making illusions so convincing as to transform domestic space into an alternate world. By donning high-tech headgear and computerized clothing, people, we are told, will be able to interact with simulated universes, commonly known as "cyberspace" or "virtual reality." As an episode of MTV's *Buzz* (1990) explained it, virtual reality is a "3-D computer generated reality. The participant is surrounded by the sights, sounds and sensations of another world. It's like jumping into your TV." Thus, just as television promised to surpass all media before it, this new technology promises to outdo television by creating a more absorbing illusion. According to *i-D* magazine, "TV, by comparison, is a low tech, low resolution flat world rooted in the '50s, a compromise that filled a necessary gap until something better came along."[12] Jaron Lanier of VPL Research even claims that virtual reality has the potential to erase the evil effects of television technology. "People," he argues, "are used to being in their little TV world, separated from each other. . . . what obviously needs to happen is technology needs to change." With virtual reality, he predicts, "It's really hard to maintain the same world view of the separation between people anymore and so I hope it will be a little bit of a tool for empathy." Cyberpunk novelist William Gibson also embraces this technology for its possible social benefits, but he has a darker vision of its effects, claiming that "it has its Orwellian potential as well."[13] If virtual reality seems farfetched, it is clearly becoming a distinct social possibility. In 1989, Mattel marketed a toy "power glove" that allowed children to clothe themselves in an alternate reality, interacting with "data" rather than people. Virtual reality is not only being extolled as an escape from the mundane social world, it is also being implemented as an improved form of "new age" domesticity where people can literally enter another world while remaining in the safety of their private homes. As *American Film* predicts, "You may be able to experience love, sexual orgasm and ultimately, death, and then remove your Walkman-size headsets, have a smoke, take a shower and go to work."[14]

Thus, the dream of merging inside and outside space is now part and parcel of discourses and design strategies integral to the innovation of consumer electronics. But, again, while the discourse on new technologies seems to proceed on familiar themes, the historical context has changed considerably. Although narrative and pictorial conventions have much in common with those of the past, the social definitions of domesticity have shifted, and modes of experiencing everyday life are also different. The disjuncture between practice and discourse—the uneven developments between social change and the ways we speak about those changes—raises fascinating questions for cultural history.

In this book, I have tried to forge various correspondences between what was said about television and the society in which those utterances were possible. Importantly, this notion of correspondence is quite different from a notion of coherence. For rather than explaining a set of discourses by using a central covering law, I have been interested in showing how the multiple, and often conflicting, middle-class ideals of postwar America gave way to contradictory responses to television in popular culture. Although popular representations cannot definitively demonstrate how people actually used television in their own homes, they do begin to reveal the discursive conventions that were formed for thinking about a new medium during the period of its installation. They begin to disclose the social construction of television as it is rooted in a mode of thought based on white middle-class concepts of gender, class, and generational difference. Ideals of interior decor and suburban lifestyles, as well as the gendered and age-related divisions of families in the home, served as a backdrop for the development of television as a cultural form.

Recent ethnographic studies of television audiences in America and overseas reveal the continued impact of gender, class, racial, and other social differences on the way in which families watch television. David Morley's work with British working-class families shows how class identity and gender divisions help to define domestic leisure, while Ann Gray's work on VCR usage among working-class families in Britain especially highlights the way that gender-based ideas about domestic technology and productive labor in the home circumscribes women's use of the new machine. James Lull's anthology, *World Families Watch Television,* and numerous studies of the global audience for *Dallas* further suggest how ethnic and racial differences in distinct cultural settings affect the ways people perceive and use television in their everyday lives.[15]

For historians, questions about the television audience pose different problems and call for other methods. The reconstruction of viewing experiences at some point in the past is an elusive project. Indeed, we will never be able to present a complete historical account of subjective experiences like watching television. Instead, by its very nature, the history of spectatorship is a patchwork history, one that must draw together a number of approaches and perspectives in the hopes of achieving a partial picture of past experiences. The approach I've taken provides insights into the way television viewing has been connected to larger patterns of family ideals and gender construction.

Popular media of the postwar years illuminate some of the central tensions expressed by the mass culture at a time when spectator amusements were being transported from the public to the private sphere. At least at the level of representation, the installation of the television set was by no means a simple purchase of a pleasure machine. These popular discourses remind us that television's utopian promise was fraught with doubt. Even more importantly, they begin to reveal the complicated processes through which conventions of viewing television in the home environment and conventions of television's representational styles were formed in the early period. Magazines, advertisements, television programming, and other popular media helped to establish rules for ways in which to achieve pleasure in television and avoid its discomforts. In so doing, they showed people how to perceive and use television at home. While the dialogue between mass culture and the public is never direct, these media discourses did help to construct ways of seeing television, some of which can now be recognized as everyday viewing practices.

As historian Carlo Ginzburg has argued, "Reality is opaque; but there are certain points—clues, signs—which allow us to decipher it." It is the seemingly inconsequential trace, Ginzburg claims, through which the most significant patterns of past experiences might be sought.[16] These discourses that spoke of the placement of a chair, or the design of a television set in a room, begin to suggest the details of everyday existence into which television inserted itself. They give us a clue into a history of spectators in the home—a history that is only beginning to be written.

Notes

Introduction

1. It took radio about thirty years to reach comparable saturation rates. Note that data on installation rates vary slightly from one source to another. These estimations are based on Cobbett S. Steinberg, *TV Facts* (New York: Facts on File, 1980), p. 142; "Sales of Home Appliances" and "Dwelling Units," *Statistical Abstract of the United States* (Washington DC: GPO, 1951–56); Lawrence W. Lichty and Malachi C. Topping, *American Broadcasting: A Source Book on the History of Radio and Television* (New York: Hastings House, 1975), pp. 521–22.

2. The period examined in this study, 1948–55, covers the years in which television became a dominant American mass medium. After 1955 there was a leveling off in the consumption of television sets, and the industry itself went through a series of important changes that marked its transition from a new medium to a mature industry with specific modes of production, distribution, and exhibition. Several significant changes crystallized in the mid-fifties. This was the point at which network prime-time programming ceased to be predominantly live and began to shift almost exclusively to telefilm (and, later to video). The shift to recorded programming also entailed a change in the production and sponsorship of prime-time programs. By mid-decade the networks began to challenge the system of program production based on single sponsorship, preferring instead a system of spot commercials where advertisers simply bought time in the network schedule. Under this plan, the networks joined forces with Hollywood film studios, which became the major prime-time program suppliers. These changes have been amply documented elsewhere, but for our purposes they constitute an important break with the early period. See, for example, Erik Barnouw, *A History of Broadcasting in the United States*, vol. 3 (New York: Oxford University Press, 1973); *Tube of Plenty: The Evolution of American Broadcasting* (New York: Oxford University Press, 1975); and his history of broadcast advertising, *The Sponsor: Notes on a Modern Potentate* (New York: Oxford University Press, 1978). See also William Boddy, "From the 'Golden Age' to the 'Vast Wasteland': The Struggles over Market Power and Dramatic Formats in 1950s Television" (Ph.D diss., New York University, 1984); Robert Vianello, "The Rise of the Telefilm and the Network's Hegemony over the Motion Picture Industry," *Quarterly Review of Film Studies* 9(3) (Summer 1984), pp. 204–18. The years 1948–55 also bracket an era of programming trends. While the pre-1948 network schedule shows a scarcity of programs, by mid-1948 the prime-time schedule was fully slotted. Furthermore, by 1955 domestic sitcoms had become one of the most lucrative and popular program types.

Although I have chosen to define the period from the point of view of industrial development and installation rates, this is not to say that the discourse on television begins in 1948 and ends in 1955. Television had been discussed in utopian writings on technology at least since Thomas Edison's and Edward Bellamy's late nineteenth-century ruminations on the idea of transmitting image and sound from a centralized source. It had also been considered in industry trade journals since the late 1920s and was discussed in the popular press in the 1930s and 1940s. For more on this, see James L. Baughman, "The Promise of American Television, 1929–1952," *Prospects* 11 (1987), pp. 119–34. There seems, however, to have been a marked shift in popular perceptions of television during 1948. At that time television was represented as a practical reality for average Americans, and in the same year advertising campaigns for television began to appear in popular periodicals. Furthermore, by 1955 there was redundancy in the representations. That is, the major representational trends seem to have been well established. Repetition at the level of representation was coupled with a more literal repetition at the level of sales. Advertisers began to promote the purchase of two television sets. Still, it would be foolish to say that there was a radical break in the discourse on television in 1955. As we know from our own experience, our culture is still thinking about television (this book is a case in point). The period examined, then, does not suggest a beginning or an end to popular debates; rather, it attempts to give the early years of installation and industrial development a certain formal coherence by taking those years as a case study.

3. Elaine Tyler May, *Homeward Bound: American Families in the Cold War Era* (New York: Basic Books, 1988).

4. *TV Guide*, 5–11 June 1953, p. 1.

5. See Carolyn Marvin, *When Old Technologies Were New: Thinking about Communication Technologies in the Late Nineteenth Century* (New York: Oxford University Press, 1988); Catherine L. Covert, "'We May Hear Too Much': American Sensibility and the Response to Radio, 1919–1924," *Mass Media between the Wars: Perceptions of Cultural Tension, 1918–1941*, ed. Catherine L. Covert and John D. Stevens (Syracuse: Syracuse University Press, 1984), pp. 199–220; John F. Kasson, *Civilizing the Machine: Technology and Republican Values in America, 1776–1900* (New York: Penguin, 1977), especially pp. 183–234; Leo Marx, *The Machine in the Garden: Technology and the Pastoral Ideal in America* (New York: Oxford University Press, 1964); James W. Carey, *Communication As Culture: Essays on Media and Society* (Boston: Unwin Hyman, 1989); Daniel J. Czitrom, *Media and the American Mind: From Morse to McLuhan* (Chapel Hill: University of North Carolina Press, 1982); Susan J. Douglas, *Inventing American Broadcasting, 1899–1922* (Baltimore: Johns Hopkins University Press, 1987), pp. 187–215 and 292–314; Warren I. Susman, *Culture As History: The Transformation of American Society in the Twentieth Century* (1973; reprint, New York: Pantheon, 1984).

6. Susman, "Culture and Communications," *Culture as History*, p. 257.

7. In addition to women's home magazines, I looked at popular weeklies (especially *Life*), the men's magazines *Popular Science* and *Esquire*, the black middle-class magazine *Ebony*, and the more downscale women's magazine *Good Housekeeping*. I examined at least half of the issues of these additional magazines from 1948 to 1955, and I used articles referred to in the *Reader's Guide to Periodical Literature* for additional sources. The home magazines, general weeklies, and *Ebony* included by far the greatest number of advertisements for television sets. Conversely, television sets were rarely advertised in the men's magazines, and they were almost never promoted to the less affluent female readers of *Good Housekeeping*. This seems to suggest, at least from the advertiser's point of view, that television sets were both a gender- and class-specific item. Importantly, however, they were heavily advertised to black consumers, so that advertisers must have considered the black middle class a significant market for the new medium. *Ebony* contained advertisements for television in almost every issue and often presented the same ads that were in magazines aimed at a primarily white constituency.

8. Since some of these magazines had regional editions, there are occasional discrepancies among issues distributed in different parts of the country. In particular, I assume, the advertisers may not always have bought space in all regional editions because television was not a national phenomenon until the mid-fifties (see chapter 1). Most typi-

cally, however, it appears that the ads for television were geared to a national audience because they often include price ranges for different parts of the country. In my random comparisons between thirty issues in Los Angeles, California, and Madison, Wisconsin, I found only one difference.

9. The first three magazines focused primarily on interior decor and home economics, whereas *Ladies' Home Journal*—often referred to as a women's service magazine—dealt with a wider array of women's issues.

10. A nationwide market research study conducted during the period shows that home magazines had anywhere from over twice to five times as many female readers as male readers. Furthermore, male readers were more often married, so that they probably read the magazines as occasional readers, not as primary consumers. See Alfred Politz Research, Inc., *The Audiences of Nine Magazines: Their Size and Characteristics: A National Study* (New York: Cowles Magazines, 1955), pp. 21–22. For the readership's class composition, see ibid., p. 17, and W. Lloyd Warner and Paul S. Lunt, *The Social Life of A Modern Community* (New Haven: Yale University Press, 1941), pp. 398–405.

11. Industry trade journals continually published reports on the class characteristics of the audience, but these reports often contradicted one another. While most agreed that middle-class income families tended to be the heaviest purchasers, there was disagreement about the extent to which upper-class and lower-class families bought television sets. As the NBC Records show, the industry kept a close eye on audience studies. The NBC Records, to which I refer in this study, are housed at the Wisconsin Center Historical Archives, State Historical Society, Madison.

12. In saying this, I wish to distance myself from trickle-down theories of popular and intellectual culture. A reigning assumption in the academy is that popular sources merely reflect a watered-down version of "high" culture and intellectual social theory. At least in the case of television, this thesis does not accurately describe the situation. In the 1950s, humanistic studies of television were few and far between; indeed television has only recently become a subject of inquiry in the humanities. While social scientists were interested in measuring television's effects and audience viewing habits in the 1950s, and while such studies did find their way into popular sources, the popular culture did not merely reflect the voices of intellectuals. In fact, the popular sources often directly debated with the "high" theories of "European intellectuals," and they often reinterpreted the findings of social science with everyday, "common sense" knowledge about homemaking, interior decor, and childrearing. In other words, even when they referred to academic sources they read them through the screen of a more popular middle-class culture. Moreover, as we shall see, the types of knowledge about the family that they produced were often completely different from the kind sought by social scientists.

13. For an example of this, see Stuart Ewen's *Captains of Consciousness: Advertising and the Social Roots of the Consumer Culture* (New York: McGraw-Hill, 1976). Although Ewen's book is in many ways one of the most interesting accounts of advertising and modern culture, its assumptions about the relationship between consumer culture and individuals need to be significantly tempered. Ewen assumes that advertisers reach into the public's psyche, persuading people to desire commodities. Although I agree that advertising works by arousing unconscious desires, I object to the way in which Ewen accounts for the notion of desire and the unconscious. He assumes that the unconscious is a vague realm of subconscious emotional life—fears, hopes, dreams—shared by a mass populace. It is, I would argue, incorrect to account for desire in terms of a generalized emotionalism shared by a mass audience. As psychoanalysis has shown, the unconscious is extremely unstable, and desire is anything but a mass emotion to be tapped by a mass market. On this basis, it seems improbable that advertising could manipulate desire in the way that Ewen argues. Furthermore, *Captains of Consciousness* does not adequately account for advertising's appeal

to conscious thought processes. In fact, as I show throughout this book, advertisers attempted to *reason* with women as much as they tried to reach them on emotional levels.

14. For a detailed study of the fate of general magazines in the postwar period, see A. J. van Zuilen, *The Life Cycle of Magazines: A Historical Study of the Decline and Fall of the General Mass Audience Magazine in the United States during the Period 1946–1972* (Vithoorn: Graduate Press, 1977).

15. For example, in a letter dated 9 August 1950, Mr. William J. Kelly of *The American Magazine* thanked NBC executive Sydney Eiges: "My many, many thanks for your efforts in arranging the television set. You can be sure of winning the undying thanks of the four I'll have to battle every inch to get a glimpse at the programs of my choice." See NBC Records, Box 160: Folder 6, Wisconsin Center Historical Archives, State Historical Society, Madison.

16. Roland Marchand, *Advertising the American Dream: Making Way For Modernity, 1920–1940* (Berkeley: University of California Press, 1985), especially pp. 1–87.

Chapter One

1. While I am concentrating on the ideological underpinnings of suburbia and family life, it should be noted that the growth of the suburbs was also the result of economic, demographic, and technological changes. In his seminal study of suburbia, Kenneth T. Jackson shows how important these changes were to the rise of the first commuter suburb, Brooklyn, New York, in the 1820s and 1830s. See Jackson, *Crabgrass Frontier: The Suburbanization of the United States* (New York: Oxford University Press, 1985). However, other historians have shown that ideological factors also encouraged the development of suburban life. See Robert Fishman, *Bourgeois Utopia: The Rise and Fall of Suburbia* (New York: Basic Books, 1987); Margaret Marsh, *Suburban Lives* (New Brunswick: Rutgers University Press, 1990); Clifford Edward Clark, Jr., *The American Family Home, 1800–1960* (Chapel Hill: University of North Carolina Press, 1986); and Henry C. Binford, *The First Suburbs: Residential Communities on the Boston Periphery, 1815–1860* (Chicago: University of Chicago Press, 1985).

2. Marsh, *Suburban Lives*, pp. 2–7. For more on the suburban ideal see Fishman, *Bourgeois Utopia*; Jackson, *Crabgrass Frontier*; and Clark, *American Family Home*.

3. Andrew Jackson Downing's *The Architecture of Country Houses* (New York, 1850) was printed nine times between 1850 and 1886. Note that even while he promoted ideals of agrarian landownership and denigrated the urban residence, Downing rarely used the word "suburb." See Jackson, *Crabgrass Frontier*, p. 64. Jackson also demonstrates how Calvert Vaux and Catharine Beecher helped shape popular conceptions about domestic architecture. See pp. 61–72.

4. Gwendolyn Wright, *Building the Dream: A Social History of Housing in America* (Cambridge, MA: MIT Press, 1981), p. 75.

5. For analyses of feminine roles and domestic ideology, see Barbara Welter, "The Cult of True Womanhood: 1820–1860," *American Quarterly* 18 (Summer 1966), pp. 151–174; Kathryn Kish Sklar, *Catharine Beecher: A Study in American Domesticity* (New York: W. W. Norton, 1973); Barbara Leslie Epstein, *The Politics of Domesticity: Women, Evangelism, and Temperance in Nineteenth Century America* (Middletown, CT: Wesleyan University Press, 1981); Karen Halttunen, *Confidence Men and Painted Women: A Study in Middle-Class Culture in America, 1830–1870* (New Haven: Yale University Press, 1982); Carroll Smith-Rosenberg, *Disorderly Conduct: Visions of Gender in Victorian America* (New York: Oxford University Press, 1985); and Marsh, *Suburban Lives*.

6. Catharine E. Beecher, *Treatise on Domestic Economy* (1841; Reprint, Source Book Press, 1843), p. 2.

7. Ibid., p. 3. Importantly, Beecher herself chose to remain single.

8. For such interpretations of domestic ideology, see Sklar, *Catharine Beecher;* Epstein, *Politics of Domesticity;* and Marsh, *Suburban Lives.*

9. Beecher, *Treatise,* p. 9.

10. Ibid.

11. Foster Rhea Dulles, *America Learns to Play: A History of Popular Recreation: 1607–1940* (New York: D. Appleton-Century, 1940), pp. 85–86. For the development of and attitudes towards commercial amusements in the early nineteenth century, see also Lawrence W. Levine, *Highbrow Lowbrow: The Emergence of Cultural Hierarchy in America* (Cambridge: Harvard University Press, 1988); Robert Lacour-Gayet, *Everyday Life in the United States before the Civil War, 1830–1860* (New York: Frederick Ungar, 1983), pp. 97–110.

12. Although taboos against women's participation in public amusements persisted even into the twentieth century, by the mid-nineteenth century entrepreneurs were attempting to entice women and children into commercial entertainment centers. See my discussion later in this chapter.

13. Beecher, *Treatise,* pp. 244–45.

14. Ibid., p. 247.

15. Dulles claims that restrictions on women's amusements were so repressive that visitors from abroad such as Frances Trollope were "incensed at an attitude which so closely restrained those of her sex" (*America Learns to Play,* p. 96).

16. Clark, *American Family Home,* especially pp. 37–41.

17. Ibid., pp. 42–45.

18. Catharine Beecher and Harriet Beecher Stowe, *The American Woman's Home* (New York: J. B. Ford and Company, 1869).

19. See Marsh, *Suburban Lives* (especially chapter 3), for a detailed explanation of this process.

20. As Gwendolyn Wright has suggested, the irregular outline of Victorian homes revealed the pursuits of the occupants: "Each bay window, porch, and other protrusion was considered evidence of some particular activity within; it made the space exactly right for playing the piano, sewing, reading, or tending a hot stove" (*Building the Dream,* p. 112).

21. In the words of Carroll Smith-Rosenberg, Victorian women were supposed to be both "innocent and animal, pure and yet quintessentially sexual" (*Disorderly Conduct,* p. 183). Also see Welter, "Cult of True Womanhood," p. 102.

22. For feminist analyses of the sexual politics of hysteria, see Smith-Rosenberg, *Disorderly Conduct;* and Elaine Showalter, *The Female Malady: Women, Madness, and English Culture, 1830–1980* (New York: Penguin, 1985). Showalter reminds us that while hysteria might have expressed anxieties with patriarchial social structure, "in its historical contexts in the late nineteenth century, hysteria was at best a private, ineffectual response to the frustrations of women's lives" (p. 161).

23. Since the new suburban home sites were small and square, however, most families would not have had the luxury of lawn games. Instead, the fantasy of pastoral bliss was kept alive through architectural solutions, most notably the addition of several porches upon which residents might convene with nature. See Clark, *American Family Home,* pp. 43–44; Wright, *Building the Dream,* p. 104; and Marsh, *Suburban Lives,* pp. 169–73. Marsh shows that by the 1920s the ideal of outdoor exercise was so popular that Palos Verdes (an elite California suburb) promoted itself with the slogan "Where Your Home is Your Playground," displaying pictures of couples on horseback, playing golf, and on the

beach. However, the residents of the community found this image too frivolous, and once they moved into their Palos Verdes estates they changed the slogan to "Palos Verdes for the Joy of Living."

24. In the 1880s, when bicycling became popular among women, one contemporary observer praised the sport as a "step toward the emancipation of woman from her usually too inactive outdoor life," and *The Wheelman* conducted a vigorous campaign to enlist ministers' and physicians' endorsement of female cycling. "Outing," *The Wheelman* 1 (1882), p. 57. Cited in Dulles, *America Learns to Play,* pp. 195–96. For more on bicycling, see Dulles, pp. 265–69.

25. For an analysis on club life and more on golf and other games, see Margaret Marsh, "Suburban Men and Masculine Domesticity, 1870–1915," *American Quarterly* 40 (June 1988), pp. 165–86.

26. For detailed studies of early department stores and women's lives, see Susan Porter Benson, *Counter Cultures: Saleswomen, Managers, and Customers in American Department Stores 1890–1940* (Urbana and Chicago: University of Illinois Press, 1986); William R. Leach, "Transformations in a Culture of Consumption: Women and Department Stores, 1890–1925," *Journal of American History* 71 (September 1984), pp. 319–42; Robert Hendrickson, *The Grand Emporiums: The Illustrated History of America's Great Department Stores* (New York: Stein and Day, 1979); Rachel Bowlby, *Just Looking; Consumer Culture in Dreiser, Gissing and Zola* (New York: Methuen, 1985).

27. For more on the reformation of theaters in the mid to late nineteenth and early twentieth centuries, see Levine, *Highbrow Lowbrow;* Kathy Peiss, "Commercial Leisure and the 'Woman Question'," *For Fun and Profit: The Transformation of Leisure in Consumption,* ed. Richard Butsch (Philadelphia: Temple University Press, 1990), pp. 105–18; Kathy Peiss, *Cheap Amusements: Working Women and Leisure in Turn-of-the-Century New York* (Philadelphia: Temple University Press, 1986), pp. 139–62; Shirley Staples, *Male-Female Comedy Teams in American Vaudeville, 1865–1932* (Ann Arbor: University of Michigan Research Press, 1984); Robert C. Allen, "The Movies in Vaudeville: Historical Context of the Movies as Popular Entertainment," *The American Film Industry,* ed. Tino Balio (Madison: University of Wisconsin Press, 1985), pp. 57–83; Robert C. Allen, "Motion Picture Exhibition in Manhattan, 1906–1912: Beyond the Nickelodeon," *The American Movie Industry: The Business of Motion Pictures,* ed. Gorham Kindem (Carbondale: Southern Illinois University Press, 1982), pp. 12–24; Russell Merritt, "Nickelodeon Theaters, 1905–1914," *The American Film Industry,* pp. 83–102; Douglas Gomery, "The Movie Palace Comes to America's Cities," *For Fun and Profit,* pp. 136–51; Lary May, *Screening Out the Past: The Birth of Mass Culture and the Motion Picture Industry* (Chicago: University of Chicago Press, 1980), pp. 147–66.

28. For research on amusement parks, see John F. Kasson, *Amusing the Million: Coney Island at the Turn of the Century* (New York: Hill and Wang, 1978); Peiss, *Cheap Amusements,* pp. 115–38; and Lauren Rabinovitz, "Temptations of Pleasure: Nickelodeons, Amusement Parks, and the Sights of Female Sexuality," *Camera Obscura* 23 (May 1990), pp. 71–89.

29. Marsh, *Suburban Lives,* p. 82. As Marsh argues, "male domesticity" might well have had the effect of giving men more authority at home at a time when they were losing power in the increasingly technocratic and bureaucratic public sphere.

30. See Clark, *American Family Home;* Wright, *Building the Dream;* and Marsh, *Suburban Lives.* Marsh includes a statistical breakdown of household spaces shown in plan books (pp. 84–86).

31. Christine Frederick, *Selling Mrs. Consumer* (New York: The Business Bourse, 1929), p. 178.

32. For more on this advertising strategy, see Marchand, *Advertising the American Dream*, especially pp. 67–188.

33. Ruth Schwartz Cowan, *More Work For Mother: The Ironies of Household Technology from the Open Hearth to the Microwave* (New York: Basic Books, Inc., 1983). Schwartz Cowan convincingly shows that the hours women spend on household work have not substantially changed with the introduction of new technologies.

34. For examples, see Clark, *American Family Home*, p. 181.

35. T. J. Jackson Lears, *No Place of Grace: Antimodernism and the Transformation of American Culture, 1880–1920* (New York: Pantheon, 1981). Lears discusses a variety of cultural movements which were intended to cure the feelings of "weightlessness" (or unreality) in the new industrial society. From my point of view, it is important here to distinguish between intention and actual cure. That is, while these cultural pastimes might have been represented in terms of their therapeutic function, it is not altogether obvious that this was their actual effect.

36. Marx, *The Machine in the Garden*, pp. 220–21.

37. For further discussion and illustration, see Arthur J. Pulos, *American Design Ethic: A History of Industrial Design* (Cambridge, MA: MIT Press, 1986), pp. 165–79; and Adrian Forte, *Objects of Desire: Design and Society from Wedgewood to IBM* (New York: Pantheon, 1986), pp. 94–99. Both of the novelty machines were designed in 1858.

38. For further discussion and illustration, see Pulos, p. 258.

39. Mary Hinman Abel, *Successful Family Life: On the Moderate Income* (Philadelphia and London: J. B. Lippincott, 1929), p. 234.

40. Robert Lynd and Helen Merrell Lynd, *Middletown: A Study in Modern American Culture* (New York: Harcourt, Brace & World, 1929), p. 257.

41. Ibid., p. 254.

42. See Robert Edward Davis, "Response To Innovation: A Study of Popular Argument About New Mass Media," (Ph.D. diss., University of Iowa, 1965).

43. Peiss, *Cheap Amusements*, pp. 67–72. Also see Elizabeth Ewen, *Immigrant Women in the Land of Dollars: Life and Culture on the Lower East Side, 1890–1925* (New York: Monthly Review Press, 1985), especially pp. 208–24.

44. For details on early reform movements, see Peiss, *Cheap Amusements*, pp. 163–84; and May, *Screening Out the Past*, pp. 43–59.

45. Lynd and Lynd, *Middletown*, p. 269.

46. See Marsh, *Suburban Lives*, pp. 140–41. As Marsh argues, the 1920s version of masculine domesticity was substantially different from that of the Progressive Era because compassionate marriage was no longer the responsibility of the husband. Women were now held responsible for making their husbands want to participate in family matters.

47. For explanations of the increasing emphasis on children, see ibid., p. 180; Paula S. Fass, *The Damned and the Beautiful: American Youth in the 1920s* (New York: Oxford University Press, 1977), pp. 53–118; and Barbara Ehrenreich and Deidre English, *For Her Own Good: 150 Years of Experts' Advice to Women* (Garden City, NY: Anchor Books, 1979), pp. 183–210.

48. Douglas, *Inventing American Broadcasting*, p. 307. Douglas also discusses the democratic ideals of radio amateurs in this book and in "Amateur Operators and American Broadcasting: Shaping the Future of Radio," *Imagining Tomorrow: History, Technology and the American Future*, ed. Joseph J. Corn (Cambridge, MA: MIT Press, 1986), pp. 35–58.

49. Covert, "We May Hear Too Much," pp. 204–5.

50. William Boddy, "The Rhetoric and Economic Roots of the American Broadcasting Industry," *Cinetracts* 6 (2) (Spring 1979), p. 43.

51. For an illustration of this advertisement, see Pulos, *American Design Ethic*, p. 282.

52. For radio's supernatural qualities, see Covert, "We May Hear Too Much," p. 202. For radio and speculations about Martians, see Douglas, *Inventing American Broadcasting*, pp. 305–7. As Douglas argues, while such predictions "would not have been taken seriously by some sectors of American society," they nevertheless were symptomatic of more general articles about radio's potential that also displayed a "hunger for contact over great distances with beings who presumably knew more and were wiser than most contemporary Americans" (p. 305).

53. For a detailed discussion, see Leslie J. Page, Jr., "The Nature of the Broadcast Receiver Market in the U.S. from 1922 to 1927," *Journal of Broadcasting* 4 (2) (Spring 1960), pp. 174–82. Reprinted in Lichty and Topping, *American Broadcasting*, pp. 467–72.

54. For more on early advertisements for radio and a general discussion of the class-based assumptions about radio in the mid-1920s, see Marchand, *Advertising the American Dream*, pp. 88–92.

55. Robert Lynd and Helen Merrell Lynd, *Middletown in Transition: A Study in Cultural Conflicts* (New York: Harcourt Brace Jovanovich, 1937), p. 263.

56. These statistics are based on Lichty and Topping, *American Broadcasting*, p. 521.

57. Aside from the major radio corporations, Philo T. Farnsworth, a private inventor, developed important parts of electronic television. He refused to sell his patents to the large corporations until RCA negotiated agreements with him in 1939.

58. William Hawes, *American Television Drama: The Experimental Years* (n.p.: University of Alabama Press, 1986). Note that I am using the popular spelling of "DuMont." The family name was actually spelled with a space between syllables, that is, as Allen B. Du Mont. However, since the trade press consistently used "DuMont," I have chosen to spell it in this way.

59. Baughman, "Promise of American Television," pp. 119–34.

60. The Hudson-Essex exhibit is described in a series of letters from Roy O. Chapin, president of the Hudson Motor Car Company, to Mr. C. W. Horn and others. See *TV Files*, 1933, NBC Records, Box 102: Folder 2, Wisconsin Center Historical Archives, State Historical Society, Madison. In a letter to Chapin, M. H. Aylesworth wrote, "Many more people were turned away from the exhibit than the theatre could hold." *TV Files*, 17 July 1933, NBC Records, Box 102: Folder 2, Wisconsin Center Historical Archives, State Historical Society, Madison. The NBC exhibit is described in *Press Clips*, 1938, NBC Records, Box 102: Folder 22, Wisconsin Center Historical Archives, State Historical Society, Madison.

61. Warren I. Susman, "The People's Fair: Cultural Contradictions of a Consumer Society," *Culture as History*, pp. 211–29.

62. *Excerpts from Daily and Trade Press: Digests of Press and Other Opinion*, 1942, NBC Records, Box 104: Folder 15, Wisconsin Center Historical Archives, State Historical Society, Madison.

63. For example, a television receiver was installed on the Airline Bus Company's Los Angeles to San Francisco "Short Line." See *Broadcasting*, 19 June 1950, p. 53. There was, however, opposition to this idea. In 1950, bills prohibiting transit television were passed in the states of Virginia and Massachusetts, and bills were also introduced in Kentucky, New York, Rhode Island, and Mississippi. See *Broadcasting*, 1 May 1950, p. 60. By 1951, the U.S. Circuit Court of Appeals in Washington had ruled transit radio unconstitutional on the grounds that transit companies did not have the right to broadcast commercial messages. See *Advertising and Selling*, September 1951, p. 122.

64. Tyler May, *Homeward Bound*, p. 165. As Tyler May also notes, in the same five years purchases for food rose only by 33 percent and clothing by 20 percent. See also U.S. Bureau of the Census, *Historical Statistics of the United States, Colonial Times to 1970* (Washington DC: GPO, 1975), pt. 1, pp. 49, 316–20.

NOTES TO PAGES 32–34

65. The biggest boom occurred between 1950 and 1951, which witnessed about a 14 percent rise in installation. Note that the data on installation rates varies slightly from one source to another. These numbers are based on Steinberg, *TV Facts*, p. 142; and Lichty and Topping, *American Broadcasting*, p. 522.

66. The north-central and western states, which had relatively similar installation rates, lagged behind the northeast, while the south and southwest mountain areas were considerably behind the rest of the country. For statistics on regional differences, see "Communications," *Statistical Abstract of the United States*, no. 668 (Washington DC: GPO, 1959); U.S. Bureau of the Census, *Housing and Construction Reports*, Series H-121, nos. 1–5 (Washington DC: GPO, 1955–58); and Leo Bogart, *The Age of Television: A Study of Viewing Habits and the Impact of Television on American Life* (New York: Frederick Ungar, 1956), p. 15.

67. In 1949, Chicago's National Television and Electrical Living Show displayed a wide array of television sets to the public, while Mayor Victor Shaw of Charlotte, North Carolina, joined forces with television dealers and broadcasters proclaiming November 13th as the beginning of "Television Week." Once more, RCA made an aggressive attempt to introduce television to the public, staging a huge fair at New York's RCA Exhibition Hall in 1948. "Radio-TV Show to Attract Half-Million," *Broadcasting*, 3 October 1949, p. 56; "Television Week Set at Charlotte Mayor," *Broadcasting*, 38 November 1949, p. 13. The RCA exhibit was advertised in *Advertising and Selling*, March 1948, p. 84. For other exhibits, see "TV-Electronics Show," *Broadcasting*, 5 June 1950, p. 51; "Whither TV?" *Newsweek*, 31 July 1950, p. 52.

68. These prices are based on "Manufactures," *Statistical Abstract of the United States* (Washington DC: GPO, 1951–55); and Christopher H. Sterling and John M. Kittross, *Stay Tuned: A Concise History of American Broadcasting* (Belmont, CA: Wadsworth, 1978), p. 290.

69. *Consumer Reports*, March 1954, p. 116.

70. Tyler May, *Homeward Bound*, p. 20.

71. Roland Marchand has observed that "most housing developments were priced out of range of those below the medium income," and that "the migration to the suburbs was primarily conducted among the top 40 percent in family income." See Marchand, "Visions of Classlessness, Quests for Dominion: American Popular Culture, 1945–1960," *Reshaping America: Society and Institutions: 1945–1960*, ed. Robert H. Bremner and Gary W. Reichard (Columbus: Ohio State University Press, 1982), p. 168. The cheaper communities such as Levittown were originally populated by a mix of young professionals and lower-middle-class, blue collar workers. See Jackson, *Crabgrass Frontier*, p. 243. Still, as Jackson asserts, the postwar suburbs were typically characterized by economic homogeneity.

72. Such redlining practices were first established during the Depression. The Home Owners Loan Corporation (HOLC), which was signed into law in 1933, "devised a rating system that undervalued neighborhoods that were mixed, dense, or aging" (Jackson, *Crabgrass Frontier*, p. 197).

73. Betty Friedan, *The Feminine Mystique* (New York: W. W. Norton, 1963).

74. The work force estimations are based on Rochelle Gatlin, *American Women Since 1945* (Jackson, MS: University of Mississippi Press, 1987), p. 25.

75. Lillian Gilbreth, et al., *Management in the Home: Happier Living through Saving Time and Energy* (1954; Reprint, New York: Dodd, Mean & Company, 1955), p. 1.

76. Tyler May details this in *Homeward Bound*. For specific case studies and interviews from the period, see, for example, pp. 27–36, 183–207.

77. Sydnie Greenbie, *Leisure For Living* (New York: George W. Stewart, 1940), p. 220.

Chapter Two

1. *Better Homes and Gardens,* September 1949, p. 38.

2. In some cases, the television set was actually placed in the fireplace. Here, the objects were made to share the same system of meaning so that the familial values traditionally attributed to the fireplace were now also attributed to the television set. See, for example, *House Beautiful,* May 1954, p. 72; *Better Homes and Gardens,* August 1953, p. 10; *American Home,* June 1954, p. 48.

3. *House Beautiful,* September 1954, p. 153.

4. Television sets were often adorned with objects that connoted intellectual pursuits and high art, values traditionally associated with the piano. See, for example, *Ladies' Home Journal,* April 1951, p. 132; *House Beautiful,* November 1954, p. 220.

5. *Better Homes and Gardens,* March 1953, p. 72.

6. *House Beautiful,* January 1953, p. 76.

7. Kathi Norris, "How Now," *TV World,* August 1953, p. 54.

8. While the home magazines recommended substituting the television set for the piano, other evidence suggests that piano ownership might still have been significant for postwar families. Sales figures for the entire market show that the sale of pianos actually rose from 136,332 in 1940 to 172,531 in 1950, and by 1960 sales had increased to 198,200. Although these sales statistics alone cannot tell us how significant this rise was for the domestic market per se, they do caution us against assuming that the piano was actually phased out during the postwar years. See *Statistical Reference Index,* Music USA: 1982 Review of the Music Industry and Amateur Music Participation/American Music Conference, Report A2275-1 (Bethesda, MD: Congressional Information Service, 1983), p. 4. Also note that the National Piano Manufacturers Association saw radio as largely responsible for a 300 percent increase in sales during the late 1930s. The Association claimed, "Millions of listeners, who otherwise might never have attained an appreciation of music, are manifesting an interest in musical culture and endeavoring to become participants themselves." Cited in Davis, "Response to Innovation," p. 138.

9. George Nelson and Henry Wright, *Tomorrow's House: A Complete Guide For the Home-Builder* (New York: Simon and Schuster, 1946), p. 80.

10. *Better Homes and Gardens,* August 1950, p. 45.

11. Marchand, *Advertising the American Dream,* pp. 248–54.

12. Tyler May, *Homeward Bound,* p. 78.

13. William H. Whyte, Jr., *The Organization Man* (1956; Reprint, Garden City, NY: Doubleday, 1957).

14. Tyler May, *Homeward Bound,* p. 88.

15. See Barbara Ehrenreich, *The Hearts of Men: American Dreams and the Flight from Commitment* (Garden City, NY: Doubleday, 1983).

16. As Maureen Honey shows in her study of women's wartime magazine fiction, the Office of War Information gave suggestions to the magazine editors on ways in which to encourage married middle-class women to work. Honey, however, shows that magazines suggested wartime work for women was temporary, to be discarded when the GIs returned. Still, as Honey also shows, many women did not want to leave their jobs when men returned home. See *Creating Rosie the Riveter: Class, Gender and Propaganda During WWII* (Amherst: University of Massachusetts Press, 1984). Also see Susan M. Hartmann, *American Women in the 1940s: The Home Front and Beyond* (Boston: Twayne, 1982), pp. 163–205; and Tyler May, *Homeward Bound,* pp. 58–91.

17. Marynia Farnham and Ferdinand Lundberg, *The Modern Woman: The Lost Sex* (New York: Harper and Bros., 1947).

18. Jean and Eugene Benge, *Win Your Man and Keep Him* (New York: Windsor Press, 1948), p. 10. Cited in Tyler May, *Homeward Bound*, pp. 80–81.

19. Although feminine ideals and attitudes toward sexuality had changed considerably since the nineteenth century, the ideal woman of the 1950s shared a common problem with her Victorian ancestors—she was placed in the impossible position of taking on several incompatible roles at the same time. The efficient housewife was somehow supposed to transform herself into an erotic plaything for her husband at night. Even mothering was presented in terms of divided consciousness. In *Their Mothers' Daughers* (1956), psychiatrists Edward Strecker and Vincent Lathbury spoke of the "dual parental performance" that the working mother had to take on, telling women that "youngsters of both sexes feel uneasy about their mother's being cast in the father role. We know of one woman, who, since the death of her husband, has been quite successful in the literary field, who makes a point of being very feminine and occasionally even a bit 'helpless' with her children." Edward A. Strecker and Vincent T. Lathbury, *Their Mothers' Daughters* (Philadelphia: J. B. Lippincott Company, 1956), p. 29. Ironically, Strecker and Lathbury were prescribing what psychiatrist Joan Reviere had previously analyzed as a female defense mechanism against negative conceptions about working women. In her seminal 1929 study "Womanliness as a Masquerade," Reviere showed how successful female professionals felt compelled to adopt a heightened veneer of femininity as a strategy for coping with their "transgression" of normative gender roles. By posing as super feminine types, these women were able to minimize anxiety about the negative reactions they anticipated from male associates. See the article reprinted in *Formations of Fantasy*, ed. Victor Burgin, et al. (London: Methuen, 1986), pp. 35–44.

20. In the early 1950s, the median marriage age ranged between twenty and twenty-one; the average family started having children in the beginning of the second year of marriage and had three to four children. For birthrates, see Rochelle Gatlin, *American Women Since 1945* (Jackson, MS: University Press of Mississippi, 1987), pp. 51, 55, 61; Hartmann, *American Women in the 1940s*, pp. 25, 91, 170, 213; Glenna Matthews, *"Just A Housewife": The Rise and Fall of Domesticity in America* (New York: Oxford University Press, 1987), p. 265; and Tyler May, *Homeward Bound*, pp. 7, 136–37; on marriage and divorce rates, see Hartmann, pp. 163–65; Gatlin, p. 51; and Tyler May, pp. 6–8, 21, 59, 117, 185. Hartmann demonstrates that the divorce rate rose among returning veterans and their wives, but levelled off in 1946 (p. 165). Tyler May explains that "college enrollments increased for women during the postwar years, but not at the same rate as for men." Since "college degrees did not guarantee the same entry into well-paying jobs and careers for women as they did for men," many "white women were likely to drop out of college in order to marry." Conversely, while much fewer black women were enrolled in college, those who were enrolled tended to finish their degrees. Black women did so, May argues, because they expected to be employed and expected that college degrees would improve their job prospects (pp. 78–79).

21. For labor force statistics, see Gatlin, *American Women Since 1945*, pp. 24–48; Julia A. Matthaei, *An Economic History of Women in America: Women's Work, the Sexual Division of Labor, and the Development of Capitalism* (New York: Schocken Books, 1982), especially p. 252; Hartmann, *American Women in the 1940s*, pp. 90–95; Tyler May, *Homeward Bound*, pp. 76–77; Matthews, *"Just A Housewife,"* p. 267.

22. A 1955 survey showed that while most women worked for financial reasons, 21 percent worked to fulfill "a need for accomplishment" or to keep busy and meet people; even the women who worked for economic purposes cited the benefits of companionship and a sense of independence. A 1958 survey showed that almost two-thirds of married women cited their jobs as their chief source of feeling "important" or "useful," while only

one-third mentioned housekeeping. See Gatlin, *American Women since 1945*, p. 33, citing Marion G. Sobol, "'Commitment to Work,'" *The Employed Mother in America*, ed. F. Ivan Nye and Lois Wladis Hoffman (Chicago: Rand McNally, 1963), pp. 40–63; Robert Weiss and Nancy Samuelson, "Social Roles of American Women: Their Contribution to a Sense of Usefulness and Importance," *Journal of Marriage and the Family* 20 (November 1958), pp. 358–66. For more on women's conceptions of work, see Tyler May, *Homeward Bound*, pp. 75–87.

23. Marchand, *Advertising The American Dream*, pp. 335–59; and T. J. Jackson Lears, "From Salvation to Self-realization: Advertising and the Therapeutic Roots of Consumer Culture, 1880–1930," *The Culture of Consumption: Critical Essays in American History, 1880–1980* (New York: Pantheon, 1983), pp. 1–38.

24. *American Home*, October 1950, p. 25. For other examples of the product-as-center motif, see *House Beautiful*, November 1949, p. 1; *Ladies' Home Journal*, October 1948, p. 115; *House Beautiful*, February 1949, p. 1.

25. For examples, see *Ebony*, March 1950, p. 7; *Ebony*, August 1953, p. 3; *Ebony*, December 1955, p. 103. Advertisements in *Ebony* also showed white viewers and white actors on screen.

26. Bogart, *Age of Television*, p. 101. As a cautionary note, I would suggest that in his attempt to present a global, synthetic picture of the television audience, Bogart often smooths over the contradictions in the studies he presents. This attempt at global synthesis goes hand in hand with Bogart's view that the television audience is a homogeneous mass and that television programming further erases distinctions. He writes, "The levelling of social differences is part of the standardization of tastes and interests to which the mass media give expression, and to which they also contribute. The ubiquitous TV antenna is a symbol of people seeking—and getting—the identical message" (p. 5). Through this logic of mass mentality, Bogart often comes to conclusions that oversimplify the heterogeneity of audience responses in the studies he presents.

27. Edward C. McDonagh, et al., "Television and the Family," *Sociology and Social Research* 40 (4) (March–April 1956), p. 117.

28. John W. Riley, et al., "Some Observations on the Social Effects of Television," *Public Opinion Quarterly* 13 (2) (Summer 1949), p. 232. This study was cosponsored by Rutgers University and CBS.

29. Raymond Stewart, cited in Bogart, *Age of Television*, p. 100.

30. Harry Henderson, "The Mass-Produced Suburbs: I. How People Live in America's Newest Towns," *Harpers*, November 1953, p. 28.

31. For more on this and other aspects of the public concern over juvenile delinquents, see James Gilbert, *A Cycle of Outrage: America's Reaction to the Juvenile Delinquent in the 1950s* (New York: Oxford University Press, 1986). Gilbert shows that while public officials, educators, psychologists, and other "experts" increasingly focused on criminal youth, "the incidence of juvenile crime does not appear to have increased enormously during this period." Gilbert goes on to show that crime statistics were imprecise and, since the definition of juvenile crime and the policing of it had changed over the course of the century, it is difficult to prove that the postwar period actually witnessed a substantial rise in teenage crimes. Given this, Gilbert argues that the perception of juvenile delinquency in the 1950s was based less on reality than it was on the way crime was labeled and reported, as well as the general worries about the future direction of American society (pp. 66–71).

32. McDonagh, et al., "Television and the Family," p. 116.

33. Stewart, cited in Bogart, *Age of Television*, p. 100.

34. *Better Homes and Gardens*, October 1955, p. 209. In the 1952 House hearings on the content of radio and television programs, Representative Joseph Byrson from South

Carolina testified to a similar domestic situation. He claimed, "My two younger children spent much of their time watching the neighbor's television. In a year or two, when my youngest son had graduated from a local junior high school, he wanted to go away to school. I believe, if I had purchased a television set at that time, he would have finished high school here in Washington." House Interstate and Foreign Commerce Committee, *Hearings before a Subcommittee of the Committee on Interstate and Foreign Commerce: Investigation of Radio and Television Programs*, 82d Cong., 2d Sess., 3 June 1952, H. Res. 278, p. 23 (hereafter cited as *Hearings: Radio and Television Programs*). Congressional witness Lloyd C. Halvorson (an economist for the National Grange, a farm organization) stated a similar problem. He told the Committee, "You may ask, why don't I turn the television set off or throw it out. If I do, the children will just go over to the neighbors, and to keep them home would make them think I was cruel. It would make an impossible family situation" (p. 93). The hearings reconvened on June 4th, 5th, and 26th, 1952; September 16th, 17th, 23d, 24th, 25th, and 26th, 1952; and December 3d, 4th, and 5th, 1952.

35. "Television Has Become a Member of the Family," *House Beautiful*, September 1951, p. 118.

36. *House Beautiful*, January 1955, pp. 39–43, 84.

37. See Kasson, *Civilizing the Machine*, pp. 183–234 and Marx, *Machine in the Garden*, pp. 227–353.

38. Susman, *Culture as History*, p. 268.

39. Joseph Wood Krutch, "Have You Caught On Yet. . . ." *House Beautiful*, November 1951, p. 221.

40. "Television: The New Cyclops," *Business Week*, 10 March 1956, reprinted in *Television's Impact on American Culture*, ed. William Y. Elliot (East Lansing, MI: Michigan State University Press, 1956), pp. 340–54; Calder Willingham, "Television Giant in the Living Room," *American Mercury*, February 1952, p. 115. This article is especially interesting since Willingham presents a kind of metacriticism of the anxieties about television during the period.

41. For discussions of this, see Jeanne Allen, "The Social Matrix of Television: Invention in the United States," *Regarding Television*, ed. E. Ann Kaplan (Los Angeles: University Publications of America, 1983), pp. 109–20 and Davis, "Response to Innovation," pp. 100–101. For examples of postwar articles, see Bill Reiche, "Television Is the Navy's School Teacher," *Popular Mechanics*, November 1948, pp. 125–27, 270, 272; Devon Francis, "TV Takes over Test Pilot's Job," *Popular Science*, March 1951, pp. 144–48; "Dismantling Bombs by TV," *Science Digest*, January 1954, inside cover.

42. Newton Minow, "The Vast Wasteland" (Address to The 39th Annual Convention of the National Association of Broadcasters, Washington DC: 9 May 1961).

43. *Look*, 21 April 1953, p. 18.

44. *American Home*, September 1953, p. 104; *House Beautiful*, March 1955, p. 78.

45. Helen Little, "How to Decorate for Television," *House Beautiful*, August 1949, pp. 66, 69.

46. It should be noted here that the term "contemporary" referred to a kind of watered-down modernism that appealed to middle-class tastes in a way that "highbrow" modernism did not. The furniture trade journal, *Home Furnishings*, was a forum for debates about the public response to modernism. The journal took a conservative attitude toward it, establishing a canon of contemporary design that was an extremely softened version of the idiosyncratic objects made by famous modernist furniture makers. The journal, in this regard, was responding to the popular skepticism about modernism during the period. In the fifties, there were various attempts to mass-produce modernist furniture, and several department stores coordinated their retail efforts with the Museum of Modern

Art's furniture exhibits. However, the popular press often scorned the extremism of modern styles, representing modernism as being contrary to middle-class family ideals. Editor Elizabeth Gordon of *House Beautiful* even called modernist design "The Threat to the Next America" in her bitter essay that argued that modernism was an international conspiracy originating in Nazi Germany with the machine aesthetics of the Bauhaus School. See *House Beautiful*, April 1953, editorial.

47. *American Home*, February 1955, p. 44; *Better Homes and Gardens*, May 1955, p. 28.

48. "Now You See It. . . . Now You Don't," *American Home*, September 1951, p. 49; *House Beautiful*, December 1953, p. 145; *American Home*, November 1953, p. 60; *Popular Science*, March 1953, p. 87.

49. Jean Baudrillard, *For A Critique of The Political Economy of the Sign*, trans. Charles Levin (St. Louis: Telos Press, 1981), pp. 53–57.

50. For examples of this sort, see *House Beautiful*, October 1953, p. 193; Beulah Donohue Hochstein, "Small Room, but Space for Living, Eating, and Sleeping," *Better Homes and Gardens*, November 1951, p. 197; *American Home*, November 1954, p. 127.

51. "Television Has Become a Member of the Family," p. 66; *American Home*, September 1951, p. 48.

52. *Better Homes and Gardens*, December 1952, p. 133.

53. Bogart, *Age of Television*, p. 97.

54. William Porter, "Is Your Child *Glued* to TV, Radio, Movies, or Comics?" *Better Homes and Gardens*, October 1951, p. 125.

55. *Ladies' Home Journal*, April 1950, p. 237. For a similar cartoon, see *Ladies' Home Journal*, December 1955, p. 164.

56. *House Beautiful*, June 1951, p. 8; *Life*, 26 November 1951, p. 11.

57. "Bang! You're Dead," *Newsweek*, 21 March 1955, p. 35.

58. See Norman Cousins, "The Time Trap," *Saturday Review of Literature*, 24 December 1949, p. 20.

59. Edward M. Brecher, "TV, Your Children, and Your Grandchildren," *Consumer Reports*, May 1950, p. 231.

60. For more on this, see Mark West, *Children, Culture and Controversy* (Hamden, CT: Archon, 1988).

61. Davis, "Response to Innovation," pp. 209–16. Davis argues that 60 percent of the discussions on television's effect on children took place in these special interest magazines (p. 170).

62. Jacqueline Rose, *The Case of Peter Pan: The Impossibility of Children's Fiction* (London: Macmillan, 1984).

63. Cited in Fredric Wertham, *Seduction of the Innocent* (New York: Rinehart, 1953), p. 377.

64. Gilbert, *Cycle of Outrage*, p. 102 also observes that the Supreme Court used Wertham's testimony and implicitly accepted his theories of media effects in the 1952 case Beauharnais vs. Illinois, 343 U.S. 250 (1952), which upheld a censorship law concerning negative portrayals of racial groups.

65. A 1954 Gallup Poll showed that 70 percent of all adults who were questioned thought that crime comics and mystery and crime programs on television were at least in part responsible for the rise in juvenile delinquency. See Bogart, *Age of Television*, p. 273.

66. Agnes Maxwell Peters to Fredric Wertham, 1 August 1948, Wertham MS, cited in Gilbert, *Cycle of Outrage*, p. 105; Margaret Mead, "Problems of the Atomic Age," *The Survey*, July 1949, p. 385, cited in Tyler May, *Homeward Bound*, p. 27.

67. Ellen Wartella and Sharon Mazzarella, "A Historical Comparison of Children's

Use of Leisure Time," *For Fun and Profit: The Transformation of Leisure into Consumption,* ed. Richard Butsch (Philadelphia: Temple University Press, 1990), pp. 183–85.

68. PTA reform reported in "Another TV Censor," *Variety,* 5 October 1949, p. 27. For early school board activities, see, for example, "TV Also Alarms Cleve. Educators," *Variety,* 22 March 1950, p. 29; "Students Read, Sleep Less in TV Homes, Ohio School Survey Shows," *Variety,* 5 April 1950, p. 38.

69. "Catholic Council Plans TV Legion of Decency Via National Monitoring," *Variety,* 29 August 1951, pp. 1, 63; "Catholic Women Attack TV for Crime Overplay," *Variety,* 25 October 1950, p. 1; "Detroit vs. TV 'Kid Abuses': City Fathers in Organized Stand," *Variety,* 20 December 1950, p. 25; "Catholics Urge Legion of Decency To Clean Up Programs For Kids," *Variety,* 14 March 1951, pp. 1, 18.

70. "TV Censorship: One Down, More to Go," *Broadcasting,* 5 March 1951, pp. 54–56. See chapter 5 for more on censorship debates.

71. The networks also tried to police themselves. As early as 1948, NBC executives considered problems of standards and practices in television. *NBC Standards and Practices Bulletin—No. 7: A Report on Television Program Editing and Policy Control,* November 1948, NBC Records, Box 157: Folder 7, Wisconsin Center Historical Archives, State Historical Society, Madison. In 1951, NBC became the first network to establish standards for children's shows, crime shows, mention of sex on programs, proper costuming, etc. See *NBC Code,* 1951, NBC Records, Box 163: Folder 1, Wisconsin Center Historical Archives, State Historical Society, Madison. For a general explanation of the code, see "Catholic Council Plans TV Legion," *Variety,* 29 August 1951, p. 63.

72. *Hearings: Radio and Television Programs,* 1952.

73. Chairman Senator Robert C. Hendrickson cited in Committee on the Judiciary United States Senate, *Hearings before the Subcommittee to Investigate Juvenile Delinquency: Juvenile Delinquency (Television Programs),* 83d Cong., 2d sess., 5 June 1954, S. Res. 89, p. 1 (hereafter cited as *Hearings: Juvenile Delinquency (Television Programs)* (Kefauver Hearings). The Committee reconvened on October 19th and 20th, 1954, and also met on April 6th and 7th, 1955, to continue the debates.

74. Newton Minow, "Is TV Cheating Our Children?" *Parents,* February 1962, pp. 52–53; "Minow Magic," *Newsweek,* 14 August 1963, p. 66.

75. Bogart, *Age of Television,* p. 268.

76. Jack Gould, "What Is Television Doing To Us?" *New York Times Magazine,* 12 June 1949, p. 7. *Popular Science,* March 1955, took the logic of human agency to its literal extreme, presenting a "lock-and-key" TV that "won't work until Mama sees fit and turns it on with her key" (p. 110).

77. *Better Homes and Gardens,* October 1955, p. 202.

78. Bogart, *Age of Television,* p. 289. In the 1954 Kefauver Hearings, similar findings about the relationship between social class and parents' attitudes toward television were made part of the official record. See Committee on the Judiciary United States Senate, *Juvenile Deliquency (Television Programs),* 5 June 1954, pp. 21–23.

79. Reverend Everett C. Parker summarizing findings from the Information Service, Central Department of Research and Survey, National Council of the Churches of Christ in the United States of America, *Parents, Children, and Television—The First Television Generation* (New York: n.p., 1954). Reprinted and summarized in Committee on the Judiciary United States Senate, *Hearings: Juvenile Delinquency (Television Programs),* 5 June 1954, p. 28. The surveys in Bogart's account include a 1955 study from the *New York Herald Tribune* that studied 1,200 school children; a 1952 and 1955 study by the American Research Bureau of children ages six to sixteen; H. H. Remmars, R. E. Horton and R. E. Mainer, *Attitudes of High School Students toward Certain Aspects of Television* (Indiana: Purdue

University, 1953). All are summarized in Bogart, pp. 252–56. See also the *Better Homes and Gardens* survey cited above and summarized in Bogart.

80. For example, in 1952, the American Research Bureau observed that by the age of seven, one child in four had stayed up to watch Berle. Bogart, *Age of Television*, p. 254.

81. "Kids Not Kidding," *Variety*, 29 March 1950, p. 33.

82. Even researchers at the time interpreted parental control in these terms. Bogart, for example, suggested that "one reason why high school teen-agers receive less supervision in their TV viewing is that their program tastes apparently are considerably closer to those of their parents" (p. 262).

83. Dorothy Diamond and Frances Tenenbaum, "Should You Tear 'Em Away from TV?" *Better Homes and Gardens*, September 1950, p. 56.

84. *Better Homes and Gardens*, March 1955, p. 173.

85. Diamond and Tenenbaum, p. 239.

86. Porter, "Is Your Child *Glued* to TV," p. 178.

87. Jacques Donzelot, *The Policing of Families* (New York: Pantheon, 1979). Donzelot discusses the history of the public regulation of families in France.

88. The housing program of Better Homes in America was formalized in its advice manual of 1931. See Blanche Halbert, *The Better Homes Manual* (Chicago: University of Chicago Press, 1931). The last chapter listed twelve governmental and educational organizations that regulated housing and home improvements. Note too that children were one of the main interests of outside agencies and reform movements. In the 1880s, childhood emerged as a distinct sociological category, something to be studied apart from other family issues, and by 1912 the category was officially recognized by the formation of a Federal Bureau of Children. For more, see Wartella and Mazzarella, "Historical Comparison." For a discussion of the development of child psychology see Fass, *The Damned and the Beautiful.*

89. Bogart, *Age of Television*, pp. 283–85 cites various psychologists who also claimed that television was a symptom of wider family problems. See also Eleanor Mac-Coby, one of the first social scientists to study children's use of television. She argued that "children will spend more time watching television if they are highly frustrated in real life than if they are not." See MacCoby, "Why Do Children Watch Television?" *Public Opinion Quarterly* 18 (3) (Fall 1954), p. 240.

90. This situation was aggravated by the fact that popular experts often blamed parents for their children's fixation to television. In 1950, Jack Gould wrote, "If they are willing to face up to the truth, the average television parents probably must concede that they themselves in part brought about their child's preoccupation with television. A television receiver becomes an exceptionally handy 'baby sitter' if parents want a little relief from youthful spirits. . . . Later they may find the habit difficult to break." See Gould, "Video and Children," *The New York Times*, 8 January 1950, sec. X, p. 15. Similarly, in "The Time Trap," Norman Cousins blamed parents for the "unspoken parental benediction" of their children's bad viewing habits.

91. Lloyd Shearer, "The Parental Dilemma," *House Beautiful*, October 1951, pp. 220, 222.

92. Sylvia O'Neill, "Are You Guilty of Juvenile Delinquency?" *Home Furnishings*, August 1954, p. 14.

93. "Video's Juvenile Audience," *Advertising and Selling*, August 1948, p. 99.

94. "Television Tempest," *Newsweek*, 27 November 1950, p. 62.

95. John Crosby, "Parents Arise! You Have Nothing to Lose but Your Sanity," *Out of the Blue: A Book about Radio and Television* (New York: Simon and Schuster, 1952), p. 115.

96. Robert Lewis Shayon, "Who Remembers Papa?" *Saturday Review*, 13 October

1951, p. 43; Bob Taylor, "What is TV Doing to MEN?" *TV Guide,* 26 June 1953, p. 15; "Daddy with a Difference," *Time,* 17 May 1954, p. 83. For additional examples, see Eleanor Harris, "They Always Get Their Man," *Colliers,* 25 November 1950, p. 34; "The Great Competitor," *Time,* 14 December 1953, p. 62; "Perpetual Honeymoon," *Time,* 22 March 1954, p. 82.

97. For example, vaudeville sketches such as "A Wife's Strategem" showed women insulting and nagging their male partners. See Staples, *Male-Female Comedy Teams,* pp. 144–45. Such scenarios could also be seen in films such as the Vitaphone serial, *The Naggers,* whose shrewish wife henpecked her ineffectual husband.

98. Andreas Huyssen, "Mass Culture as Woman: Modernism's Other," *After the Great Divide: Modernism, Mass Culture, Postmodernism* (Bloomington and Indianapolis: Indiana University Press, 1986), p. 47.

99. Douglas discusses this in "Amateur Operators and American Broadcasting" and in *Inventing American Broadcasting,* pp. 187–215.

100. Covert, "'We May Hear Too Much,'" p. 205.

101. Philip Wylie, *Generation of Vipers* (1942; Reprint, New York: Holt, Rinehart and Winston, 1955), pp. 199–200.

102. Ibid., pp. 214–15.

103. Ibid., pp. 213–14.

104. As William Lafferty has pointed out to me, Bruce is actually watching the previous week's episode of *Fireside Theatre,* a western melodrama entitled, "His Name is Jason."

105. This is not to say that Hollywood movies always presented strong male characters. In fact, the figure of the dandy was a popular male type in twenties and thirties films. What I am arguing here is that the episode represents the dichotomy between Hollywood and television through the opposition between virile and passive male heroes.

106. Robert Lewis Shayon, "Daddy Pinza and Daddy Thomas," *Saturday Review,* 1 November 1953, pp. 54–55.

107. Eleanor E. MacCoby, "Television: Its Impact on School Children," *Public Opinion Quarterly,* 15 (3) (Fall 1951), pp. 421–44. This kind of research filtered down to the industry trade journals, which reported on the decline in family interaction in television households.

108. Jack Gould, "TV Daddy and Video Mama: A Dirge," *The New York Times Magazine,* 14 May 1950, p. 56; *Better Homes and Gardens,* September 1950, p. 56; *TV Guide,* 21 August 1953, p. 11. MacCoby, "Television," p. 438, and Bogart, *Age of Television,* p. 261, also summarized numerous other studies that suggested television was interfering with meals.

109. John Crosby, "What's Television Going to Do To Your Life?" *House Beautiful,* February 1950, p. 125. This is one of the rare occasions in which a popular television critic wrote for a woman's home magazine. It is also one of the few articles that was addressed to a male reader.

110. Phil Hiner, "Television as You Like It," *Popular Science,* May 1954, p. 216.

111. Goodman Ace, "A Man's TV Set Is His Castle," *The Saturday Review,* April 1953, reprinted in Ace, *The Book of Little Knowledge: More Than You Want to Know about Television* (New York: Simon and Schuster, 1955), pp. 165–67.

112. Nelson and Wright, *Tomorrow's House,* p. 76.

113. *House Beautiful,* October 1951, p. 168.

114. Alfred Politz Research, Inc., *National Survey of Radio and Television Sets Associated with U.S. Households* (New York: The Advertising Research Foundation, 1954), p. 71.

115. *Better Homes and Gardens,* November 1951, p. 263.

116. *Better Homes and Gardens*, June 1953, p. 126.

117. *American Home*, September 1955, p. 17.

118. Nancy Crawford, "Young Home Builders," *Ladies' Home Journal*, November 1953, p. 182.

119. *Better Homes and Gardens*, October 1955, p. 139.

120. For examples of advertisements depicting divided families, see *Better Homes and Gardens*, November 1953, p. 40; *Better Homes and Gardens*, December 1952, p. 30; *American Home*, November 1951, p. 10.

121. *American Home*, December 1953, p. 84.

122. Phil Hiner, "Television As You Like It," *Popular Science*, May 1954, pp. 216-18. A similar device was marketed by Philco.

123. "Two-Headed TV Set Displays Different Shows at Once," *Popular Science*, March 1954, p. 156.

Chapter Three

1. This stove was mentioned in *Sponsor*, 4 June 1951, p. 19. It was also illustrated and discussed in *Popular Science*, May 1952, p. 132. The *Popular Science* reference is interesting because this men's magazine did not discuss the TV component of the stove as a vehicle for leisure, but rather showed how "a housewife can follow telecast cooking instructions step-by-step on the TV set built into this electric oven." Perhaps in this way, the magazine allayed men's fears that their wives would use the new technology for diversion as opposed to useful labor.

2. Nancy Folbre, "Exploitation Comes Home: A Critique of the Marxist Theory of Family Labour," *Cambridge Journal of Economics* 6 (1982), pp. 317-29.

3. Henri Lefebvre, foreward, *Critique de la Vie Quotidienne* (Paris, L'Arche, 1958), reprinted in *Communication and Class Struggle*, ed. Armond Mattelart and Seth Siegelaub, trans. Mary C. Axtmann (New York: International General, 1979), p. 136.

4. See David Morley, *Family Television: Cultural Power and Domestic Leisure* (London: Comedia, 1986); and Ann Gray, "Behind Closed Doors: Video Recorders in the Home," *Boxed In: Women and Television*, ed. H. Baehr and G. Dyer (New York: Pandora, 1987), pp. 38-54.

5. Tania Modleski, "The Rhythms of Reception: Daytime Television and Women's Work," *Regarding Television*, pp. 67-75. See also the fourth chapter in Modleski, *Loving With A Vengeance: Mass-Produced Fantasies for Women* (New York: Methuen, 1984).

6. Nick Browne, "The Political Economy of the Television (Super) Text," *Quarterly Review of Film Studies* 9 (3) (Summer 1984), p. 176.

7. William Boddy, "The Rhetoric and Economic Roots of the American Broadcasting Industry," *Cinetracts* 6 (2) (Spring 1979), pp. 37-54.

8. William Boddy, "The Shining Centre of the Home: Ontologies of Television in the 'Golden Age'," *Television in Transition*, ed. Phillip Drummond and Richard Paterson (London: British Film Institute, 1985), pp. 125-33.

9. For a detailed analysis of the rise and fall of the DuMont Network, see Gary Newton Hess, *An Historical Study of the DuMont Television Network* (New York: Arno Press, 1979).

10. Cited in "DuMont Expansion Continues," *Radio Daily*, 12 April 1949, p. 23. See also "DuMont Skeds 7 A.M. to 11 P.M.," *Variety*, 22 September 1948, p. 34; "Daytime Tele As Profit Maker," *Variety*, 27 October 1948, pp. 25, 33; "Round-Clock Schedule Here to Stay As DuMont Programming Makes Good," *Variety*, 10 November 1948, pp. 29, 38.

11. Cited in "Daytime Video: DuMont Plans Afternoon Programming," *Broadcasting-Telecasting*, 28 November 1949, p. 3. See also "WTTG Gives Washington Regular Daytime Video with New Program Setup," *Variety*, 19 January 1949, p. 30; "Video Schedule on Co-ax Time," *Variety*, 12 January 1949, p. 27; "DuMont's 'Mother' Goes Network in Daytime Spread," *Variety*, 27 November 1949, p. 27.

12. "ABC, CBS, NBC Cold to Full Daytime Schedule; DuMont to Go It Alone," *Variety*, 6 October 1948, p. 27.

13. "CBS All-Day TV Programming," *Variety*, 26 January 1949, p. 34; "Video Schedule on Co-Ax Time," *Variety*, 12 January 1949, p. 27; "WNBT, N.Y., Swinging into Line as Daytime Video Airing Gains Momentum," *Variety*, 19 January 1949, p. 24; Bob Stahl, "WNBT Daytime Preem Has Hausfrau Pull but Is Otherwise Below Par," *Variety*, 9 February 1949, p. 34; "Full CBS Airing Soon," *Variety*, 2 March 1949, p. 29; "Kathi Norris Switch to WNBT Cues Daytime Expansion for Flagship," *Variety*, 1 March 1950, p. 31.

14. Cited in "Daytime TV," *Broadcasting-Telecasting*, 11 December 1950, p. 74.

15. *Sponsor*, 4 June 1951, p. 19.

16. *Newsweek*, 24 September 1951, p. 56.

17. *Televiser*, September 1951, p. 20.

18. In the early 1950s, many of the shows were sustaining vehicles—that is, programs that were aired in order to attract and maintain audiences, but that had no sponsors.

19. "DuMont Skeds 7 A.M. to 11 P.M.," *Variety*, 22 September 1948, p. 25.

20. "Pat 'N' Johnny," *Variety*, 1 March 1950, p. 35. This example bears interesting connections to Rick Altman's more general theoretical arguments about the aesthetics of sound on television. Altman argues that television uses sound to signal moments of interest, claiming that, "the sound track serves better than the image itself the parts of the image that are sufficiently spectacular to merit closer attention on the part of the intermittent viewer." See Altman, "Television/Sound," *Studies in Entertainment: Critical Approaches to Mass Culture*, ed. Tania Modleski (Bloomington and Indianapolis: Indiana University Press, 1986), p. 47.

21. Robert C. Allen, *Speaking of Soap Operas* (Chapel Hill: University of North Carolina Press, 1985).

22. See "Daytime Video: DuMont Plans Afternoon Program" and "DuMont Daytime 'Shoppers' Series Starts," *Broadcasting-Telecasting*, 12 December 1949, p. 5.

23. As I discuss in chapter 5, some variety programs included fifteen minute sitcoms and soap operas.

24. "TV's 'Stars in the Afternoon'," *Variety*, 3 October 1951, p. 29.

25. "Women's Magazine of the Air," *Variety*, 9 March 1949, p. 33; "Women's Page," *Variety*, 1 June 1949, p. 34.

26. NBC had particular problems securing sponsors and, especially during 1951 and 1952, many of its shows were sustaining programs. So critical had this problem become that in fall of 1952 NBC temporarily cut back its schedule, giving afternoon hours back to affiliates. Affiliates, however, complained that this put them at a competive disadvantage with CBS affiliates. See "NBC-TV's 'What's the Use?' Slant May Give Daytime Back to Affiliates," *Variety*, 3 September 1952, p. 20; "Daytime TV—No. 1 Dilemma," *Variety*, 24 September 1952, pp. 1, 56; "NBC-TV to Focus Prime Attention on Daytime Schedule," *Variety*, 24 December 1952, p. 22; "NBC—TV Affiliates In Flareup," *Variety*, 6 May 1953, p. 23.

27. Weaver's concept was adopted by CBS executives who in 1952 instituted the "12 plan" that gave sponsors a discount for buying twelve participations during the daytime schedule. "Day TV Impact," *Broadcasting*, 3 November 1952, p. 73; Bob Stahl, "CBS-TV's Answer to 'Today,'" *Variety*, 12 November 1952, pp. 23, 58.

28. John H. Porter, memo to TV network salesmen, 11 June 1954, NBC Records, Box 183: Folder 5, Wisconsin Center Historical Archives, State Historical Society, Madison.

29. George Rosen, "Garroway 'Today' Off to Boff Start As Revolutionary News Concept," *Variety,* 16 January 1952, p. 29.

30. Joe Meyers and Bob Graff, cited in William R. McAndrew, confidential memo to John K. Herbert, 23 March 1953, NBC Records, Box 370: Folder 22, Wisconsin Center Historical Archives, State Historical Society, Madison.

31. *Daytime Availibilities: Program Descriptions and Estimates,* 1 June 1954, NBC Records, Box 183: Folder 5, Wisconsin Center Historical Archives, State Historical Society, Madison.

32. "Early Morning Inserts Get WNBT Dress-Up," *Variety,* 13 August 1952, p. 26.

33. "For the Girls at Home," *Newsweek,* 15 March 1954, p. 92. NBC's advertising campaign for *Home* was unprecedented for daytime programming promotion, costing $976,029.00 in print, on-air promotion, outdoor advertising, and novelty gimmicks. See Jacob A. Evans, letter to Charles Barry, 28 January 1954, NBC Records, Box 369: Folder 5, Wisconsin Center Historical Archives, State Historical Society, Madison.

34. Jacob A. Evans, letter to Charles Barry, 28 January 1954, NBC Records, Box 369: Folder 5, Wisconsin Center Historical Archives, State Historical Society, Madison.

35. In a promotional report, NBC boasted that on *Today's* first broadcast, Kiplinger received 20,000 requests for a free copy of the magazine. Matthew J. Culligan, sales letter, 27 January 1953, NBC Records, Box 378: Folder 9, Wisconsin Center Historical Archives, State Historical Society, Madison.

36. The report cited here was commentary for a slide presentation given by Coffin to about fifty researchers from ad agencies and manufacturing companies in the New York area. *Commentary for Television's Daytime Profile: Buying Habits and Characteristics of the Audience,* 10 June 1954, NBC Records, Box 183: Folder 5, Wisconsin Center Historical Archives, State Historical Society, Madison. For the actual survey, see W. R. Simmons and Associates Research, Inc., *Television's Daytime Profile: Buying Habits and Characteristics of the Audience,* 15 September 1954, NBC Records, Box 183: Folder 8, Wisconsin Center Historical Archives, State Historical Society, Madison. A short booklet reviewing the findings was sent to all prospective advertisers; *Television's Daytime Profile: An Intimate Portrait of the Ideal Market for Most Advertisers,* 1 September 1954, NBC Records, Box 183: Folder 5, Wisconsin Center Historical Archives, State Historical Society, Madison. For NBC's exploitation of the survey, see also Ed Vane, letter to Mr. Edward A. Antonili, 7 December 1954, NBC Records, Box 183: Folder 5, Wisconsin Center Historical Archives, State Historical Society, Madison; Hugh M. Bellville, Jr., letter to Robert Sarnoff, 27 July 1954, NBC Records, Box 183: Folder 5, Wisconsin Center Historical Archives, State Historical Society, Madison; Thomas Coffin, letter to H. M. Beville, Jr., 21 July 1954, NBC Records, Box 183: Folder 5, Wisconsin Center Historical Archives, State Historical Society, Madison. The survey also made headlines in numerous trade journals, newspapers, and magazines. For press coverage, see NBC's *clipping file,* NBC Records, Box 183: Folder 5, Wisconsin Center Historical Archives, State Historical Society, Madison.

37. Edward Stasheff, *The Television Program: Its Writing, Direction, and Production* (New York: A. A. Wyn, 1951), p. 47.

38. Consumer spectacles were further achieved through rear-screen projection, an "aerial" camera that captured action with a "telescoping arm," and mechanical devices such as a weather machine that adorned products in a mist of rain, fog, sleet, or hail. *Daytime Availabilities: Program Descriptions and Cost Estimates,* 1 June 1954, NBC Records, Box 183: Folder 5, Wisconsin Center Historical Archives, State Historical Society, Madison.

39. Charles C. Barry, memos to Richard Pinkham, 2 March 1954, 3 March 1954, and 4 March 1954, NBC Records, Box 369: Folder 5, Wisconsin Center Historical Archives, State Historical Society, Madison.

40. Franklin Sisson, *Thirty Television Talks* (New York, n.p., 1955), p. 144. Cited in Giraud Chester and Garnet R. Garrison, *Television and Radio* (New York: Appleton-Century-Crofts, Inc., 1956), p. 414.

41. Caroline Burke, memo to Ted Mills, 20 November 1953, NBC Records, Box 377: Folder 6, Wisconsin Center Historical Archives, State Historical Society, Madison; Arlene Francis, cited in Earl Wilson, *The NBC Book of Stars* (New York: Pocket Books, 1957), p. 92.

42. Cited in Wilson, *The NBC Book*, p. 94.

43. Sylvester L. Weaver, memo to Harry Bannister, 10 October 1952, NBC Records, Box 378: Folder 9, Wisconsin Center Historical Archives, State Historical Society, Madison.

44. Joe Meyers, cited in William R. McAndrew, confidential memo to John K. Herbert, 23 March 1953, NBC Records, Box 370: Folder 22, Wisconsin Center Historical Archives, State Historical Society, Madison.

45. A. A. Schechter, "'Today' As An Experiment Bodes Encouraging Manana," *Variety,* 16 July 1952, p. 46. NBC also advertised *Today* by claiming that "people are actually changing their living habits to watch 'Today.'" See *Sponsor,* 25 February 1952, pp. 44–45.

46. *Daytime Availabilities: Program Descriptions and Cost Estimates,* 1 June 1954, NBC Records, Box 183: Folder 5, Wisconsin Center Historical Archives, State Historical Society, Madison.

47. Walter Benjamin, "The Work of Art in the Age of Mechanical Reproduction," in *Illuminations: Essays and Reflections,* ed. Hannah Arendt (New York: Schocken, 1969), pp. 217–51.

48. *Ladies' Home Journal,* April 1955, p. 130. See also *Ladies' Home Journal,* February 1955, p. 95; *Good Housekeeping,* July 1955, p. 135.

49. *The New Yorker,* 3 June 1950, p. 22.

50. Crosby, "What's Television Going to Do to Your Life?" *House Beautiful,* February 1950, p. 125.

51. *American Home,* October 1955, p. 14.

52. Walter Adams and E. A. Hungerford, Jr., "Television: Buying and Installing It Is Fun; These Ideas Will Help," *Better Homes and Gardens,* September 1949, p. 38; *American Home,* December 1954, p. 38.

53. *American Home,* May 1955, p. 138. The cartoon was part of an advertisement for the *Yellow Pages.*

54. *House Beautiful,* June 1952, p. 59.

55. W. W. Ward, "Is It Time To Buy Television?" *House Beautiful,* October 1948, p. 220.

56. *Ladies' Home Journal,* May 1953, p. 148.

57. "The Wonderful Anti-Statics," *House Beautiful,* January 1955, p. 89; *Ladies' Home Journal,* November 1948, p. 90.

58. Gertrude Brassard, "For Early Tea and Late TV," *American Home,* July 1952, p. 88.

59. In August 1949, for example, *House Beautiful* suggested that a swiveling cabinet would allow women to "move the screen, not the audience" (p. 69). Although portable sets were not heavily marketed in the early 1950s, they were sometimes presented as the ideal solution to the problem of moving the heavy console set.

60. *House Beautiful,* May 1952, p. 138.

61. Wright, *Building the Dream,* p. 172.

62. *House Beautiful*, June 1951, p. 121.

63. Vivian Grigsby Bender, "Please a Dining Room!" *American Home*, September 1951, p. 27.

64. *Better Homes and Gardens*, December 1952, p. 144; *Better Homes and Gardens*, February 1953, p. 169; see also *American Home*, September 1953, p. 102.

65. *House Beautiful*, November 1948, p. 5.

66. Edith Ramsay, "How to Stretch a Day," *American Home*, September 1949, p. 66; *House Beautiful*, December 1950, p. 77.

67. *American Home*, February 1954, p. 32.

68. *House Beautiful*, November 1954, p. 158. For additional examples, see *American Home*, November 1953, p. 60; *Better Homes and Gardens*, December 1951, p. 7; *TV Guide*, 18 December 1953, p. 18.

69. *Better Homes and Gardens*, October 1952, p. 177.

70. Laura Mulvey, "Visual Pleasure and Narrative Cinema," *Screen* 16 (3) (1975), pp. 6–18. Since the publication of Mulvey's article, numerous feminists—including Mulvey—have theorized ways that women might find subjective pleasures in classical cinema, and feminists have also challenged the idea that pleasure in the cinema is organized entirely around scenarios of "male" desire. For a bibliography on this literature and a forum on contemporary views on female spectatorship in the cinema, see *Camera Obscura* 20–21 (May–September 1989).

71. W. W. Ward, "Is It Time to Buy Television?" *House Beautiful*, October 1948, p. 172.

72. *House Beautiful*, May 1955, p. 131.

73. *Better Homes and Gardens*, October 1953, p. 151. There is one exception to this rule of male body posture, which I have found in the fashionable men's magazine *Esquire*. While *Esquire* depicted the slovenly male viewer, it also showed men how to watch television in fashion by wearing clothes tailored specifically for TV viewing. In these cases, the male body was relaxed, and the men still smoked and drank liquor, but they were posed in more aesthetically appealing ways. See "Town-Talk Tables and Television," *Esquire*, January 1951, pp. 92–93; and "Easy Does It Leisure Wear," *Esquire*, November 1953, p. 74. The figure of the fashionable male television viewer was taken up by at least one male clothing company, The Rose Brothers, who advertised their men's wear by showing well-dressed men watching television and by promising, "You Can Tele-Wise Man by His Surretwill Suit." See *Colliers*, 1 October 1949, p. 54.

74. Robert M. Jones, "Privacy Is Worth All That It Costs," *Better Homes and Gardens*, March 1952, p. 57.

75. This is not to say that television was the only domestic machine to disrupt representations of gender. Roland Marchand, for example, has argued that advertisements for radio sets and phonographs reversed traditional pictorial conventions for the depiction of men and women. Family-circle ads typically showed husbands seated while their wives were perched on the arm of the chair or sofa. In most of the ads for radios and phonographs in his sample, the opposite is true. Marchand argues that "in the presence of culturally uplifting music, the woman more often gained the right of reposed concentration while the (more technologically inclined) man stood prepared to change the records or adjust the radio dials." See *Advertising the American Dream*, pp. 252–53. When applied to television, Marchand's analysis of radio does not seem to adhere since men were often shown seated and blatantly unable to control the technology.

76. I am borrowing Natalie Zemon Davis's phrase with which she describes how women in preindustrial France were able to invert gender hierarchies during carnival festivities and even, at times, in everyday life. See "Women On Top," *Society and Culture in Early Modern France* (Stanford, CA: Stanford University Press, 1975), pp. 124–51.

77. *Popular Science,* May 1954, p. 177; *Esquire,* March 1951, p. 10; Jack O'Brien, "Offsides in Sports," *Esquire,* November 1953, p. 24.

78. Marsh, *Suburban Lives,* p. 82.

79. Greenbie, *Leisure for Living,* p. 210. Greenbie, in fact, presented a quite contradictory account of mechanization in the home, at times seeing it as the man's ally, at other times claiming that modern machines actually took away male authority.

80. "Home is for Husbands Too," *Esquire,* June 1951, p. 88.

81. In addition, companies that produced home-improvement products and workshop tools continually used television sets in their illustrations of remodeled rooms. Typically here, the Masonite Corporation promoted its do-it-yourself paneling in an advertisement that displayed a television set in a "male room" just for Dad. See *Better Homes and Gardens,* August 1951, p. 110. For similar ads, see *American Home,* June 1955, p. 3; *Better Homes and Gardens,* February 1953, p. 195; *American Home,* November 1952, p. 105. It should be noted that some of these ads also showed women doing the remodeling work.

82. "From Readers' Albums of Television Photos," *Popular Science,* December 1950, p. 166. See also "TV's Images Can Be Photographed," *Popular Science,* August 1950, pp. 184–85; R. P. Stevenson, "How You Can Photograph the Fights Via Television," *Popular Science,* February 1951, pp. 214–16.

Chapter Four

1. Gary Simpson, cited in William I. Kaufman, ed., *How to Direct for Television* (New York: Hastings House, 1955), p. 13.

2. S. C. Gilfillan, "The Future Home Theater," *The Independent,* 17 October 1912, pp. 836–91.

3. Daniel J. Boorstin, *The Americans: The Democratic Experience* (New York: Vintage Books, 1973), p. 393.

4. In 1954, *Fortune* magazine estimated that over the course of the past decade, nine million people had moved to suburban towns across the nation. Cited in Jackson, *Crabgrass Frontier,* p. 238. Jackson also shows that much of this migration to suburbia had to do with the fact that building in the postwar years was heavily concentrated in suburban areas. The Bureau of Labor Statistics survey of 1946–47 determined that at least 62 percent of residential construction took place in the suburbs.

5. For example, in *Crabgrass Frontier* Jackson argues that "the single-family tract house—post-World War II style—whatever its aesthetic failings, offered growing families a private haven in a heartless world" (p. 244). Often this "haven in a heartless world" logic sees television as the cultural indicator of the return to Victorian domestic ideals. In *The American Family Home,* Clifford Edward Clark, Jr., argues that "many families conceded that the television, by bringing entertainment into the home, strengthened a sense of family cohesiveness and self-interest. . . . Almost without thinking, middle-class suburbanites took the protected-home vision of the nineteenth-century reformers and turned it into their central preoccupation" (p. 31). Clark does acknowledge that the new suburbanites held to "an implicit ideal of community" and often became active in civic affairs. While he recognizes this interest in community at the level of social activity, he maintains that the haven model for the home persisted at the ideological level. My argument, on the other hand, maintains that the ideology of suburbanization was not merely a return to the nineteenth-century ideal; instead, it contained within it the terms of the contradiction between community involvement and domestic privacy. In other words, the ideal was that one could be alone in one's home, but still be attached to the community.

6. In "The Mass-Produced Suburbs, I" *Harpers*, November 1953, p. 26, Henderson argued that being involved in organizations was a way to gain status in the community: "Since no one can acquire prestige through an imposing house, or inherited position, activity—the participation in community or group affairs—becomes the basis of prestige. In addition, it is the quickest way to meet people and make friends." In his follow-up article, he explored community associations more fully, stating that "nearly everyone belongs to organizations," and concluding again that "one becomes a 'wheel' or personage of some importance and influence, only in one way: by working hard in organizations, accepting responsibility, and speaking up in meetings." See "Rugged American Collectivism: The Mass-Produced Suburbs, Part II" *Harpers*, December 1953, pp. 81, 86. Similarly, Tyler May, *Homeward Bound*, p. 25, observes that there were sixty-six adult organizations in Chicago's suburb, Park Forest.

7. Henderson, "The Mass-Produced Suburbs," p. 26.

8. For popular books on architecture and interior decor, see, for example, *Sunset Homes for Western Living* (San Francisco: Lane Publishing Co., 1946); Robert Woods Kennedy, *The House and the Art of Its Design* (Huntington, NY: Robert E. Krieger, 1953); Cliff May, *Western Ranch Houses* (Menlo Park, CA: Lane Book Co., 1958); Katherine Morrow Ford and Thomas H. Chreighton, *The American House Today* (New York: Reinhold, 1951).

9. *Sunset Homes for Western Living*, p. 11.

10. Morrow Ford and Chreighton, *The American House Today*, p. 139.

11. *Architectural Digest* 14 (2) (ca. 1955), p. 23; *Architectural Digest*, June 1948, p. 47. See also *Architectural Digest* 15 (3) (ca. 1957), p. 17; and *Architectural Digest*, June 1948, p. 90.

12. Boorstin, *The Americans*, p. 345. Boorstin sees this "leveling of place" as part of a wider "ambiguity" symptomatic of the democratic experience.

13. *Sunset Homes for Western Living*, p. 14.

14. Thomas H. Hutchinson, *Here Is Television, Your Window On the World* (1946; reprint, New York: Hastings House, 1948), p. ix.

15. Charles Siepmann, *Radio, Television and Society* (New York: Oxford University Press, 1950), p. 340.

16. Marx, *Machine in the Garden*, see especially pp. 194–96.

17. Beecher and Beecher Stowe, *American Woman's Home*, pp. 91, 96.

18. Wright discusses this in *Building the Dream*, p. 107.

19. For an interesting discussion of how modern architecture and interior decor were popularized through the cinema, see Donald Albrecht, *Designing Dreams: Modern Architecture in the Movies* (New York: Harper & Row, 1986).

20. See, for example, "Home Without Compromises," *American Home*, January 1952, p. 34; *Better Homes and Gardens*, September 1955, p. 59; *Good Housekeeping*, September 1951, p. 106. The use of maps and globes as a decorative accessory was typical. See *Good Housekeeping*, September 1952, pp. 79, 83; *Architectural Digest* 15 (ca. 1957), p. 153. Domestic objects such as lamps were designed to look like globes. See, for example, *Home Furnishings*, November 1953, p. 59.

21. *Theatre Arts*, October 1948, p. 1.

22. *Better Homes and Gardens*, October 1953, p. 48; *Better Homes and Gardens*, December 1953, p. 21.

23. *Better Homes and Gardens*, March 1953, p. 130. For other examples of celestial/sky imagery, see *Better Homes and Gardens*, October 1953, p. 135; *Newsweek*, 19 April 1954, p. 8; *Better Homes and Gardens*, October 1952, p. 35.

24. The longevity of this convention is perhaps best demonstrated by the twelve-year-long run of *The Love Boat*, a program that revolved around the adventures of a cruise

ship and its visits to exotic tourist traps. Think too of the longstanding use of large window views or mural landscapes for the backdrops in talk shows such as *The Tonight Show* and *Late Night With David Letterman.*

25. Fortune editors, "$30 Billion for Fun," *Mass Leisure,* ed. Eric Larrabee and Rolf Meyersohn (1955; Reprint, Glencoe, Il: The Free Press, 1958), pp. 162–68.

26. *House Beautiful,* February 1950, p. 126. If, however, the television theater was figured to replace the movie palace, the television and movie industries were not necessarily at odds in the women's magazines. Instead, various advertisements show cooperative marketing strategies. Although Hollywood producers often attempted to keep their stars out of television in the early years, they did allow a number of appearances on television and in advertisements which promoted both the television and the film product. In 1952, for example, Sylvania and RKO cosponsored an advertisement in which movie actress Jane Russell endorsed Sylvania television tubes. The caption beneath her picture read, "Miss Russell is co-starring in *The Las Vegas Story,* an RKO Radio Picture." In *Better Homes and Gardens,* April 1952, p. 180.

27. *Better Homes and Gardens,* October 1953, p. 8.

28. *Home Furnishings,* November 1950, p. 42; "TV Ups Furniture Sales," p. 64. For more on television's influence on furniture sales, see John Meck, "Appliance Buyers— Here's How to Up Your Television Sales 40%," *Home Furnishings,* September 1950, p. 27; "Video Steals Chi Show on Summer Home Furnishings; See Banner Year," *Variety,* 28 June 1950, p. 31; and W. J. Baxter, *The Future of Television: How It Will Affect Different Institutions,* Bulletin 11A (New York: Baxter International Economic Research Bureau, 12 March 1949), NBC Records, Box 106: Folder 13, Wisconsin Center Historical Archives, State Historical Society, Madison. The report states: "We find, in our survey, there are more and more families who give 'television parties' and have to buy more of what are called 'occasional chairs.' They are also more inclined to look for new lamps, new rugs and other items of furniture" (p. 13).

29. See, for example, the advertisement for Wilson Jump furniture from which this citation was taken. In *House Beautiful,* May 1955, p. 12.

30. *House Beautiful,* September 1954, p. 10. The Kroehler Company referred to its retail outlets as "TV Centers." Other companies that offered complete television furnishing ensembles include Flexsteel Furniture and the Valley Upholstery Corporation. See *House Beautiful,* March 1955, p. 6; and "With an Eye . . . On the Viewer," *Televiser,* April 1950, p. 16.

31. *House Beautiful,* August 1949, p. 66.

32. "Where Shall We Put the Television Set?" *Good Housekeeping,* August 1951, p. 107.

33. Kennedy, *House and Art of Its Design,* p. 181.

34. *Popular Science,* August 1950, pp. 174–81.

35. *American Home,* May 1951, p. 40.

36. The October 1949 issue of *House Beautiful* was entirely devoted to this subject, and it displayed television sets in the new climate-controlled rooms.

37. *Better Homes and Gardens,* October 1952, p. 41. For other examples of tie-ins between television and temperature-regulating household products, see *American Home,* July 1955, p. 16; *American Home,* November 1950, p. 123; *Better Homes and Gardens,* June 1953, p. 157; *House Beautiful,* October 1955, p. 235; and *Better Homes and Gardens,* July 1953, p. 36.

38. Television Research Institute, *TV vs. Movie Competition,* 10 September 1948, NBC Records, Box 106: Folder 12, Wisconsin Center Historical Archives, State Historical Society, Madison.

39. *House Beautiful*, September 1955, p. 97. Hopalong Cassidy wallpaper, a Roy Rogers chuckwagon, a Howdy Doody chair, and Lone Ranger juvenile furniture were also available. See "TV Ups Furniture Sales," *Broadcasting*, 26 June 1950, p. 64.

40. *Time*, 19 February 1951, p. 74.

41. James W. Carey and John J. Quirk, "The Mythos of the Electronic Revolution," *Communication As Culture*, pp. 113-41. For related issues see Marx, *Machine in the Garden;* Kasson, *Civilizing the Machine;* and Wolfgang Schivelbusch, *Disenchanted Night: The Industrialization of Light in the Nineteenth Century*, trans. Angela Davies (Berkeley: California University Press, 1988).

42. Marvin, *When Old Technologies Were New*, pp. 200-01.

43. See Carey and Quirk, "The Mythos of the Electronic Revolution" and "The History of The Future," *Communication As Culture*, pp. 173-200; Andrew Feldman, "Selling the 'Electrical Idea' in the 1920s: A Case Study in the Manipulation of Consciousness," (MA thesis, University of Wisconsin-Madison, 1989).

44. Douglas, *Inventing American Broadcasting*, pp. 306-9.

45. President of Adam Hat Stores, Inc., letter to Mr. Niles Trammell, ca. July 1935, NBC Records, Box 104: Folder 5, Wisconsin Center Historical Archives, State Historical Society, Madison; *Continuing Study of Television Homes* cited in *Variety*, 26 January 1949, p. 38.

46. Sylvester L. (Pat) Weaver, "The Task Ahead: Making TV the 'Shining Center of the Home' And Helping Create A New Society of Adults," *Variety*, 6 January 1954, p. 91. The hope for a new democratic global village was also expressed by other industry executives. David Sarnoff, chairman of the Board of RCA, claimed: "When television has fulfilled its destiny, man's sense of physical limitation will be swept away, and his boundaries of sight and hearing will be the limits of the earth itself. With this may come a new horizon, a new philosophy, a new sense of freedom and greatest of all, perhaps, a finer and broader understanding between all the peoples of the world." Cited in William I. Kaufman, *Your Career In Television* (New York: Merlin Press, 1950), p. vii.

47. Cited in Bogart, *Age of Television*, p. 98.

48. David Riesman, "Recreation and the Recreationist," *Marriage and Family Living* 16 (1) (February 1954), p. 23.

49. *Hearings: Radio and Television Programs*, 5 June 1952, p. 83.

50. Ibid., p. 84.

51. Eugene David Glynn, "Television and the American Character—A Psychiatrist Looks at Television," *Television's Impact on American Culture*, ed. William Y. Elliot (East Lansing, MI: Michigan State University Press, 1956), p. 177.

52. Jay B. Nash, *Spectatoritis* (New York: Holston House, 1932), p. 5.

53. A similar scene is found in *The Three Stooges* comedy short, "Scheming Schemers" (ca. 1946), when the Stooges, posing as plumbers, mistakingly squirt a gush of water through the television set of a wealthy matron who is showing her guests a scene of Niagara Falls on television.

54. Levine, *Highbrow Lowbrow*.

55. George Lipsitz, *Time Passages: Collective Memory and American Popular Culture* (Minneapolis: University of Minnesota Press, 1990), p. 8. See also Kasson, *Amusing the Million*.

56. Harry Hershfield, "Humorist's Warm Slant On That New Robot—TV," *Variety*, 2 January 1952, p. 105.

57. *American Home*, January 1951, p. 89.

58. "If You Want to Camouflage Your Television Set," *Good Housekeeping*, November 1954, pp. 70-71. This decorative suggestion solved two aesthetic problems. The window

shade camouflaged the set while the map brought an illusion of the outside world into the home.

59. Robert M. Yoder, "Be Good! Television's Watching!" *Saturday Evening Post,* 14 May 1949, pp. 29, 131.

60. Even before the postwar period, this fear was conveyed by films such as Fritz Lang's science-fiction classic, *Metropolis* (1927), which pictured the evil ruler/father of a fascist society who used a television monitor to survey his subjects as they labored in a fantastic underground factory. Similarly, Charlie Chaplin's *Modern Times* (1937) presented a chilling (if humorous) depiction of a factory worker who, during a trip to the bathroom, was monitored on large screen television by his evil boss.

61. Calder Willingham, "Television Giant in the Living Room," *American Mercury,* February 1952, p. 117.

62. See chapters 2 and 5 for more on this.

63. *Esquire,* July 1952, p. 87.

64. *Ladies' Home Journal,* May 1949, p. 30.

65. *Broadcasting,* 22 March 1954, p. 110.

66. *Better Homes and Gardens,* February 1952, p. 154.

67. *TV Guide,* January 1955, back cover.

68. *Better Homes and Gardens,* September 1953, p. 177.

69. See, for example, an advertisement for Durall window screens that shows a housewife blocking her husband's view of a bathing beauty on the television set in *Good Housekeeping,* May 1954, p. 187. See also the cartoon from *Collier's* that appears in this chapter on p. 124.

70. *The New York Times Magazine,* 11 December 1949, p. 20; *TV Guide,* 6 November 1953, p. 14.

71. In focusing on this sense of female isolation, I also want to point out the problems with Joshua Meyrowitz's theoretical account of television's "merging of masculinity and femininity" in *No Sense of Place: The Impact of Electronic Media On Social Behavior* (New York: Oxford University Press, 1985), pp. 187–225. Meyrowitz argues that television was one of the factors leading to the women's movement because it brought traditionally male spaces to the home and thus allowed women to participate in the masculine sphere from which they were typically excluded. "Television's first and strongest impact is on the perception that women have of the public male world and the place, or lack of place, they have in it. Television is an especially potent force for integrating women because television brings the public domain to women. . . ." (p. 224). There are several problems with Meyrowitz's position. Firstly, although he is making a historical-causal argument about television's impact on women's lives, he lacks historical perspective. In his attempt to provide a general theory of the social effects of electronic media, he elides historical evidence that would make his argument problematic. Secondly, he doesn't explain why other communication technologies that brought public space into the home did not have the effects he assumes television did, and he doesn't consider the popular fears about television's potential to confine women to their homes. The final and most crucial problem with his argument is that he bases his claims on an essentialist notion of space. In other words, he assumes that public space is male and private space is female. But public spaces like the office or the theater are not simply male; they are organized according to categories of sexual difference. In these spaces certain social positions and subjectivities are produced according to the placement of furniture, the organization of entrances and exits, the separation of washrooms, the construction of partial walls, and so forth. Thus, television did not bring "male" space into "female" space; instead, it transposed one system of sexually organized space onto another.

72. *Better Homes and Gardens,* November 1951, p. 218.

73. *Ladies' Home Journal,* January 1952, p. 64.

74. McDonagh, et al., "Television and the Family," *Sociology and Social Research* 40 (4) (March–April 1956), pp. 117, 119.

75. Survey cited in Betty Betz, "Teens and TV," *Variety,* 7 January 1953, p. 97.

76. *Good Housekeeping,* September 1955, p. 137.

77. *House Beautiful,* November 1955, p. 126. For other examples of this sort, see *The New York Times Magazine* 12 June 1949, p. 6; *Colliers,* 9 December 1950, p. 58; *Life,* 6 December 1948, p. 3.

78. W. J. Baxter, Baxter International Economic Research Bureau, *The Future of Television: How It Will Affect Different Industries,* Bulletin 11A (New York, 12 March 1949), p. 12. In NBC Records, Box 106: Folder 13, Wisconsin Center Historical Archives, State Historical Society, Madison. Similarly, after reviewing numerous studies from the fifties, Bogart claims in *The Age of Television,* "In the early days, 'guest viewing' was a common practice" (p. 102). For a summary of the actual studies, see Bogart, pp. 101–7. For additional studies that show the importance of guest viewing in the early period, see Riley, et al., "Some Observations on the Social Effects of Television," *Public Opinion Quarterly* 13 (2) (Summer 1949), pp. 223–34 (this article was an early report of the CBS-Rutgers University studies begun in the summer of 1948); McDonagh, et al., "Television and the Family," p. 116; "When TV Moves In," *Televiser,* October 1950, p. 17 (this is a summary of the University of Oklahoma surveys of Oklahoma City and Norman, Oklahoma); Philip F. Frank, "The Facts of the Medium," *Televiser,* April 1951, p. 14; and "TV Bonus Audience in The New York Area," *Televiser,* November 1950, pp. 24–25.

79. McDonagh, et al., "Television and the Family," p. 116.

80. *Esquire,* July 1953, p. 110; Bob Taylor, "Let's Make Those Sets Functional," *TV Guide,* 21 August 1953, p. 10.

81. Herbert J. Gans, "The Sociology of New Towns: Opportunities for Research," *Sociology and Social Research* 40 (4) (March–April 1956), p. 238. Later, in *The Levittowners: Ways of Life and Politics in a New Suburban Community* (New York: Pantheon, 1967), Gans suggested that residents had a less pessimistic view of the new suburbs. While he acknowledged women's boredom and isolation, he argued that home ownership gave many Levittowners a sense of pride.

82. Whyte, *Organization Man,* p. 314. An advertisement for Levittown also evoked the idea of friendship, telling prospective residents that they would "enjoy life, for here in Levittown all of our 37,000 men, women, and children have a common purpose: to be happy, friendly, neighborly." See *The New York Times,* 25 September 1949, sec. R, p. 3.

83. Henderson, "Rugged American Collectivism, The Mass-Produced Suburbs, Part II," *Harpers,* December 1953, p. 80.

84. John Keats, *The Crack in the Picture Window* (1956; Reprint. Boston: Houghton Mifflin Company, 1957), p. 80.

85. *NBC Promo for Ethel and Albert for Use on The Golden Windows,* 31 August 1954, NBC Records, Box 136: Folder 15, Wisconsin Center Historical Archives, State Historical Society, Madison.

86. Gilbert Seldes, "Domestic Life in the Forty-ninth State," *Saturday Review,* 22 August 1953, p. 28.

87. George Lipsitz, "The Meaning of Memory: Family, Class and Ethnicity in Early Network Television," *Time Passages,* pp. 39–76.

88. *I Married Joan's* Aunt Vera, *My Favorite Husband's* Gillmore and Myra Cobbs, *Burns and Allen's* Harry and Blanche Morton, and *Ozzie and Harriet's* Thorny Thornberry

were among the faithful companions in the early 1950s sitcoms. Later in the 1950s and in the early 1960s, sitcoms extended this convention (e.g., *Leave It To Beaver*'s Eddie Haskell and *Donna Reed*'s Midge and Dave Kelsy). Although set in urban locales, early sitcoms that focused on middle-class families also included neighbor characters (e.g., *I Love Lucy*'s Fred and Ethel Mertz, *My Little Margie*'s Mrs. Odetts, and *Make Room For Daddy*'s Benny).

89. Madelyn Pugh Davis, interview, *I Love Lucy: The Very First Show,* CBS, 30 April 1990.

90. Horace Newcomb makes a distinction betwen situation comedies—that is, comedies based on situations, complications, and confusions that take place in a relatively closed space—and domestic comedies that he sees to be more realistic in their spatial articulations of the home and in their portrayal of family life. He also claims that the domestic comedy provided glimpses of the neighborhood outside. See the second chapter in Newcomb, *Television: The Most Popular Art* (Garden City, NY: Anchor Press/Doubleday, 1974).

91. *Better Homes and Gardens,* November 1951, p. 162.

92. *Better Homes and Gardens,* October 1952, p. 215.

93. *House Beautiful,* November 1949, p. 77.

94. *Life,* 27 April 1953, p. 12. For other examples of this sort, see *Life,* 26 October 1953, p. 53; *Life,* 22 November 1948, p. 59; *Life,* 5 October 1953, p. 87. A related advertising motif was the phone call. Here, advertisers gave the illusion that television was a form of interpersonal communication by depicting a television screen on which a person was engaged in a phone conversation. Since the human figure always seemed to acknowledge the reader with a sideways glance, the ads suggested that television would involve potential consumers in a kind of unmediated dialogue. See *Better Homes and Gardens,* November 1953, p. 53; *Life,* 27 April 1953, pp. 16–17; *American Home,* November 1954, p. 127.

95. *Advertising and Selling,* January 1951, p. 101.

96. Sylvester L. Weaver, "Thoughts on the Revolution: Or, TV Is a Fad, Like Breathing," *Variety,* 11 July 1951, p. 42.

97. "NBC to Project 'American Family' in 3-Hour Saturday Night Showcase," *Variety,* 3 August 1949, p. 31.

98. *Variety,* 6 August 1952, p. 26.

99. For a review of the show, see *Variety,* 30 January 1952, p. 31. Note that the particular episode I have seen is aimed clearly at a female audience, with its pitch for women's stockings and its promise of a date with Cesana; however, Cesana addresses the home viewer as if she were a man, specifically his pal who has been stood up for a double date. Note, as well, that there was a radio version of this program in which a female host courted male viewers in the late night hours. Entitled *Two at Midnight,* the program was aired locally on WPTR in Albany and is reviewed in *Variety,* 22 October 1952, p. 28.

100. "DuMont Daytime," p. 5 (see ch. 3, n. 22).

101. "CBS-TV's 'Studio Without Walls' New Gitlin Entry," *Variety,* 24 September 1952, p. 43.

102. "Guest In the House," *Newsweek,* 12 October 1953, p. 64.

103. This article appeared in John Crosby's popular anthology, *Out of the Blue: A Book about Radio and Television,* pp. 170–72.

Chapter Five

1. *The Television Code of the National Association of Radio and Television Broadcasters,* 2d ed., March 1954. Reprinted in *Hearings: Juvenile Delinquency (Television Programs),* 5 June 1954, p. 45.

2. This program was reviewed in *Time*, 9 December 1949, p. 55; *Variety*, 21 December 1949, p. 28.

3. This chapter is based on over 1,000 family comedy episodes. I refer to the genre by its various appellations: family comedy, family sitcom, and domestic sitcom.

4. The earliest prime-time network offerings include *Mary Kay and Johnny* (which was successively aired on DuMont, NBC, and CBS between 1947 and 1950), *Wren's Nest* (ABC, 1949), *Growing Paynes* (DuMont, 1948–49), *Mixed Doubles* (NBC, 1949), *The O'Neills* (DuMont, 1949–50), *The Life of Riley* (NBC, 1949–58), *One Man's Family* (NBC, 1949–55), *The Aldrich Family* (NBC, 1949–53), *The Ruggles* (ABC, 1949–52), and *The Goldbergs* (which was successively aired on DuMont, CBS, and NBC 1949–55).

5. *Variety*, 25 August 1948, p. 32.

6. Edward Stasheff, *The Television Program: Its Writing, Direction, and Production* (New York: A. A. Wyn, 1951), p. 25. This book had a chart showing how television deviated from theater, film, and radio (p. 26); Caroll O'Meara, *Television Program Production* (New York: Ronald Press, 1955), p. 174.

7. My research concentrates on critical reviews in national magazines and *The New York Times* (which chiefly expressed the views of east coast critics), as well as the Hollywood industry trade journal, the weekly *Variety* (which, it should be noted, was read by television executives in numerous parts of the country, but also originated in the east). Future research might locate nuances in national tastes by comparing television criticism in local newspapers throughout the country.

8. Gilbert Seldes, *Writing For Television* (Garden City, NY: Doubleday, 1952), p. 32; Jack Gould, "Live vs. 'Canned,'" *The New York Times Magazine*, 5 February 1956, p. 27. For more on critical commentary, see Boddy, "From the 'Golden Age' to the 'Vast Wasteland,'" pp. 104–15.

9. For an analysis of the connections between vaudeville and motion picture comedies, see Henry Jenkins, III, "'What Made Pistachio Nuts?': Anarchistic Comedy and the Vaudeville Aesthetic," (Ph.D. diss., University of Wisconsin, Madison, 1989). Jenkins shows how anarchistic comedy's integration of the vaudeville aesthetic helped to undermine the style of classical realism used in the majority of big-budget Hollywood films. He also shows how this cycle of films worked to transgress middle-class tastes in humor. For related issues, see Steve Seidman, *Comedian Comedy: A Tradition in the Hollywood Film* (Ann Arbor: UMI Research Press, 1981).

10. Stasheff, *Television Program*, p. 21.

11. Boddy, "From the 'Golden Age' to the 'Vast Wasteland,'" pp. 104–15.

12. *Lobby Ceremonies*, 1950, NBC Records, Box 162: Folder 10, Wisconsin Center Historical Archives, State Historical Society, Madison.

13. "ABC Sets Ragtime Teeoff Splash for WJZ-TV; Reprise Palace Vaude," *Variety*, 4 August 1948, p. 26.

14. Jack Benny, cited in Walter Kingson, et al., *Broadcasting Television and Radio* (New York: Prentice Hall, 1955), pp. 3–4; Delbert Mann, cited in William I. Kaufman, ed., *How to Direct For Television* (New York: Hastings House, 1955), p. 70; Kingson, et. al., *Broadcasting*, p. 107.

15. Samuel Chotzinoff, "The Future of Music on Television," *House Beautiful*, August 1949, p. 113.

16. See, for example, Jack Gould, "Durable Burns and Allen," *The New York Times*, 3 December 1950, sec. X, p. 13; Jack Gould, "Inside U.S.A.," *The New York Times*, 9 October 1949, sec. X, p. 11; Jack Gould, "Ed Wynn on TV," *The New York Times*, 16 October 1949, sec. X, p. 11; Grace and Paul Hartman, "Is There a Doctor in the House?" *Variety*, 26 July 1950, p. 40; Nat Kahn, "TV Must Develop Camera Technique," *Variety*, 3 March 1949, pp. 29, 40; William Molyneux, "Less Than Meets the Eye," *Theatre Arts*, August

1953, pp. 69–72; Mordi Gassner, "Advancing Television Technique," *Televiser*, May 1950, pp. 9–11; D. P. Bowles, "What's Ahead in TV Programming and Production?" *Advertising and Selling*, April 1950, p. 136.

17. Orrin E. Dunlap, *The Future of Television* (New York: Harper and Brothers, 1947), p. 87.

18. This wasn't simply a taste standard; it was also motivated by economic factors. As Robert Vianello has argued, the networks saw live-origination as an ideal way in which to compete for hegemony over the airwaves. Since live-origination was a distinct capability of the networks, it allowed them to compete successfully with numerous telefilm producers and packagers during the early period. By promoting the superiority of live television, the networks, in effect, could maintain power over affiliates and advertisers. See Vianello, "The Power Politics of 'Live' Television," *Journal of Film and Video* 37 (Summer 1985), pp. 26–40 and "The Rise of the Telefilm and the Network's Hegemony over the Motion Picture Industry," *Quarterly Review of Film Studies* 9 (3) (Summer 1984), pp. 204–18.

19. "Defense of Staying Live," *Variety*, 5 January 1955, p. 92. By this point, Pat Weaver clearly recognized the industry trend for film and even expressed his willingness to compromise, admitting that "recording a live show on film can be good." However, he asserted that it could never be "as good as a live show." In this particular case, he was promoting his new idea of live spectaculars, what we might now call specials, with which he hoped to exploit his parent company's color system. In his study of Pat Weaver, Vance Kepley, Jr., also argues that Weaver's preference for live-origination over filmed programming was directly related to his attempt to court affiliate stations. Broadcasters, Weaver feared, would have no reason to sign network-affiliate contracts if the programs they received from the network could also be purchased from movie producers or telefilm syndicators. See Kepley, "The Weaver Years at NBC," *Wide Angle* 12 (2) (April 1990), pp. 46–62.

20. The reasons for the industry's switch from live to filmed formats has been documented by Boddy, "From the 'Golden Age' to the 'Vast Wasteland'"; Barnouw, *Tube of Plenty*; and Tino Balio, ed., *Hollywood in the Age of Television* (Boston: Unwin Hyman, 1990). Production costs, production schedules, and changes in the structure of network-advertiser relations, as well as shortages of talent, teleplay properties, and studio space, all provided good reasons for the networks to move to Hollywood and use film. Furthermore, as William Lafferty has shown, the early efforts of independent syndicators and program packagers proved the viability of filmed television—especially its potential for extra profits in reruns. See Lafferty, "No Attempt at Artiness, Profundity, or Significance: Fireside Theatre and the Rise of Filmed Television Programming," *Cinema Journal* 27 (1) (Fall 1987), pp. 23–47. In 1953, when the fledgling ABC network merged with United Paramount Theaters, the wedding of film and television was given network status. Filmed programming, produced by Hollywood studios, was particularly set in place in 1955 when ABC cooperated with Disney to produce *Disneyland*. See William Boddy, "The Studios Move into Prime Time: Hollywood and the Television Industry in the 1950s," *Cinema Journal* 24 (4) (Summer 1985), pp. 23–37. Situation comedies, action adventures, and westerns produced by both Hollywood majors and, to a lesser degree, independents, became a staple of network television by the end of the decade.

21. David Swift, "OZZIEMAMAPEEPERS-VILLE," *Variety*, 29 July 1953, p. 40.

22. *Variety*, 19 January 1949, p. 27; *Variety*, 27 October 1948, p. 26.

23. "Just a Radio Hangover: Few Properties Built for Video," *Variety*, 8 April 1953, p. 1.

24. J. R. Poppele, "Moral Responsibility Cited as Challenge to Television," *Variety*, 28 July 1948, p. 28.

25. Peter Lind Hayes, "Stay in the Parlor," *Variety,* 3 January 1951, p. 104.

26. For an analysis of the critical discourses on anthology dramas, see Boddy, "From the 'Golden Age' to the 'Vast Wasteland,'" pp. 104–15.

27. The notable exception to this was *Gulf Playhouse* (also called *1st Person*), which used subjective camera to place the viewer in the position of the leading character. Furthermore, it should be noted that theater directors who moved into television were interested in developing forms of experimental theater on the new medium. *Theatre Arts* sometimes spoke of experimental techniques, such as theater-in-the-round, that producers hoped to adapt to television. By 1953, however, the magazine stopped considering such possibilities and, more generally, the whole field of avant-garde techniques was marginalized as television increasingly moved to Hollywood, where major studios developed factory methods of production.

28. Stasheff, *The Television Program,* p. 22.

29. For the development of bourgeois theater and the creation of genteel audiences see Levine, *Highbrow Lowbrow.* For the audience composition and class/ethnic address of the vaudeville theater, see Albert F. McLean, Jr., *American Vaudeville as Ritual* (Louisville: University of Kentucky Press, 1965); Robert C. Allen, *Vaudeville and Film, 1895–1915: A Study of Media Interaction* (New York: Arno Press, 1980); and Staples, *Male-Female Comedy Teams.*

30. Barnouw argues that the anthology drama fell from grace in the 1954–55 season when sponsors and their agencies began to demand control of scripts. He details how sponsors revised the political content of "Thunder on Sycamore Street," whose script dealt with the topic of racism. See *Tube of Plenty,* pp. 154–68.

31. "Inside Television," *Variety,* 21 April 1948, p. 31. In fact, there was even a television show called *Palace Theater of the Air,* which tried "to revive as much as possible the atmosphere of the Palace, N.Y." See *Variety,* 31 March 1948, p. 31.

32. As Arthur Frank Wertheim has shown, radio variety comedy began to take a back seat to slick Hollywood-produced domestic comedies of the 1940s—programs such as *The Aldrich Family.* See Wertheim, *Radio Comedy* (New York: Oxford University Press, 1979), pp. 263–82. By the postwar period, critics often expressed disapproval for the stale jokes and hackneyed routines of variety comics. In this context, numerous radio comics began emigrating to the television screen where their variety formats were given new life through the addition of sight to sound. Moreover, this emigration was precipitated in 1948 when CBS wooed away NBC headliners. See Wertheim, *Radio Comedy,* pp. 314–34 and Robert Metz, *CBS: Reflections in A Bloodshot Eye* (Chicago: Playboy Press, 1975), pp. 137–45.

33. David Marc has elaborated on this in his book *Comic Visions: Television Comedy and American Culture* (Boston: Unwin Hyman, 1989). He also shows how the tradition of variety humor continued to give voice to unconventional and controversial comics such as Lenny Bruce, who appeared on Steve Allen's program in 1959.

34. *Variety,* 21 July 1948, p. 37; *Variety,* 26 January 1949, p. 36; *Variety,* 2 April 1952, p. 37.

35. Jack Gould, "Ed Wynn on TV," *The New York Times,* 16 October 1949, sec. X, p. 11.

36. *Variety,* 24 September 1952, p. 31; *Variety,* 3 December 1952, p. 23.

37. "Illness Rampant from Overwork," *Variety,* 24 December 1952, pp. 21–22; for Berle, see "Danger—TV Comics at Work," *Variety,* 15 December 1954, p. 1.

38. Bob Hope, "Getting So a TV Comic Doesn't Know What to Steal First," *Variety,* 16 July 1952, p. 43.

39. George Rosen, "Berle Comeback," *Variety,* 3 December 1952, p. 23, reported that

Berle sometimes paid for talent out of his own pocket because Texaco refused to raise the budget.

40. Arthur Frank Wertheim, "The Rise and Fall of Milton Berle," *American History/American Television*, ed. John E. O'Connor (New York: Ungar, 1983), pp. 55–78.

41. Irwin A. Shane, "20 Points For Checking TV Production Ideas: Part I," *Televiser*, October 1950, p. 17.

42. Jack Gould, "Television Comedy," *The New York Times*, 24 September 1950, sec. X, p. 11.

43. *Hearings: Radio and Television Programs*, 25 September 1952, pp. 335, 344. Some respondents on the survey found Berle suitable for children, but the general thrust of the survey (and particularly the way Mrs. Smart interpreted it for the Committee) was negative. Arthur J. Klein, a member of the Federal Communications Subcommittee at the hearings, crossexamined Mrs. Smart for what he considered to be her skewed interpretations of the data (p. 350).

44. *NBC Standards and Practices Bulletin—No. 7: A Report on Television Program Editing and Policy Control*, November 1948, NBC Records, Box 157: Folder 7, Wisconsin Center Historical Archives, State Historical Society, Madison.

45. Mr. Kemp, letter to T. McAvity, 25 February 1953, NBC Records, Box 368: Folder 61, Wisconsin Center Historical Archives, State Historical Society, Madison. The NBC Records include a set of documents that concern Gertrude Berg's appearance on Berle. Included is a wire from the Spring Valley Village Board of Spring Valley, New York, which reads: "Mollie added much entertainment to the Milton Berle Show. Would that we had more of her." Letter written to president of NBC, 3 March 1953, NBC Records, Box 368: Folder 61, Wisconsin Center Historical Archives, State Historical Society, Madison.

46. *Variety*, 11 March 1953, p. 23.

47. Poppele, "Moral Responsibility," p. 28.

48. "Prelate Blasts TV Comics for 'Committing (Video) Suicide,'" *Variety*, 28 February 1951, p. 26; "Television Posts Danger Signs," *Variety*, 7 March 1951, p. 1.

49. Donald E. Deyo, letter to the editor, From the Radio-TV Mailbag, *The New York Times*, 6 February 1949, sec. X, p. 11; J. P. C., letter to the editor, From the Radio-TV Mailbag, *The New York Times*, 6 February 1949, sec. X, p. 11.

50. *Hearings: Radio and Television Programs*, 25 September 1952, pp. 344–45.

51. Cited in Jack Gould, "Let's Slow Down: TV 'Clean-Up' Threatens to Get Out of Hand," *The New York Times*, 9 April 1950, sec. X, p. 11. As the title of this article suggests, Gould was against government censorship, calling instead for the industry to police itself and for parents to take more control over their children's viewing. Also see his "Video and Children," *The New York Times*, 8 January 1950, sec. X, p. 15; "TV Censorship Board Proposed," *Variety*, 7 March 1951, p. 36.

52. *Hearings: Radio and Television Programs*, 5 June 1952, pp. 81–82.

53. Ibid., 25 September 1952, p. 350. In this testimony, Mrs. Smart was responding to a question from Arthur Klein, who made specific allusions to the comedian that broadcasts on "Tuesday night at 8 o'clock" (i.e., Milton Berle).

54. *Hearings: Radio and Television Programs*, 3 June 1952, pp. 10–11.

55. Ibid., p. 9.

56. "Low State of TV Comedy Blamed on Censorship, Pressure Groups," *Variety*, 25 February 1953, p. 1.

57. Arthur Gelb, "Why's and Wherefore's for a Revised Format," *The New York Times*, 6 September 1953, sec. X, p. 9.

58. For a review of the 1954 format, see *Variety*, 29 September 1954, p. 27.

59. *Variety*, 31 March 1954, p. 1. Similarly, variety show director Jack Van Nostrand

observed that "while television variety shows started off in exactly the same vein [as radio], with the Milton Berle and Ed Sullivan shows as examples, there is a definite tendency among the better shows to get away from the run-them-on-and-run-them-off technique. . . . I believe that the story, thematic or so-called 'book' show will finally replace the disjointed hangover from vaudeville." Cited in O'Meara, *Television Program Production*, p. 228.

60. Staples details this in *Male-Female Comedy Teams in American Vaudeville*. Also see Linda Martin and Kerry Segrave, *Women in Comedy: The Funny Ladies from the Turn of the Century to the Present* (Secaucus, NJ: Citadel Press, 1986).

61. For background on female comics in early radio and film, see Martin and Segrave. For more on female film comics, see Jenkins, "What Made Pistachio Nuts?"

62. Jack Gould, "TV's Top Comediennes," *The New York Times Magazine*, 27 December 1953, pp. 16–17.

63. Ibid.

64. Publicity and magazine articles further encouraged audiences to perceive these women as nonglamorous types, often comparing the Hollywood "glamorpuss" to the ordinary looks of the TV heroine. For example, *Life*, 18 February 1952, pp. 93–94, ran a two-page spread on Lucille Ball's transition from film to television entitled "Beauty into Buffoon." When writing of Marjorie Reynolds, the female lead in the working-class sitcom *The Life of Riley*, *TV Guide* printed before and after photographs that compared her Hollywood image to her television role. The first was a studio portrait of Reynolds shot in glamor photography style with a caption that read, "Then: a blonde glamor girl of the films." The second was a candid shot of Reynolds as she sat (ambiguously in her home or in her dressing room) reading a script. The caption read, "Now: Marjorie, attractive, brunette and a housewife as well as a television star." See *TV Guide*, 9 October 1953, p. 18. Here as elsewhere, the female television star was tailored to suit the image of a family medium. For more on the deglamorization of television stars in publicity and fan discourses, see Denise Mann, "The Spectacularization of Everyday Life: Recycling Hollywood Stars and Fans in Early Television Variety Shows," *Camera Obscura* 16 (January 1988), pp. 49–77. For more on Ball's average housewife image, see Alexander Doty, "The Cabinet of Lucy Ricardo: Lucille Ball's Star Image," *Cinema Journal* 29 (4) (Summer 1990), pp. 3–22.

65. Ralph Levy, cited in Cheryl Blythe and Susan Sackett, *Say Goodnight Gracie!: The Story of Burns & Allen* (New York: E. P. Dutton, 1986), p. 35.

66. Indeed, this innovation must have been extremely important to the producers and creative personnel since the process of filming in front of a live audience necessitated extensive labor. Sets, sound facilities, and elaborate lighting schemes had to be devised so that film cameras could shoot action continuously. The multiple camera system allowed the Desilu production team to achieve variation in camera angle and distance without retaking scenes. As David Bordwell has suggested to me, this system was similar to that used in the first sync-sound films of the late 1920s and early 1930s, and many of the people that shot early television programs were familiar with the multiple camera techniques employed in these early sound films. In fact, Karl Freund, the German emigre cinematographer who worked on numerous Lubitsch musicals in the early sound period, invented the system of high-key, even lighting that was first used in *I Love Lucy*. Over the course of the 1950s, the multiple camera system that Desilu perfected would become a standard television industry practice used both by independent companies such as George Burns's Mcfadden Productions and Hollywood majors such as Screen Gems.

67. By 6 November 1953, *TV Guide* reported that "only one or two of all the situation comedies made in Hollywood are filmed before audiences" (p. 1). Programs such as *I Married Joan* and *Burns and Allen* retained the multiple camera system as a means of shooting

continuous action, but alleviated the additional costs and labor entailed by shooting in front of studio audiences. As Marc Daniels (director of both *I Love Lucy* and *I Married Joan*) claimed, "While I was able to use the cameras pretty freely in the Lucy Method, I was still bound to the studio audience. In the Joan Method, I was able to put into practice what I had envisioned four years ago. We rehearsed for three days and then filmed the half hour in one day's shooting with plenty of coverage for comedy." Cited in Louis D. Snader, "Resolving Some Major Vidpix Issues," *Variety,* 29 July 1953, p. 37.

68. *Variety,* 22 September 1948, p. 26; *Variety,* 16 November 1949, p. 42.

69. *Variety,* 19 January 1949, p. 26.

70. *Variety,* 28 September 1955, p. 38; *Variety,* 9 September 1953, p. 34. Similarly, a *Variety* review praised the "warmth" with which *Life With Luigi* depicted Italian immigrants. See *Variety,* 24 September 1952, p. 30.

71. *Variety,* 29 April 1953, p. 33; *Variety,* 10 June 1953, p. 32; *Variety,* 23 September 1953, p. 32; *Variety,* 2 September 1953, p. 27.

72. "Perpetual Honeymoon," *Time,* 22 March 1954, p. 82; "A Homey Little Thing," *Time,* 19 December 1949, p. 55; Gilbert Seldes, "Domestic Life in the Forty-ninth State," *Saturday Review,* 22 August 1953, p. 28.

73. "Lucille Ball Baby Shatters Ratings," *Variety,* 21 January 1953, p. 1.

74. "Desilu Formula for Top TV: Brains, Beauty, Now a Baby," *Newsweek,* 19 January 1953, p. 56.

75. Bart Andrews discusses the popularity of Lucy merchandise in *Lucy & Ricky & Fred & Ethel: The Story of I Love Lucy* (New York: Popular Libary, 1977), pp. 17–18. He claims, for example, that one "furniture manufacturer sold a whopping one million *I Love Lucy* bedroom suites in just ninety days," and that "three thousand retail outlets carried Lucille Ball dresses, sweaters and blouses." For more on the conflation of life and text in *I Love Lucy,* see Patricia Mellencamp, "Situation Comedy, Feminism and Freud: The Discourses of Gracie and Lucy," in *Studies in Entertainment: Critical Approaches to Mass Culture,* pp. 80–95; Richard de Cordova, "Enunciation and Performance in *I Love Lucy,*" paper presented at University of Wisconsin-Madison, Department of Communication Arts, 12 November 1987; and Doty, "Cabinet of Lucy Ricardo."

76. *Variety,* 9 March 1949, p. 33.

77. "Normality and $300,000," *Newsweek,* 17 November 1952, p. 66.

78. "The Great Competitor," *Time,* 14 December 1953, p. 62; Gilbert Seldes, "Domestic Life in the Forty-ninth State," *Saturday Review,* 22 August 1953, p. 28; "Two-Family Man," *Newsweek,* 15 April 1954, p. 86.

79. For a description of the development of classical film and its techniques of realistic storytelling, see David Bordwell, Kristin Thompson, and Janet Staiger, *The Classical Hollywood Cinema: Film, Film Style and Mode of Production to 1960* (New York: Columbia University Press, 1985). Again, it should be noted that anarchistic comedies and the lesser known "vaudefilms" did break the rules of classic story construction. See Jenkins, "What Made Pistachio Nuts?" and Seidman, *Comedian Comedy.*

80. It also included two episodes in which the Ricardos appear on radio shows ("The Quiz Show" [1951] and "Lucy Gets Ricky on the Radio," [1952]) and three episodes in which they appear in magazines ("Men Are Messy" [1951], "Ricky's Life Story" [1953] and "Fan Magazine Interview" [1954]).

81. A similar plot was used in a 1952 sketch of "The Honeymooners" on *Cavalacade of Stars.*

82. These episodes are untitled.

83. In *I Married Joan* (untitled, 1955), Joan and her husband go on a panel show; in *Make Room For Daddy* ("The Opera Singer," 1953), the Williams family helps a young Italian girl get on a variety show (see the discussion later in this chapter); in *The Honeymooners*

("Better Living through TV," 1955), Ralph and Norton attempt to become rich by selling a kitchen gadget on a TV commercial; in *I Married Joan* (untitled, 1952), Joan tries to be a star by getting a job on a TV commercial (see the discussion later in this chapter); and in *I Love Lucy* ("Lucy Does a Commercial," 1952 and "The Million-Dollar Idea," 1954), Lucy does television commercials (see the discussion later in this chapter).

84. Halttunen, *Confidence Men and Painted Women*, pp. 184–85.

85. Louise Pinkey Sooy and Virginia Woodbridge, *Plan Your Own Home* (Stanford: Stanford University Press, 1940), p. 1.

86. Nelson N. Foote, "Family Living As Play," *Marriage and Family Living* 17 (4) (November 1955), pp. 297, 299. We might see Foote's thesis as a precursor to Erving Goffman's *The Presentation of Self in Everyday Life* (New York: Anchor, 1959). Goffman explains social interaction through a theatrical model of self-presentation, in which people perform roles as if in a play, fluctuating between "backstage" and "onstage" behavior.

87. Henderson, "Rugged American Collectivism," p. 81 and "The Mass-Produced Suburbs," p. 27.

88. Whyte, *Organization Man*, p. 333.

89. Ibid., pp. 343–45.

90. Kennedy, *House and Art of its Design*, p. 42.

91. "Theatrical Designers Assist in Planning New Colony of Residence at Great Neck," *The New York Times*, 2 October 1949, secs. VIII and IX, p. 1.

92. The episode, for which I have no title, deals with a spat between Uncle David and his brother.

93. Note, however, that many of the sitcoms did utilize offscreen sound effects and dialogue, which added to the narrative a more realist dimension of space. For an early consideration of creating realistic sound in television, see Richard Hubbell, *Television Programming and Production* (1945; reprint, New York: Rinehart & Company, Inc., 1956), pp. 154–64.

94. Serafina Kent Bathrick, "The True Woman and the Family Film: The Industrial Production of Memory," (Ph.D. diss., University of Wisconsin, Madison, 1981).

95. *Variety*, 19 October 1949, p. 35.

96. "Daddy Pinza and Daddy Thomas," *Saturday Review*, 21 November 1953, p. 55. Another critic wrote similarly of *The Danny Thomas Show*: "It doesn't require deep probing to fathom the reason for its success. Being honest is the prime payoff, staying within the bounds of reasonable caricature of what could happen around any home with two youngsters about. The premise is rarely strained for the sake of a big laugh and if a line or situation doesn't evoke chuckles there is no begging with extraneous gags of a broad physical nature." See *Variety*, 21 September 1955, p. 37.

97. *Variety*, 17 October 1951, p. 31.

98. Mellencamp, "Situation Comedy," especially pp. 87–94.

99. It is motivated by intertextual references to Lucille Ball's prior career in the movies, i.e., the routine is a comedic reference to Ball's film performances as a Ziegfeld girl.

100. *Variety*, 8 October 1952, p. 28.

101. Mary Beth Haralovich, "Sitcoms and Suburbs: Positioning the 1950s Homemaker," *Quarterly Review of Film and Video* 11 (1) (Spring 1989), pp. 61–83.

102. Peterson also sang "She Can't Find Her Keys" on a January 1962 episode that featured Jeff dreaming that he was a rock star. The recording of the song was a top hit in 1962.

103. As I have argued elsewhere, by 1965 this trend toward realism had subsided as numerous "fantastic family sitcoms" (*Bewitched, Mr. Ed, My Favorite Martian, I Dream of Jeannie*, etc.) took center stage. See my "From Domestic Space to Outer Space: The 1960s Fantastic Family Sit-com," *Close Encounters: Film, Feminism and Science Fiction*, ed. Con-

stance Penley, Elisabeth Lyon, Lynn Spigel, and Janet Bergstrom (Minneapolis: University of Minnesota Press, 1991), pp. 205–35.

Epilogue

1. Roger Dressler, technical director, Licensing Group, Dolby Laboratories, cited in interview/press release, Electronic Industries Association Consumer Electronics Group, Washington DC, 6 April 1990, p. 2.

2. Tom Hundley, "Assignment: Levittown: American Dream Has Aged Well, Appreciated Too," *Chicago Tribune,* 6 September 1989, sec. 1, p. 6.

3. *Current Population Reports,* "Household and Family Characteristics," series P20, no. 424 (Washington DC: GPO, 1987).

4. Richard Noakes, Sales Manager, Harman-Kardon/JBL, interview/press release, Electronic Industries Association Consumer Electronics Group, Washington DC, 6 April 1990, p. 2.

5. Hans Fantel, video columnist for *The New York Times,* cited in interview/press release, in *Your Home Can Be a Theater,* Electronic Industries Association Consumer Electronics Group, Washington DC, 6 April 1990, p. 2; Don Metzger, equipment manager for Memtek Products, interview/press release, in *Your Home Can Be a Theater,* p. 4; Steve Cladero, national sales manager for Yamaha, interview/press release, in *Your Home Can Be a Theater,* p. 5.

6. Frank Vizard, "Bring the Big Picture Home," *American Home,* Fall/Winter 1990, p. 100.

7. Mark Fleischmann, "Puttin' on The Ritz: Bringing a New Meaning to 'Home' Movies," *Audio/Video Interiors,* Summer 1990, pp. 76–88.

8. *Sound and Image,* Summer 1990, p. 113; *Audio/Video Interiors,* Summer 1990, p. 35.

9. Ted Rozylowicz, manager of marketing and sales, LCD products for Sharp, cited in interview/press release, in *Your Home Can Be A Theater,* p. 7.

10. *Sound and Image,* Summer 1990, p. 33.

11. *Life,* February 1989, p. 67.

12. Mark Heley, "Cyberspace," *i-D,* December 1989/January 1990, p. 37.

13. Jaron Lanier and William Gibson, interview, *Buzz,* MTV, ca. April 1990.

14. Gregory Solman, "Through the Looking Glass," *American Film,* September 1990, p. 50.

15. David Morley, *Family Television: Cultural Power and Domestic Leisure* (London: Routledge, 1986); Ann Gray, "Behind Closed Doors: Video Recorders In the Home," *Boxed In: Women On and In Television,* ed. Helen Baehr and Gillian Dyer (London: Pandora, 1986), pp. 38–54; James Lull, ed., *World Families Watch Television* (Newberry Park, CA: Sage, 1988). For examples of research on *Dallas,* see Ian Ang, *Watching Dallas* (London: Methuen, 1985) and Elihu Katz and Tamar Liebes, "Decoding Dallas: Notes from a Cross-Cultural Study," *Television: The Critical View,* ed. Horace Newcomb, 4th ed. (New York: Oxford University Press, 1987), pp. 419–32.

16. Carlo Ginzburg, "Morelli, Freud and Sherlock Holmes: Clues and Scientific Method," *History Workshop* 9 (Spring 1980), p. 27.

Index

(Page numbers in **boldface** denote illustrations)

INDEX

Glynn, Eugene, 114
Godey's Lady's Book, 13
Godfrey, Arthur, 78, 129, 149–50
Goebbels, Hermann, 62
Goffman, Erving, 224n. 86
Goldbergs, The, 129–31, 148–49, 157, 160, 168–**69,** 218n. 4
"Golden Age" of television. See anthology drama; television, and live theater.
Good Housekeeping, 18, 82, 85–86, 117–18, 190n. 7
Gordon, Elizabeth, 201–9n. 46
Gould, Jack, 55, 66, 138, 140–41, 146–48, 152, 154, 204n. 90, 221n. 51
Gray, Ann, 186–87
Great Neck, N.Y., 165
Greenbie, Sydnie, 34, 97, 211n. 79
Growing Paynes, 141, 218n. 4
Guiding Light, A, 78
Gulf Playhouse, 220n. 27

Halttunen, Karen, 162–63, 166
Halvorson, Lloyd C., 200–201n. 34
Hamlet, 65
Hanley, Helen, 156
Hansen, Katherine, 154
Harmon, Homer, 165
Harpers, 101
Harvey, Paul, 114
Hatful of Rain, A, 41
Haymarket Riot, 18
Heavens to Betsy, 155–57
Henderson, Harry, 128–29, 164, 212n. 6
Hennock, Frieda, 54
Here Is Television, Your Window on the World, 102
Hershfield, Harry, 117
Hitchcock, Alfred, 94
Hollywood, 81, 83, 94, 146, 165, 185; gradually dominates television, 147, 172, 189n. 2, 220n. 27
Home, 81–85, 208nn. 33, 38
Home Craftsman, 97
Home Furnishings, 59, 106–7, 201–2n. 46
home magazines. *See* women's magazines
"home theater" and video technology, 181–87
Honey, Maureen, 198n. 16
Honeymooners, The, 88–89, 96, 125–26, 129, 137, 160, 171, 223–24n. 83

Hoover, Herbert, 27, 58
Hopalong Cassidy, 90
Hope, Bob, 147
Horwich, Frances, 85
House and the Art of Its Design, The, 108
House Beautiful, 5, 18, 38, 45–50, 59, 66, 67, 88–91, 94–95, 106, 108, 140, 201–2n. 46, 209n. 59
house design and layout, 1; and "contemporary" design, 48–49; and domestic space, 67–69, 89–94; and modernism, 201–2n. 46, 212n. 19; and privacy, 94–98, 101–5; in postwar period, 1, 33–35, 65–69, 89–95, 101–5, 107–9; in Progressive era, 19–24; in Victorian period, 12–18, 67, 193n. 20; plan books, 12–13, 15, 194n. 30
Housing Act of 1949, 33
housework, 18, 21–23, 73–75, 199–200n. 22; and consumerism, 17, 82–92; and isolation, 91–93; and labor-saving technology, 18–24, 77, 82, 89–93, 195n. 33; and leisure, 14–15, 17, 19–26, 75, 86–90; and television, 87–90, 93–95
How To Do It, 82
Huckleberry Hound, 56
Hudson, Rock, 123
Hudson-Essex Corporation, 30
Hutchinson, Thomas H., 102
Huyssen, Andreas, 61
hysteria, 19, 193n. 22

i-D, 185
I Love Lucy, 105–6, 120–21, 130, 141, 146, 151–52, **153**–55, 160, 162–63, 168, 172–77, 222–23nn. 66, 67, 223–24n. 83; and show-related merchandise, 158, 223n. 75
I Married Joan, 153–55, 160, 176, **177,** 222–24nn. 67, 83
Impelleteri, Vincent R., 139
Independent, The, 99
Indianapolis, 146
Inness, George, 24
International House, 115
"International Style," 104

Jackie Gleason Show, The, 160
Jackman, Alonzo, 110

230

INDEX